George Washington

George Washington

The Wonder of the Age

JOHN RHODEHAMEL

Yale UNIVERSITY PRESS

NEW HAVEN & LONDON

Published with assistance from the Annie Burr Lewis Fund.

Yale University Press books may be purchased in quantity for educational, business, or promotional use. For information, please e-mail sales.press@yale.edu
(U.S. office) or sales@yaleup.co.uk (U.K. office).

Designed by James J. Johnson and set in Miller and Cochin types
by Integrated Publishing Solutions.
Printed in the United States of America.

Library of Congress Control Number: 2016939283
ISBN 978-0-300-21997-5 (hardcover : alk. paper)

A catalogue record for this book is available from the British Library.

This paper meets the requirements of
ANSI/NISO Z39.48-1992 (Permanence of Paper).

10 9 8 7 6 5 4 3 2 1

Jack, Sam, Catherine, Anna

Contents

George Washington

≫ 1 ≪

Look Around You

Georg e Washington never took much interest in his ancestors. When he was an old man, and the new president of the new United States of America, he would reply politely to an aristocratic English genealogist who had written for help in tracing the Washington family tree. Courtesy, however, did not disguise Washington's pointed little lecture on the promise of the great experiment then under way in America. For the Americans had set out to create a new society, one guided by the faith that a person's rank should be grounded on attainment rather than ancestry—by the faith that all people were created equal.

His own ancestry was "a subject," President Washington wrote the genealogist, "to which I confess I have paid very little attention. My time has been so much occupied in the busy and active scenes of life from an early period of it that but a small portion of it could have been devoted to researches of this nature. . . . We have no Office of Record in this Country in which exact genealogical documents are preserved; and very few cases, I believe, occur where a recurrence to pedigree for any considerable distance back has been found necessary to establish such points as may frequently arise in older Countries."[1]

Washington's subtext might have read: In republican society, people, though born equal, still sought the honors supplied elsewhere by the trappings of aristocracy. A kind of republican peerage might exist, but entry into its ranks did not require fortunate birth but rather demonstrated talent, ambition, and a virtuous devotion to the public good. Washington had been too busy winning honor to study his lineage.

So much honor did he win that His Excellency General George Washington may seem an unlikely champion of the revolutionary principle that all people are created equal. In death as in life, Americans have revered Washington as a mythic figure, remote in his icy majesty. We cannot forget that he was the master of three hundred slaves. He was commander of officers and men in their thousands—the generalissimo awarded quasi-dictatorial powers by the Continental Congress in 1776. He was a consummate political actor who became America's first elected head of state. Washington was also a high-living Virginia gentleman possessed of vast tracts of land and of all the luxuries wealth could command. He was an authentic classical hero—"the American Cincinnatus"—said to have countless admirers but not a single friend. He was a proud but insecure man who could confuse dissent with disloyalty.

Yet this same George Washington was a revolutionary, for a quarter-century the central figure in a radical revolution that aimed at nothing less than the transformation of Western civilization. When Washington was born, in 1732, the British colonies in North America were obscure and inconsequential outposts. The courts of Europe had long been the focus of the Atlantic world. All the principal European states were ruled by hereditary monarchs—kings and queens, emperors and czars—who reigned by virtue of their carefully recorded pedigrees. In Britain the king was constrained by a constitution that compelled him to govern with the consent of Parliament. But even in England the king was the unquestioned head of state. Just beneath royalty revolved the glittering constellations of aristocracy—proud lords and highborn ladies. They too were exalted by birth far above the common run of men and women. Government-by-birth appeared the most satisfactory model for ordering society, one that had prevailed for centuries and promised to persist into the remote future.

When Washington died, in 1799, the eighteenth century was coming to a close, while the age of hereditary power, the very notion of government-by-birth, had been started down the road to extinction. And the United States of America, overleaping its small beginnings on the margins of European civilization, would one day thrust itself into the forefront of world history. The little republic would become a gigantic continental democracy—a nation unlike any that had come before. The promise of equality may never be realized. Nevertheless, the American Revolution made the theory of popular government a reality for the first time, furnishing a compelling alternative to the ancient tyranny of kings. American success marked a fundamental turning point in human affairs.

That success may have been out of reach without Washington's leadership. Of course, George Washington did not make the Revolution: it was the work of the American people. The man who described himself as "a figure upon the stage" in the "greater Drama . . . now acting on this Theatre" emerged as a flawless performer, taking his cues from his audience—the people themselves.[2] Although many Americans were shut out of the political process, participation by white men was widespread. They could draw on ideals born in the classical republics of antiquity. Many had studied the political theorists of the Enlightenment. They took pride in the venerable constitution of Britain itself, the set of traditions that, Britons and their British-American cousins boasted, made England the most free nation on earth. The Americans drew as well on their own unique heritage as inhabitants of fluid, quasi-republican colonial societies.

Still, at every stage of the drama, George Washington played the leading role. Thomas Jefferson supposed that to Washington belonged "the singular destiny and merit, of leading the armies of his country successfully through an arduous war for the establishment of its independence; of conducting its councils through the birth of a government, new in forms and principles, until it settled down into a quiet and orderly train; and of scrupulously obeying the laws through the whole of his career, civil and military, of which the history of the world furnishes no other example."[3]

Revolution is a perilous enterprise. You have a republic, but only if you can keep it, Benjamin Franklin had warned after the delegates signed the new Constitution in 1787. Would it prove, as philosophers predicted and history had confirmed, that the republican government demanded by the principle of equality could never provide the bonds of power needed to hold together a large and diverse nation? Was it inevitable that, in a few years or decades, the United States would be forced to abandon popular representation and resort to despotism? Would the infant republic fragment into a set of squabbling petty sovereignties?

We know the outcome of the experiment. Those living through its early years could not. But they did understand what was at risk. They were contending for what Washington called "a blessing to Millions yet unborn."[4] No one felt the gamble more keenly than he did. "The sacred fire of liberty, and the destiny of the Republican model of Government . . . [is] staked, on the experiment entrusted to the hands of the American people," he declared at his first inauguration in 1789.[5] Jefferson remembered, years after the older man's death, that Washington had "often declared to me that he considered our new constitution as an experiment on the practicability of republican government, and with what dose of liberty man could be trusted for his own good; that he was determined the experiment should have a fair trial, and would lose the last drop of his blood in support of it."[6]

It was not Washington's blood, however, but his enormous prestige, the trust Americans held for him, that had carried the experiment safely through so many hazards.

He had won that trust in the Revolution. He had won it, most of all, by the extraordinary act of resigning his command at the end of the war. General Washington had led the American states to independent nationhood through eight and a half years of war and diplomacy. But history had seen many victorious generals—many Caesars and Cromwells. What set this general apart was the way that, when the war was over, he willingly, even eagerly, gave up power to return to Mount Vernon as a private citizen in 1783.

The astonishing renunciation deeply impressed the entire Western world, as Washington had surely known it would. In Europe as well as America, George Washington was widely regarded as the greatest man alive—the shining republican hero. In an age that believed power corrupted its possessors, Washington was the wonder of the age.

Revolutions have a way of going bad—tyrants are often supplanted by other tyrants. The greatest revolution of the eighteenth century broke out in Paris in 1789, the year Washington became president. Fifteen years later, the French Revolution succeeded in replacing a king with an emperor when Napoleon Bonaparte crowned himself in 1804. In America the outcome had been different. Jefferson concluded that "the moderation and virtue of a single character has probably prevented this revolution from being closed as most others have been, by a subversion of that liberty it was intended to establish."[7]

Washington called the American Revolution "the last great experiment, for promoting human happiness."[8] He was wrong. The creation of the American republic would not be the last experiment for benefiting humankind by the remaking of government. There would be more such experiments. The least successful came to pass in the twentieth century—carnivorous tyrannies that murdered innocents in their tens of millions, reduced the survivors to slavery, and unleashed catastrophic wars.

Throughout his life George Washington had been engaged in another experiment. While still a boy, he had begun a process of self-invention. On the success of the one endeavor would ultimately hinge the success of the other. For the result of the personal experiment was Washington's deliberate creation of the public character that gave him the moral authority to lead the quarrelsome collection of former colonies into sturdy nationhood.

The American people themselves contributed to the creation of the Washington monument. Monarchy was still the only model they had. As soon as independence was proclaimed in July 1776, a mob of riotous New Yorkers toppled the equestrian statue of His Britannic Majesty George III from its pedestal in a Manhattan public square. (The leaden likeness was quickly melted down to make some forty-two thousand musket balls to fire at His Majesty's soldiery.) In 1792, citizens of the United States placed a statue of their first president on the same pedestal. The Americans had cast aside European pomp and heraldry. As they began to gather about their new republic the emblems of nationhood, they chose instead certain noble words, an eagle, and a flag. But General Washington was the earliest symbol of their cause. "God save great Washington," the rebels sang. "God damn the king!" When the first president-elect crossed the Hudson River on the way to his inauguration in New York in 1789, a choir of schoolgirls embarked on a flower-bedecked sloop welcomed him to their city with an "Eloquent Ode." Insipid indeed were the lyrics of their little song, but "God Save the King" was the tune. It was safe enough to treat this man like a king because he didn't want to be one.

The mythmaking began with Washington's election as general of the Continental Army in 1775. From the moment he accepted command, he became the vessel of America's hope. The same projection would have attended the appointment of another man, but the lofty, impassive Virginian seemed perfectly suited to assume such symbolic stature. The conscious blending of his own ambitions with the future of the United States only became stronger as the struggle of nation building continued. His identification with the new republic was so complete, and his heroic character so carefully contrived, that it is unlikely that the "real" Washington will ever escape the obscuring embrace of myth. As Marcus Cunliffe observed fifty years ago, "we may suspect that myth and man can never be entirely separated, and that valuable clues to Washington's temperament, as well as his public stature, lie in this fact."[9]

Many of those who have studied the paragon have hoped to reveal the living Washington hidden behind the mythical hero. None has really succeeded. Parson Mason Locke Weems, the great man's earliest and most popular biographer, insisted that it was not "in the glare of *public,* but in the shade of the *private life,* that we are to look for the man."[10] The good parson could write like a manic angel, but his flights often carried him far beyond the realms of literal truth. In his insistence on the primacy of his subject's private life, Weems was simply mistaken. George Washington's greatness is to be found in his public achievements, and those achievements are authentically monumental. So the man must remain a monument.

From horizon to horizon, the first of fathers ranges across the firmament of American memory in hazy ubiquity, at once familiar and out of focus. His genius escapes us. Jefferson had insisted that the "world furnishes no other example" to stand with Washington's. And yet, thanks to generations of hymn singers, the most successful statesman in American history is often best remembered as a boy with a hatchet or as a simpleminded prig kneeling in the snow to pray. A tawdry mythological excrescence oozing Victorian pieties and wooden teeth has gained a greater hold on the national imagination than the epic of Washington's indispensable leadership in the making of the great nation that probably would not have come to be without him.

It hardly matters. As Cunliffe suggested, the true Washington monument is the United States of America. Look around you if you want to see it.[11] He remains the greatest figure in American history. As Gordon Wood has written, "Washington was truly a great man and the greatest president we ever had. . . . Washington was an extraordinary man who made it possible for ordinary men to rule. There has been no president quite like him, and we can be sure we shall not see his like again."[12]

⁂ 2 ⁂

Powerful Ambitions, Powerful Friends

G EORGE WASHINGTON did not start out as a statue on a pedestal. His act of self-creation may have been the most comprehensive in all America's long procession of self-made men. He was born a fourth-generation Virginian, and like many Americans his knowledge of his family extended back only as far as his immigrant ancestor, in Washington's case a great-grandfather. "In the year 1657, or thereabouts," he told the English genealogist, "and during the Usurpation of Oliver Cromwell John and Lawrence Washington, Brothers Emigrated from the north of England, and settled at Bridges Creek, on Potomac river, in the County of Westmoreland."[1] In the early winter of 1657, the little *Sea Horse of London* had ascended Chesapeake Bay and sailed into the ten-mile-wide mouth of the great tidewater river. Along the distant shores of Maryland and Virginia stretched a landscape that dwarfed Europe in scale and richness.

It was the first American voyage of the mate, John

Washington, the son of an Oxford-educated clergyman whose prospects in England had been darkened by the Puritan revolution. In setting out on the return voyage, the tobacco-laden ketch ran onto a Potomac shoal and split its seams. The sailors went ashore. The mate must have liked what he saw there: when the crew refloated *Sea Horse* and set sail for the Chesapeake Capes, Washington stayed behind in Virginia. He soon married the daughter of a prosperous Maryland planter and entered enthusiastically into the cycle of land, tobacco, and politics, displaying the acquisitive drive that elevated men in the fifty-year-old colony.

Land and cash from his father-in-law gave the immigrant a solid start in his new world. Soon he was importing indentured servants from England, with Virginia granting him fifty acres for every new inhabitant he landed in the colony. If seventeenth-century Virginians were lucky enough to survive more than a few years in that harsh land, they were likely to outlive several less fortunate spouses. John Washington married three times. With each union, he picked up a little more property. Washington also gained offices. He became county coroner, vestryman of his church, justice of the peace, and a ranking officer in the militia. The local parish was named for him. He was elected one of Westmoreland County's delegates to the colonial assembly, the Virginia House of Burgesses.

John Washington died twenty years after landing in Virginia, aged about forty-five. The man who had come ashore empty-handed could leave his heirs eight thousand acres, much of it laid out in tobacco plantations. His sons and grandsons followed the immigrant's example. They married well, gathered in land and slaves and county offices, grew tobacco, and died in early middle age.

John Washington's grandson Augustine died in 1743, a year short of his fiftieth birthday. He left behind his widow and seven children, the two oldest the issue of his first marriage to Jane Butler. Eldest of the five children of his union with Mary Ball was eleven-year-old George.

George had been born on February 22, 1732 (New Style), in a little farmhouse set near the point where Popes Creek pours its waters into the Potomac. This record of the child's birth is carefully inscribed in Mary Washington's Bible: "George Washington Son to Augustine & Mary his Wife was Born the 11th. Day of February 1731/2 about 10 in the Morning & was Baptised the 5th. of April Following."[2] But the item in the old book was not composed at the time of the event it records. Though the writing has been described by Washington's preeminent biographer Douglas Southall Freeman as that of an "unknown hand," examination reveals the penmanship of George Washington himself, exhibiting the handwriting style he used in his early twenties.[3] That the young man should register his own birth was emblematic of his emerging character. George Washington was a record-keeping animal—he noted and measured and wrote almost as naturally as he breathed. And by the time he inscribed his mother's Bible, Washington had already begun to make something of a name for himself, for this he did at an uncommonly early age. He always believed that his life was important, that it was a drama that required a proper opening scene. W. W. Abbot has observed that "an attentive reader [of Washington's

papers] has to be struck by the man's uncommon awareness of self: his strong sense that what he decided and
what he did, and how others perceived his decisions and
deeds, always mattered. These things mattered to Washington not because he had any grand sense of destiny as
many have surmised, or that he had a nasty itch for power
as some might suspect, but because he saw life as something a person must make something of. More than most,
Washington's biography is the story of man constructing
himself. . . . Washington at work on Washington."[4]

His father's estate amounted to about ten thousand
acres and fifty slaves. It was a respectable holding, but
hardly conspicuous in a colony where great families like
the Lees and Byrds and Carters numbered their slaves in
the hundreds and their acres in the many tens of thousands. George Washington had been born into the middle
ranks of Virginia gentry. And, as a younger son by a second
marriage, he was due at age twenty-one only a modest portion of his father's property—just a few hundred worn-out
acres and ten slaves.

So the future champion of liberty became a slaveholder
at age eleven. The legacy of slavery would attend him all his
life. There were probably slaves in the room where he was
born; slaves stood by quietly as he lay dying sixty-seven
years later. John Washington had relied mostly on white
indentured servants to work his tobacco fields. But in the
half-century between the emigrant's death and the birth
of his great-grandson, the Virginia colony had been transformed by the importation of tens of thousands of captive
people from West Africa. By the time George Washing-

ton's childhood ended, Virginia's population approached a quarter million, and as many as a third were enslaved blacks. Conditions of servitude were harsh. Coerced labor would allow some Virginians of the revolutionary generation to live well and devote their energies to the pursuit of honor through public service. But the enslavement of these new Americans from Africa presented a tragedy that would haunt all Americans far into the future.

We know nothing of the circumstances of Augustine Washington's death, and the son barely spoke of his father. It is certain only that the consequences were far-reaching. George's father and two older brothers had gone to school in England; his own expectations of following them there were now dashed. The choicest portions of Augustine Washington's estate went to his two oldest sons. George's inheritance was too meager to establish him as an independent planter. He would have to make his own way in the world.

After Augustine Washington's death, George found himself at Ferry Farm with his mother and his four younger siblings. Fortunately, he did not lack a male figure on whom to model himself. His half-brother Lawrence, fourteen years his senior, must have been the glorious embodiment of everything George hoped to be. Lawrence had worn a scarlet uniform, had sailed the ocean-sea, heard the big guns roar, and seen men die in battle. He was an English-educated gentleman who had married into northern Virginia's most important family. Lawrence had inherited the bulk of Augustine Washington's estate. He was also an able and highly ambitious man. He held the rank of major and served as adjutant general of the colony's militia. Fairfax

County had sent him to the House of Burgesses. He was president of the Ohio Company, a vast western land speculation. Lawrence Washington must have seen promise in his little brother, for he set out to train him for success, starting George on the road he so eagerly followed to fame, wealth, and power.

In 1740, Lawrence Washington had served as an officer of the Virginia regiment in the disastrous British attack on Spanish Cartagena, a sorry episode in the War of Jenkins' Ear. Only six hundred of the thirty-five hundred Americans who sailed to the Caribbean with the Royal Navy ever came home. The survivors were left with bitter memories of mistreatment at the hands of supercilious British regulars. But Lawrence Washington did gain a captain's commission in the regular army. A royal commission was a far greater prize than the appointments as colonial militia officers that the Washington men had held in the past. A regular officer was commissioned for life. In many regiments, officers' commissions were hard assets that could be sold for cash. Even if the regiment were disbanded, even if the man never donned his uniform again, he was entitled to half pay until the day he died. Lawrence undoubtedly impressed the distinction between royal and colonial commissions on his brother. The pursuit of rank in the British Army became the reigning goal of George Washington's first military career.

His formal education ended by the time he was fifteen or sixteen, adding up to no more than eight years in all. Since he was not destined for the privileged life of a gentleman planter, his were not the opportunities accorded more fortunate Virginians of the time. He did not go to school in England like his older brothers. He did not attend Virginia's College of William and Mary or a northern university, as did men like Thomas Jefferson and James Madison. His training was largely practical, as befitted one who must soon be earning a living. Surviving copybooks and school papers reveal that he studied mathematics, surveying, and geography along with the legal forms and accounting methods used in plantation business. Washington's lifelong love of harmony and order is evident in his earliest manuscripts. He learned to write in an imposing hand that is still lovely to see. His lines lay perfectly straight across the paper. He liked elegant capital letters, and his first surveys were embellished with ornamental flourishes. His penmanship could impart charm to documents as uninspiring as crop rotation tables. George Washington also mastered language itself, probably teaching himself to write by emulating the prose he read. Though the adolescent produced dreadful poetry on the agonies of unrequited love, the man became a forceful writer, capable of compelling passages. For as long as he lived, this man of action spent a good portion of his waking hours at his desk, pen in hand. Some twenty thousand documents written by George Washington still exist, and the common assumption that his great papers were the work of other minds is much mistaken. As Edmund S. Morgan has written, Washington "had a great many amanuenses, and the quality of his writing is often attributed to them, but the consistent force and clarity have to be the expression of a single mind."[5]

Reading also helped Washington absorb the code of conduct that was as essential to his advancement as were his native drive and talent. Most famous of his bids to gain a gentleman's polish was the boy's exercise of copying out the 110 "Rules of Civility and Decent Behaviour in Company and Conversation," a collection of maxims originally compiled in 1595 by French Jesuits. While giving moral and religious guidance, the "Rules" also gently instructed those most in need of help not to handle their privates or pick lice when people were watching. Young men eager to please their betters were advised to "bedew no mans face with your Spittle." But more advanced students could acquire a good grounding in the diplomatic skills a beginner needed to get ahead—those ceremonies of respect and deference due the powerful, the kind of behavior that won a man respect for himself.

Brother Lawrence may have been his friend and patron, but Mary Ball Washington was George's legal guardian until he came of age. Canonized by the Victorians as MARY MOTHER OF WASHINGTON—these are the only words cut into the obelisk that rises above her grave in Fredericksburg—her reputation has suffered a precipitous decline. The current mother of Washington is a grim, pipe-smoking harridan who spent her days frightening small children and making miserable the life of her oldest son. Caricatures are formed around an element of truth, and there must be some truth to this one. It can be surmised that George Washington never much liked his mother, even though he probably inherited some of his stubborn strength from her. Both of them were proud, strong-willed characters. Washington soon grew into a man who would have recalled with little fondness the time when another person, even a parent, had controlled him. After he left home, he saw her only rarely, even though she lived until he was nearly sixty. She humiliated him during the Revolution by lobbying for a pension from the Virginia House of Delegates. Never once, at least in her correspondence, did she offer a word of praise or pride for her son's enormous success. She seemed to regard his public service as distraction from his true duty of attending to her needs. When she was old and claimed distress, Washington explicitly disinvited her from coming to live at Mount Vernon. His house, he said, with its constant company of strangers, would never suit her. It wasn't that he disliked old women. A few years earlier, he had warmly invited his mother-in-law to make Mount Vernon her permanent home.

Lawrence Washington had come away from the harrowing siege of Cartagena with enough admiration for his commander, Admiral Edward Vernon, to name his new home Mount Vernon in the old seaman's honor. Here Lawrence and his bride lived in his father's house, with its sweeping Potomac vistas. Like many of his family, this ambitious man had made the kind of advantageous marriage that his society regarded as a perfectly honorable way to get ahead. (Wedding notices in the Williamsburg press sometimes featured an estimate of the bride's net worth.) Lawrence's new wife was Anne Fairfax, daughter of Colonel William Fairfax of Belvoir, who was himself first cousin and Virginia agent of that great man, Thomas, sixth Baron Fairfax of Cameron. Lord Fairfax, on the strength of his lucky birth and a dead king's gift, was master of his own Virginia kingdom, the Northern Neck Propriety. Lawrence Washington's election to the House of Burgesses and his appointment as adjutant general of the militia followed swiftly on his marriage to William Fairfax's daughter. He was now poised to take a place in the highest ranks of Virginia society, that airy realm no Washington had yet attained.

George was soon spending much of his time with Lawrence's family at Mount Vernon. Mount Vernon was half a day's ride from his mother's modest farm outside Fredericksburg. It must have seemed a world away. Life at Mount Vernon was bathed in the gorgeous light of Belvoir, the Fairfax family's grand Georgian mansion just downriver. George Washington was delighted to be drawn into the aristocratic Fairfax orbit. He quickly became a favorite of his brother's father-in-law, William Fairfax, and absorbed a higher education within the Belvoir's elegant rooms. The Fairfax alliance was to be of the utmost importance in his progress as a gentleman, soldier, politician, and landholder.[6]

The most important member of the family was Baron Fairfax. His new world empire contained between five million and six million acres, close to nine thousand square miles—roughly the size of Wales. The eccentric Lord Fairfax also took to George Washington. Their connection was tenuous. Washington was merely the younger half-brother of the husband of the daughter of the dependent cousin that His Lordship often treated contemptuously. The Virginian had little education and no experience with the world, had never seen a city or traveled outside his rural Chesapeake neighborhood. But the fatherless Washington had a knack for winning the favor of powerful older men.

Lord Fairfax encountered a striking personage the day he first met the compelling youth. By the time George Washington reached manhood, everyone agreed that he had been gifted with the physical attributes of a classical hero. The legends of Augustine Washington's tremendous strength gain credibility from the undisputed fact that his son was one of the biggest, strongest, and most vigorous men of his day. In his manhood, he stood over six feet. A head taller than most men, Washington seemed born to command them. His 220 pounds looked to be all bone and muscle. Many remarked on the length of his powerful arms and the amazing size of his hands and feet. With such arms, it was no surprise that Washington could hurl missiles like rocks and iron bars farther than any contestant who cared to challenge him. Yet he moved with uncanny grace. His bearing was majestic, even arresting. People stopped in their tracks just to watch the big man cross a street or a parade ground. He was a superb dancer in a place where that skill brought a man honor. And when Washington mounted a horse, no one could take his eyes off him. Another Virginia rider from that country of proud horseman captured Washington's prowess. Thomas Jefferson said Washington was the "best horseman of his age, and the most graceful figure that could be seen on horseback."[7] Above all things, Lord Fairfax loved riding to the hounds. He spent much of his life in Virginia pursuing the fox across the countryside. A shared love of the hunt and

Fairfax's admiration for Washington's horsemanship may have been bonds that brought the unlikely pair together.

But it would have taken more than horsemanship and strength of arm to impress the sophisticated nobleman and the other influential men who would soon vie to help the young Washington. Even at an early age, George Washington must have given off glimpses of the singular genius of his character. Courteous, deferential, soft-spoken, Washington followed the gentleman's code he had studied so attentively. But at the core of his being lived a steely will in which gentleness played little part. As a few of the best portraits show, Washington's blue-gray eyes projected a shaft of icy power that must have turned aside many a milder gaze. The engine driving this tireless prodigy was his consuming ambition to excel. He could never rest until he had won the admiration of the world.

Of course there had been English aristocrats living at Belvoir long before Lord Fairfax's arrival. George had been welcomed into the big brick house soon after his brother's marriage in July 1743, just three months after Augustine Washington's death. The patriarch of Belvoir, Lawrence's new father-in-law, was William Fairfax, the agent of the Northern Neck. The Northern Neck agency had made its former holders rich. Fairfax's immediate predecessor was the legendary Robert Carter. "King" Carter had amassed much of his 300,000 acres by serving his own interests at least as assiduously as he served those of the Northern Neck proprietary. Now, two years after Robert Carter's death, the golden mantle of the office descended on William Fairfax's shoulders. From the moment he came ashore, he was one of the leading figures in Great Britain's principal colony. The highest offices naturally came his way—a seat on the Governor's Council, a colonel's rank in the militia. In 1743, Colonel Fairfax summoned from England his son, George William. Though he was seven years older than George Washington, the two would remain close friends for thirty years. George William Fairfax soon brought home the former Miss Sarah Cary, the young bride he had won on the banks of the James River. Her friends called her Sally. (Long after she had retired within her tomb, Sally Fairfax would become famous when giddy novelists and sober historians alike told the beguiling story of George Washington's dark passion for his best friend's wife.)

The Fairfax men were British nobility by birth and education, and the ambiance at Belvoir was much like that of an aristocratic home in England.[8] George was driven to understand and to master his world. Fortune had greatly favored him—there could be no better instructor than his own brother's father-in-law. William Fairfax was as glad to teach as the student was to learn. He came to love George Washington like a son. His patronage was crucial to Washington's early success.[9]

From the old gentleman and his own brother, from a few important books, and from the Anglo-Virginian society he moved in, Washington absorbed the creed shared by the English-speaking gentry of the Enlightenment. The pillar of that creed was an eighteenth-century strain of classical stoicism. It taught the wise man to accept that fate was all-powerful. ("There is a Destiny," Washington would

maintain, "which has Sovereign control of our Actions—
not to be resisted by the efforts of Human nature.")[10] In the
kind of paradox beloved of mystics, the acceptance of pow-
erlessness gave rare powers. The wise man had mastered
his passions. He was beyond the sway of fear and desire.
He could look on death without blinking, even though he
might suspect that all he saw there was the consumma-
tion of nothingness. Self-mastery made him master of the
larger world, and the proof of that mastery was his civic
virtue. His honor was inflexible. The good man used the
courage and integrity engendered by his act of will to pursue glorious fame and leave an example to inspire future
generations. Of course Washington himself was a person
of the enormous passions, chief among them ambition.
He was also subject to outbursts of uncontrollable anger.
Many of the lessons did not really take hold for years—
after his teachers had gone down to death, and the student
himself had passed through many trials. Over time his will
proved stronger than his passions. He eventually won the
victory that one fellow revolutionary characterized as his
victory over himself.[11]

For after he had outgrown the overwrought egotism of
his early years, George Washington's ambition became that
noble aspiration that was so distinctive of his age. Like his
great contemporaries, Washington came to desire above
all else the kind of fame that meant a lasting reputation
as a man of honor. At age sixteen he copied this "Query"
into his earliest diary: "What's the Noblest Passion of the
Mind?" The answer is that the love of fame is the noblest
passion of the mind. George Washington would answer

that query with the conduct of his life. Although he av-
idly sought high office and though he remained the most
powerful man in America for many years, it was not really power that Washington wanted. Not an end in itself,
exalted rank was essential for both the respect it brought
and for the chance it provided to perform glorious acts
that would be remembered long after the actor himself
had passed from the scene.

Thoughtful people of Washington's time believed that
all humans were born with a malignant lust to dominate
their fellows. Political power corrupted those who wielded
it; tyrants bestrode the earth. But people were also convinced that ambition—the love of fame—offered an alchemy
that could transmute the base appetite for power into a
pursuit of the honor that would endure after marble monuments had subsided into dust. Ambition in this formulation was not a selfish motive, but a willingness to sacrifice
one's own happiness for the welfare of the many. The love
of fame was the greatest gift a good man could give his
country.[12] George Washington would consume his life in
the quest for such living honor, and he would win as much
of immortality as fame can ever give.

In 1748, William Fairfax gave Washington his introduction to Virginia's western frontier. Two weeks past his
sixteenth birthday, he joined a monthlong expedition to
survey some of the proprietor's Shenandoah land. On the
trip, Washington started the first of his many diaries. He
called it the "Journal of my Journey over the Mountains."
The party spent one of the first nights out in a pioneer's
cabin. "I being not so good a Woodsman as the rest of my

Company striped my self very orderly & went in to the Bed
as they call'd it when to my Surprize I found it to be nothing only one Thread Bear blanket with double its Weight
in Vermin such as Lice Fleas &c. I was glad to get up . . . &
put on my Cloths & Lay as my Companions." Washington
was appalled by the frontier settlers he encountered. He
considered them filthy, ignorant, lice- and vice-ridden savages, a contempt he continued to hold until the end of his
life. A few days later, the surveyors met a band "of thirty
odd Indians coming from War with only one Scalp."[13]

The journey was a revelation. Here, not much more
than a day's ride from the scenes of his boyhood, was a
fresh country of almost unimaginable richness. The vision
of a spacious western destiny would absorb Washington
until the day he died. The West would shape his judgment
as a land speculator and canal builder, and later as an advocate of American nationhood.

The next year, Fairfax clout handed Washington the
lucrative post of surveyor of Culpeper County. In a place
where the number of a man's acres was the final arbiter of
his wealth and prestige, surveying was a highly respectable, as well as profitable, profession. Surveyors were gentry who ranked with lawyers, doctors, and planters. Boys
of seventeen did not get appointments as county surveyor.
But George Washington did. He had earned the job the
old-fashioned way—through the interest of powerful
friends. Although he would show that he was highly qualified for the work, the appointment was unprecedented for
one so young as he, a mark of his growing stature.[14] The
salary was only £15 a year, but an industrious man could

earn much more in fees and bonuses. Washington made the most of the opportunity. He traveled indefatigably through the Shenandoah frontier, his saddlebags stuffed with choice assignments funneled to him by the proprietor's office. A woodsman's life hardened the tough young man, and here he laid the foundations of his fortune, clearing as much as £150 a year. By 1750 the eighteen-year-old was able to buy his first tract of land, about two thousand Shenandoah acres.

Lawrence Washington had a cough. George Washington's earliest surviving letter begins "Dear Brother I hope your Cough is much mended since I saw you last."[15] But Brother never mended—probably he had tuberculosis. Whatever he had would kill him before he turned thirty-five. In 1751, hoping tropical air might prove restorative, Lawrence and George took ship to Barbados. The trip was George Washington's only blue-water voyage and the only time he would leave North America. The island gentry entertained the brothers. The two marveled at the exotic sights, but were much oppressed by heat. George attended the theater for the first time, beginning a lifelong love affair with playacting.

Then smallpox attacked the younger man, laying him out for three weeks in a stifling room with lizards scuttling across the walls. Washington's strength brought him through the trial that brought an end to many. His face would always be lightly scarred by the distinctive pockmarks—then a common disfigurement. More important was the mark the sickness had left on his immune system: he was now safe from the scourge of eighteenth-century armies.

But Lawrence Washington had gained nothing from the voyage. He was living away his last days on earth. Lawrence went on to Bermuda, sending his brother back to Virginia. In January 1752, George landed at Yorktown and rode to Williamsburg, where the nineteen-year-old boldly called on the colony's newly arrived royal governor, Robert Dinwiddie. A few lines of Washington's handsome script in a fragment of a badly damaged diary record his meeting with the jowly, sixty-year-old Scotsman: "I waited upon and was received graciously, he enquired kindly after the health of my Brother and invited me to stay and dine."[16] Although the next page is missing, one may assume that Governor Dinwiddie was as impressed as the Fairfaxes had been. Washington knew that fulfilling his ambitions in a hierarchical world required the favor of powerful men. The youth who had lost his father probably also yearned to recapture some of the paternal guidance that death had snatched away. George Washington would cultivate a series of father figures until he attained a stature that lifted him beyond the need for patrons.

Among other matters, Dinwiddie and Washington probably talked about the coming vacancy of the adjutant generalship of the Virginia militia. The incumbent, Major Lawrence Washington, was obviously too sick to perform his duties. If the younger Washington asked the governor for his dying brother's place, it is certain that he did so with the deferential charm he had read about in the "Rules of Civility" and seen practiced within the halls of Belvoir. A few months later, pressing his case in a letter, he assured Dinwiddie, "If I could have the honour of obtaining [the appointment] I should take the greatest pleasure in punctually obeying from time to time, your Honours commands; and by a strict observance of my Duty render myself worthy of the trust reposed in Me."[17]

Of course he had no military or executive experience. He was still a minor, the ward of his mother. All he had to recommend him was his gentry status, his Fairfax connection, and his imposing person. Those assets proved sufficient. Anyone could see that he would look splendid in uniform. He clearly knew how to deal with his superiors. In November 1752, the Council followed the governor's recommendation and named him adjutant of militia for the Southern District, one of the four posts into which his brother's office had been divided. Before long he transferred to the command of his own Northern Neck district. The commission came with the rank of major and a yearly salary of £100, no trifling sum. He quickly spent a third of it on a dress uniform ordered from London, the "rich crimson" coat glorious with gold braid and forty-eight gold-gilt buttons.[18]

In Dinwiddie, Washington had gained a new patron. But he soon lost his greatest patron and his best friend. Lawrence Washington returned from the islands and died at Mount Vernon in July 1752. Survivors included his wife, an infant daughter, and his sorrowing younger brother. The widow remarried. The little girl died. George Washington cleared out the tomb dug into the bluff above the river at Mount Vernon and laid his brother's coffin on the earthen floor.

3

War for North America

In THE SPRING OF 1754, far off in the green gloom of the western forests, Lieutenant Colonel George Washington of the Virginia Regiment fired the first shots of one of history's great wars, a world war that decided the future of a continent and set the stage for the American Revolution.

War had been a long time coming. As some Virginians patented lands in the Northern Neck and as the surveyor of Culpeper County laid out their new tracts, visions of far greater wealth beckoned in the West, beyond the mountains that hemmed in Lord Fairfax's Shenandoah Valley. A band of influential Anglo-Virginians had secured King George II's grant to a vast stretch of the Ohio Valley. Virginia partners in the Ohio Company included William Fairfax and Governor Dinwiddie himself. Washington's own lamented brother had been the president of the Ohio Company. The partners stood to gain 500,000 acres, nearly eight hundred square miles.

London had not placed Britain's hopes in the hands of a band of mere self-interested speculators. These were the colony's leaders—of the twenty-five Virginia partners, twenty served in the House of Burgesses, and half of those on the Governor's Council. Patriotism and ancestral hatred for the French papists, as well as hope of profit, had turned their eyes on the Ohio. While they certainly intended to make fortunes, the partners also advanced their country's imperial ambitions. British diplomacy was best served by working through private companies: the ink was scarcely dry on the 1748 peace treaty that had closed the latest installment in the centuries-long war that would finally end at Waterloo in 1815. The charter required that, to win its empire, the Ohio Company must build a fort and settle one hundred families on the land before seven years had passed. The Company had not only to beat the time limit but also to confront an array of rivals—Indians of many tribes, French Canadians, Pennsylvanians, even competing Virginia land syndicates.

The land itself was a formidable adversary. In the Mohawk tongue Ohio meant the beautiful river. That beauty mingled with danger and mystery. The Ohio country lay beyond the most distant outposts of English settlement, across the parallel rows of the Allegheny Mountains that ranged west past the horizon, one blue ridge after another. Some English maps labeled them the Endless Mountains. Everywhere the land flaunted a profligate abundance. Shaggy bison grazed the long meadows burned clear by Indian hunters, but deer, elk, panthers, wolves, and bear were all more common. Sky-darkening flocks of passenger pigeons passed over the landscape like weather systems. Yellow-green Carolina parakeets glittered in stands of trees so massive that the seedlings might have sprouted at the beginning of the world.

White men called the country wilderness and knew that to go there was to risk everything. Men simply vanished, without witness or grave. Of all the dangers it had pleased God to place upon the land, nothing surpassed the terror that the Indians inspired. For generations Indians had used the Ohio more as a hunting ground than an area of permanent settlement, but by the early eighteenth century, the West had become a haven for tribes fleeing the burgeoning English presence east of the Appalachians. These were true American pioneers—Delaware and Shawnee driven from western Pennsylvania, Iroquois migrating from New York. All sought new homes in the Ohio. Most of all they sought the independence that would allow them to preserve their traditional way of life. Throughout the bloody decade of 1750s, as France and Britain continued their great war for empire, the native Americans were contending for nothing less than survival as a people. Theirs was a bitter legacy of defeat and dispossession. A soul-crushing dread of cultural extinction hung over their camps. The Ohioans regarded white intruders with suspicion so intense that the threat of violence crackled around every encounter like an electrical current.

Into this cauldron plunged the Ohio Company. In 1750, a year after the royal charter reached Virginia, the company dispatched Christopher Gist, a Maryland surveyor and Indian trader, on the first of his two explorations of the Ohio

Valley. Gist was a shrewd, tough frontiersman who could boast as much western experience as any English colonial. After a hard winter in the forests, Gist returned to Williamsburg with his maps and journals. He was lucky to return at all. The people he traveled among instinctively feared new usurpations by English-speaking expansionists. Soon, Gist wrote, the Indians "began to suspect me, and said, that I was come to settle the Indian's Lands and they knew I should never go Home again safe." Gist hardly needed to add, "I found this Descourse was to be of ill Consequence to me."[1] He quickly took refuge behind a fictitious diplomatic mission and decided to shun the Indian villages and sleep in the woods thereafter.

At the time of Gist's explorations, however, most of the Ohio Indians regarded an invasion from Canada as the more alarming threat to their autonomy. The French had begun to move aggressively into the region, extending their trading posts and trying to strengthen alliances with bribes, threats, and punishing raids. They had not hesitated to make bold claims of French sovereignty in the hearing of outraged tribesmen. These forays shocked the native Americans. Disturbed as well were officials in Philadelphia, Williamsburg, and London. But as long as Britain hoped to maintain the armed truce with France, the Anglo-Americans would bide their time. The Indians could not take up the hatchet without English backing. When France began to build forts on the waters of La Belle Rivière, however, the challenge could no longer be ignored.

Though the French had seized the initiative, their prospects in a North American conflict were poor. Sixty thousand French Canadians were hugely outnumbered by 1.3 million British colonials. (The population of British America was growing faster than any other in the world, doubling itself, Benjamin Franklin calculated, every twenty-five years.) Everyone knew that the surest path to an Indian alliance was paved with trade goods—guns and ammunition, rum, steel knives and iron kettles, glass beads and wool blankets. The British produced and delivered trade goods France could never hope to match in quality, quantity, or price. Many of the tribes, however, were deeply attached to the French.

Everyone knew that only force of arms could bestow clear title to the American interior. In the spring of 1753, the new governor general of Canada, Ange de Menneville, Marquise Duquesne, sent out a force of two thousand commanded by Captain Paul Marin de la Malgue. Captain Marin's command amounted to a few infantry regiments. In Europe, this would have been a trifling force. But as it moved south into the upper Ohio Valley, Marin's expedition constituted a mighty host—certainly the strongest army ever seen in the interior up to that time.[2]

The British colonies did not command sufficient power to turn back a French invasion. Pennsylvania's pacifist Quaker government had always been reluctant to practice war. Most Virginians also opposed an expensive war in a western wilderness that seemed more remote than Europe. The House of Burgesses had always resisted new taxes imposed by the governor. They suspected that the war scare had been conjured up to protect the investments of certain rich men in high positions. Dinwiddie was disgusted with his elected assembly. He apprehended that the Virginians were infected with that darkest of villainies. "The people here," the governor wrote, "are too much bent on a republican spirit."³ British officials in America would continue to voice such complaints until the time came when there were no more British officials in America.

The governor's critics may have been too harsh. Robert Dinwiddie's call to arms probably stemmed more from his vision of Britain's imperial destiny than from fear for his stake in the Ohio Company. As the governor put it, "British dominions on this continent . . . if properly protected" would one day form the "western and best empire in the world."⁴ When news came that a French army was building forts, he appealed to his superiors in London: France had insolently invaded British soil.

George II's royal command reached Williamsburg in October 1753. Dinwiddie was to order all "Europeans not our subjects . . . peaceably to depart" the Ohio country. Should they refuse, the Virginians must "drive them off by Force of Arms."⁵ To reach the French, however, the king's ultimatum had to be carried in the dead of winter through hundreds of miles of hostile country. Still, one Virginian saw his great opportunity approaching in this long-awaited collision of empires on the River Ohio. Freeman guessed that it was Major Washington's great patron, Colonel William Fairfax of Belvoir, a man who sat on the Governor's Council, who told him of the need for a diplomatic courier. He rode straight to Williamsburg and volunteered. Dinwiddie accepted.

Washington would later agree that "it was deemed by

some an extraordinary circumstance that so young and in-experienced a person should have been employed on a ne-gotiation with which subjects of the greatest importance were involved."[6] But Dinwiddie's choice was not so strange. No crude pioneer or Indian trader would do to carry the king's message to the French commandant. George Wash-ington was a gentleman—perhaps no Virginian of equal social standing had as much personal knowledge of the frontier. He was one of the colony's ranking militia officers. His late brother had been president of the Ohio Company.

Some have observed that Washington did not even speak French, and was completely unversed in the intrica-cies of native American diplomacy. The importance of those deficiencies has been overstated. No great diplomatic skills were needed: French response to the British ultimatum was a foregone conclusion. By sending Marin's army south, France had already demonstrated a willingness to fight for the Ohio. The real purpose of delivering Dinwiddie's letter was to clear the way for a vigorous Anglo-American prosecu-tion of a war that was already inevitable. Dinwiddie needed news of French defiance to silence his critics in Virginia, galvanize leaders of the other colonies, and assure the home government's support. The courier would also have a chance to bring back valuable intelligence on enemy strength and intentions. In all these respects, Washington succeeded.

Major Washington was less than successful in achiev-ing another of the governor's objectives—securing the al-legiance of the Ohio Indians. But again, by 1753, it would have required a reversal of British policy, not a more ca-pable negotiator, to satisfy the region's inhabitants. The

Indians wanted to keep their country free of all Europeans except a few traders. They hoped to use the power that
George Washington represented to drive the French back to
Canada, not to establish British hegemony. To play one European power against the other had been the cornerstone of
native American strategy for generations. "To preserve the
Balance between us & the French," one British official had
written, "is the great Ruling Principle of Modern Indian
Politics."[7] Governor Dinwiddie's campaign to fill the Ohio
country with Virginia settlers was not likely to win any
Indian allies, and it demeans the chiefs' sophistication to
suggest that a cleverer man than Washington could have
tricked them into acting against their own interests.

But if the mission's objective was to deliver the ultimatum and live long enough to bring a French response
back to Williamsburg, Major Washington was well qualified. He certainly looked as though he might survive the
dangers that lay ahead. The king's messenger faced a nine
hundred–mile winter journey through country that most
Virginians regarded as a howling wilderness. As he would
soon demonstrate, this young man hardly knew fear. When
Dinwiddie first met Washington, he had surely detected
the iron in his backbone, just as he must have sensed his
intelligence and ambition. Forty years later, Gilbert Stuart
would look into Washington's eyes and capture their pierc-
ing challenge on canvas. Stuart was then convinced that
had George Washington "been born in the forests he would
have been the fiercest man among the savage tribes."[8] The
painter must have been right. A considerable measure of
ferocity would be required for the ordeal that awaited the

emissary as he hurriedly left Williamsburg, heading north by northwest into the teeth of the approaching winter.

Thirty years later George Washington described the two-month journey in a single understated sentence: "At a most inclement Season, [I] travelled over the Apalacheon Mountains, and passed 200 miles thro an uninhabited Country (except by a few tribes of Indians settled on the Banks of the Ohio) to Presque Isle within 15 miles of Lake Erie in the depth of winter while the face of the Earth was covered with snow and the waters covered with Ice; the whole distance from Wmsburg the then seat of government at least 500 miles."[9]

He was to seek out the commandant of French forces on the Ohio, deliver Dinwiddie's letter, wait for a reply, and return to Williamsburg "with all convenient & possible Dispatch."[10] The letter began, "The Lands upon the River Ohio . . . are so notoriously known to be the Property of the Crown of Great Britain, that it is a Matter of equal Concern & Surprize to me, to hear that a Body of French Forces are erecting Fortresses."[11]

Washington hired a few woodsmen and enlisted Christopher Gist as guide. Old enough to be his commander's father, Gist's western experience greatly exceeded that of the officer who had never crossed the Endless Mountains. By the middle of November 1753, the seven men had left behind the last Virginia settlements. Hard rains, swollen creeks, and a "vast Quantity of snow" slowed their march. Deep snow already mantled the mountains ahead as the Ohio country fell into the grip of the coldest winter in memory.[12]

By the end of the month, the travelers had reached their first objective—the Forks of the Ohio. Here the Monongahela plunged into the Allegheny and their mingled waters flowed on together as the Ohio. Washington put his surveying skills to use as he explored the site that he quickly recognized as the geographical linchpin of the coming war. Dinwiddie had planned to build a fort two miles downstream. But Washington saw that a fort placed at the confluence would dominate both rivers, and with them, the upper Ohio Valley. For the next five years, Washington would be caught up in Britain's struggle to control the Forks of the Ohio. The shifting destiny of North America can be traced through the successive names given the forts and settlements built there. Virginia's first fort, never finished, was called Fort Prince George in honor of the eighteen-year-old royal heir who would soon be crowned King George III. For the next five years it was Fort Duquesne, the French stronghold that cast its grim shadow far east into Virginia and Pennsylvania. On the ashes of Duquesne, the redcoats raised Fort Pitt. Outside the fort's walls rose "Pittsboro," a frontier town in the English colony of Pennsylvania, and finally smoky Pittsburgh, a city in the United States of America.

They traveled on to Logstown, an Indian settlement a few days beyond the Forks. The orders were to seek out the Iroquois chief the English called the Half King. The man's name was Tanaghrisson. An experienced warrior-diplomat in his mid-fifties when he first encountered the green Virginia major, he had emerged as the region's most important leader, claiming to speak on behalf of many tribes.[13] Tanaghrisson was an English ally, known on occasion to fly British colors from his canoe. He hated the French. He said that Frenchmen had boiled and eaten his father.

Half King was a title that the English had made up. They believed that the Grand Council of the Iroquois Six Nations in New York controlled the Ohio Indians and that the Council had appointed Tanaghrisson to rule over them. But the true situation was more subtle than this simpleminded white man's formulation. Seneca though Tanaghrisson was, his loyalties as well as the source of his power were rooted in the soil he defended. What united the Ohio Indians was not Iroquois dominance but a shared determination to save their land. Much of the influence Tanaghrisson did have with the other Indians sprang from the hope that he might be able to use his alliance with the Virginians to keep the Ohio country free.[14]

The chief had alarming news for his new friend. The French army had left Montreal in February 1753 with orders to build a chain of forts south from Lake Erie to the Ohio-Mississippi confluence. By June, the French had finished Fort Presque Isle on the southern shore of Lake Erie. In July, Captain Marin's soldiers raised Fort Le Boeuf, fifteen miles below the lake. There Tanaghrisson, leading a delegation of Iroquois, Delaware, and Shawnee chiefs, confronted the French officer. Washington recorded Tanaghrisson's account of the confrontation that had taken place three months earlier. And so the angry words of the Indian chief and the French captain came to be preserved for history in the pages of that celebrated pamphlet *The Journal of Major George Washington*.

Tanaghrisson had rebuked the French. "NOW FATHERS, it is you that is the Disturber of the Land, by coming & building your Towns. . . . FATHERS Both you & the English are White. We live in a Country between, therefore the Land does not belong to either one or the other; but the GREAT BEING above allow'd it to be a Place of residence for us; so Fathers, I desire you to withdraw, as I have done our Brothers the English, for I will keep you at Arm's length. I lay this down as a Tryal for both, to see which will have the greatest regard to it."

Captain Marin had replied contemptuously. "I am not afraid of Flies or Musquito's; for Indians are such as those; I tell you down the River will I go according to my Command: if the River was ever so block'd up, I have Forces sufficient to burst it open, & tread under my Feet all that stand in Opposition together with their Alliances; for my Force is as the Sand upon the Sea Shoar."[15] Marin had spoken from strength. Tanaghrisson could only throttle his rage. Now the Seneca hoped that this tall Virginian might bring the power the Indians needed to fight back the invaders.

Of course Tanaghrisson was not only recounting his meeting with the French but also giving a pointed warning to Washington and the government he represented. That message—that the Ohio, the "Country between," belonged to the Indians—was utterly incompatible with the purposes that had propelled Washington into the wilderness in the first place. Soon Tanaghrisson and three other chiefs called on Washington in the privacy of his tent. They asked to know "what Business we were going to the

French about?"[16] He could hardly tell them he was carrying a letter that declared that all the Ohio was British territory. For days before the question came, Washington had been struggling to concoct an answer, apparently without much success. "This was a Question I all along expected, & had provided as satisfactory Answers as I cou'd, which allay'd their Curiosity a little."[17] The halfhearted support the Indians accorded him thereafter suggests that his answers were less than satisfactory. The major had asked for a strong party of warriors to convey him the rest of the way to the French commandant. But the Indians refused to provide the armed escort—only Tanaghrisson, a hunter, and two other old chiefs would go along.

The seventy-mile march from Logstown to the nearest French post consumed four more days of deep cold. The officers at Venango received Washington cordially but told him they had no authority to treat with an ambassador. They sent him on to their superior at Fort La Boeuf, though not before drunkenly favoring him with the intelligence that "it was their absolute Design to take Possession of the Ohio, & by G— they would do it."[18] The party continued on in "excessive rains, Snows, & bad weather, through many Mires & Swamps" before Washington finally faced Captain Jacques Le Gardeur, sieur de Saint-Pierre, commandant of French forces on the Ohio.[19] If the major elected to observe European protocol, it would have been a chilly task to strip off his knee-length fur matchcoat and buckskins to change into a dress uniform. But that done, and with Governor Dinwiddie's letter retrieved from its waterproof pouch, Major Washington could present himself as an emissary of His Britannic Majesty to His Most Christian Majesty as he entered the stockade of fresh-cut timber.

He was greeted with ceremony befitting his ambassadorial status. Captain Saint-Pierre was a veteran soldier. He impressed Washington, who wrote that the fifty-two-year-old captain was an "elderly Gentleman, & has much the Air of a Soldier."[20] When the French officers retired to translate Dinwiddie's letter, Washington boldly paced off the dimensions of their fort and counted its men and cannon. Presently Captain Saint-Pierre gave the major a letter for Governor Dinwiddie. It was sealed, but the courier knew the import. When his words were translated in Williamsburg a month later, Captain Saint-Pierre mildly advised Dinwiddie "as to the summons you send me to retire, I do not think myself obliged to obey it." Less mildly, the Frenchman continued, his orders were to fight if he had to, "and I entreat you, Sir, not to doubt one moment, but that I am determined to conform myself to them with all the exactness and resolution which can be expected from the best of officers."[21]

News of French defiance needed to reach Williamsburg as soon as possible. The journey home was a nightmarish ordeal. Leaving Fort La Boeuf, the party hoped to make better time going downriver by canoe. But though the march upriver had taken four days, floating downstream used up a week, so difficult was the passage through rapids, and across ice and shoals. Wet, frozen, and exhausted, the men reached Venango three days before Christmas. Here they reclaimed their horses and pushed on the next day. Soon the horses gave out. The land was locked in the hardest of winters—streams were frozen solid and the animals could find neither water nor forage. Gist, who had spent two previous winters in the Ohio, described the cold as unbearable. Washington decided that he and Gist would press ahead alone, on foot. When Gist argued that his commander was too inexperienced to make such a rigorous trek, Washington overruled him. "I took my necessary Papers, pull'd off my Cloths; tied My Self up in a Match Coat; & with my Pack at my back, with my Papers and Provisions in it, & a Gun, set out with Mr. Gist."[22]

They covered eighteen miles the first day. When night came, Gist wrote, "the Major was much fatigued." They rested a few hours and set out again at two in the morning. The next day "the Major's feet grew very sore, and he very weary."[23] But there was no rest for the weary that day and night, or all the day that followed. They were now traveling in the company of a strange Indian who had promised to show them the shortest route to the Allegheny. But the warrior apparently had another purpose. Washington recorded in his *Journal* that the man "fired at Mr. Gist or me, not 15 Steps, but fortunately missed."[24]

Gist's account is more thorough, but does nothing to dispel the mystery that surrounds the incident. Gist had "mistrusted" the Indian, and soon, he wrote, Major Washington "mistrusted him as much as I. . . . The Major saw him point his gun toward us and fire. Said the Major, 'Are you shot?' 'No,' said I. Upon which the Indian ran forward to a big standing white oak, and to loading his gun; but we were soon with him. I would have killed him; but the Major would not suffer me to kill him." They let the man go

and then marched all night to put a safe distance between
the would-be assassin and themselves. They kept going
until dark the following day. Tired and footsore, Washington had marched without rest for more than thirty-six
hours through deep snow and subfreezing temperatures.
Gist must have been impressed.

A discouraging sight greeted them on the banks of
the Allegheny. The cold weather had given hope that they
would find the quarter-mile river bridged by an ice sheet
strong enough to cross. Instead they found a chaos of tur-
bulent water pushing grinding slabs. Working "with but
one poor Hatchet," the pair spent an entire day building
a raft to carry them across. Darkness was falling by the
time they shoved their frail vessel into the flood. Disaster quickly overtook them. "We were jammed in the Ice
in such a Manner," Washington wrote, "that we expected
every Moment our Raft wou'd sink & we Perish; I put out
my setting Pole, to try to stop the Raft, that the Ice might
pass by, when the rapidity of the Stream threw it with so
much Violence against the Pole, that it Jirk'd me into 10
Feet Water, but fortunately I saved my Self by catching
hold of one of the Raft Logs."[25] When the current carried
them past an island, the two men floundered ashore. They
were now soaked and freezing, shipwrecked in the middle
of the river. Morning revealed that Gist's fingers and toes
were frostbitten. But, Gist wrote, "the cold did us some
service, for in the morning it was frozen hard enough for
us to pass over on the ice."[26]

Major Washington strode into the Governor's Palace
in Williamsburg on January 16, 1754, eleven weeks after

his departure. Dinwiddie had kept a fast packet riding at anchor on the York River, ready to carry dispatches to London. The governor wanted a written report at once. Washington probably got little rest during the day and night he spent composing the seven thousand–word account of his adventure. Governor Dinwiddie rushed it into print as *The Journal of Major George Washington, Sent . . . to the Commandant of the French Forces on the Ohio.*[27] Reprinted in London and throughout the colonies, the little book soon made Washington's name known on both sides of the Atlantic—a most uncommon distinction for any American. Like Franklin before him, and Jefferson and Hamilton after him, Washington first attracted the notice of the world through his writing.

If style is character, the sturdy prose of Washington's *Journal* revealed its author as a brave and intelligent officer driven by an unwavering determination to prevail. When the *Gentlemen's Magazine* of London published the narrative, the editors identified him as a veteran soldier, hardly suspecting the green age of the youth who had penetrated the wilderness. The perilous mission had yielded shining success. Major Washington was promoted lieutenant colonel, second in command of the Virginia Regiment. He had just turned twenty-two.

But he had failed to win over the Indians. Historian David L. Preston has revealed that the natives complained that "Col Washington whom we had convoyed to the French Fort, left us there, came through the Woods, and never thought it worth his while to come to Logs Town, or near us and give us any Account of the Speeches that passed between him and the French at the Fort which he promised to do." Moreover, the Half King "complained very much of the behavior of Colonel Washington to him . . . saying he took upon him to command the Indians as his slaves."[28] The chief's remark may well have been an accurate reflection of Washington's instinctive contempt for dark-skinned people he was accustomed to dominating. No wonder the tribesmen soon deserted him.

Washington had counted hundreds of canoes ranged along the river bank outside the walls of Fort La Boeuf. When the spring breakup sent rotten ice drifting downstream, those canoes would follow, carrying French soldiers to the Forks of the Ohio. Virginia must outrace the enemy. Before the snows had melted from the mountainsides, the new lieutenant colonel was headed west with a detachment of 159 volunteers and orders to occupy the Forks. If carrying Britain's ultimatum had won him a reputation, this chance to exercise an independent military command was more dazzling still. Washington was leading an expedition sure to attract the notice of the entire Atlantic world. He had orders to fight if the French opposed him.

By April 1754, "sorrowful News" had arrested Washington's westward progress—he learned that a French army had already occupied the vital confluence. They were busy building Fort Duquesne, using timber cut by the Ohio Company work party they had driven off. Washington's militiamen could hardly hope to dislodge a thousand soldiers. Still, he decided to push on toward the Forks. Then came a letter dictated to an interpreter by his friend Tanaghrisson. Enraged by the French advance, the chief pleaded for help from Virginia and Pennsylvania. The Half King promised many warriors to fight alongside the English. Washington replied with his own assurances that a great army was coming from Virginia. Neither man would be able to deliver on his promise.

Washington had made his headquarters at Great Meadows, about forty miles south of Fort Duquesne. Here he waited for the reinforcements promised by Virginia, Maryland, New York, and the Carolinas, and by his Indian allies. What came instead was another warning from Tanaghrisson. His scouts had discovered a company of French soldiers hidden in the woods not far from Washington's camp. The enemy must be planning an ambush.

Near midnight, Washington led forty men into the black forest to rendezvous with the Indians and ambush the ambushers. All night long they stumbled through the dark under a hard rain, losing their way, falling over one another, groping on their hands and knees for a path. Washington had hoped for a dawn attack, but by the time he could deploy his men and Tanaghrisson's warriors, the French were moving around their camp set against the face of a cliff. Still, the attackers managed to take positions on the surrounding high ground before a sentry cried out and the muskets began to fire. A newly discovered account reveals that it was Washington himself who first discharged his musket, perhaps giving him literal credit for firing the first shot of the Seven Years' War.[29]

The fifteen-minute battle was already over when death claimed the day's most important victim. Tanaghrisson had done all he could to bring about open warfare be-

tween his English allies and his French enemies. Perhaps
it is the Half-King who deserves the real credit for starting
the Seven Years' War. The warrior was not fighting with
a firearm. He wielded a tomahawk, which he now used
to split the skull the French commander, Joseph Coulon
de Villiers, sieur de Jumonville. Then he reached into the
shattered cranium, scooped out the dead man's brains,
and washed his hands in them. A militiaman's account
of the fight, presented for the first time in historian Fred
Anderson's *Crucible of War*, tells how Tanaghrisson approached the hapless officer and mockingly addressed him
in French—"Tu n'es pas encore mort, mon père" (You are
not dead yet, my father)—before bringing down his tomahawk.[30] Tanaghrisson had been enraged by a report that
the French soldiers meant to murder his family. The Indians finished off the wounded and moved to kill the prisoners. Washington stopped the slaughter and conducted
twenty terrified captives back to Great Meadows. They left
thirteen scalped corpses to rot. Jumonville's own brother
saw the wreckage lying there two months later. An Indian
had mounted one of the heads on a stake, where its eyeless
gaze looked out across the indifferent forest.

One French soldier had escaped the trap, glad enough
to get away without his boots. He staggered into Fort
Duquesne a few days later, his bare feet in tatters, to tell
the French command of the horror in the gloomy hollow.
News of the little fight soon electrified Europe. From opposite sides of the Channel, observers as eminent as Voltaire
and Horace Walpole would marvel that a few shots fired by
an obscure youth in the backwoods of America had struck a

spark that "set the world on fire." That fire was to consume
hundreds of thousands of lives in battles fought around the
globe. Although war had already been inevitable, and although it was not formally declared until 1756, the great
struggle commenced at the moment Washington attacked
the luckless Frenchmen. The Seven Years' War—known
as the French and Indian War in America—would involve
not only Britain and France and their colonies but also
Austria, Russia, Spain, Portugal, and Prussia and most of
the German states.

Washington's letter to his brother Jack, in which he
bragged that "I heard Bulletts whistle and believe me there
was something charming in the sound," was published in
the London press.[31] On reading it, the veteran soldier King
George II sniffed, "He would not say so, if he had been
used to hear many."[32] It would not be the last time that
George Washington would attract the attention of a British monarch. But the fight was the last victory he would
enjoy for some time to come.

Dinwiddie presently commissioned George Washington a full colonel commanding the Virginia Regiment.
He thanked the governor effusively, though he did harbor doubts about his inexperience. And all of the power
at the newly minted colonel's command could not avert
French vengeance. Nor did his little victory seem to be as
quite as splendid as he might have hoped. The captured
Frenchmen insisted that theirs had been a peaceful diplomatic mission—the mirror image of Washington's six
months earlier—to deliver an ultimatum demanding British withdrawal from territory claimed by France. Papers

taken from Jumonville's body seemed to confirm the story. Though he continued to maintain that the French officer had been a skulking spy, Washington stood accused of murdering an ambassador.

Only a few of the promised reinforcements trickled into Washington's headquarters. Ordinary Virginians showed little enthusiasm for dying in a rich man's war in the wilderness. The Burgesses were still unwilling to vote adequate funds. Moving supplies over the mountains was as difficult as ever. Washington's men had laid the track that opened the Ohio Valley to wheeled vehicles for the first time in history, but it was a mighty poor road. Colonel Washington's camp at Great Meadows, where he was building the little stockade he called Fort Necessity, lacked food, tools, gunpowder, artillery, uniforms, and the rum and trade goods he needed to keep his Indian allies happy.

Worse yet, Washington began to fear that he no longer had Indian allies. Tanaghrisson had brought in only a dozen warriors, who seemed more interested in securing English rations than French scalps. Hoping to rally the hundreds of fighters he must have to defend Fort Necessity, Washington summoned Iroquois, Delaware, and Shawnee chiefs to a grand council. Lying to the Indians was official policy, and, in the Indians' own country, often a matter of self-preservation. George Washington was perfectly capable of the practice. He addressed the assembled chiefs through an interpreter. The French, Washington did not blush to tell them, "drove you off from your Lands, declaring you had no Right on the Ohio. The English, your real Friends . . . sent an Army to Maintain your Rights; to Put you in Possession of your Lands. . . . It is for the Safety of your Wives and Children that we fight; and this is the only Motive of our Conduct."[33] Such promises had become formulaic—Washington's speech convinced no one. Many of the Delaware and Shawnees went over to the French, while the Iroquois declared their neutrality. Even Tanaghrisson abandoned Washington, convinced that the Virginians were about to be beaten by the advancing enemy. The Ohio Indians now understood that both sides meant to take their land—they wanted to stay clear of the war or at least fight on the winning side.

The French appeared the likely winners. Washington had received all of the men Virginia could scrape up, just 181 untrained militiamen. One hundred South Carolina troops had also joined his force. More than a third of the soldiers were too sick for duty.[34] The rest were worn out and chronically hungry. Others had simply vanished. They reckoned the charge of desertion and the risks of a lonely trek through the woods preferable to the chance of death or capture. Nevertheless, Washington began an ill-considered advance from Fort Necessity toward the Forks of the Ohio. He scurried back to Fort Necessity when scouts reported that the French were marching against Great Meadows with a thousand men. The last of Washington's Indians slipped away. A prudent officer might have refused battle under such disadvantages. Perhaps the soldiers' exhaustion prevented a timely retreat from Fort Necessity; perhaps it was their commander's pride.

When the attack came, on July 3, 1754, Washington got his introduction to the kind of military disaster that would become all too familiar to him. Instead of assaulting across open ground as Washington had expected, the enemy prudently took cover on the heights around the badly sited fort. They began to pour a deadly fire into the stockade. Men dropped all around the conspicuous commander, who, though he exposed himself recklessly, was again untouched. A few hours into the battle, the heavens opened and a terrific rain came down. It soon became apparent that, in addition to its other shortcomings, the fort was located in the bottom of the meadow's drainage basin. The trenches quickly flooded. Gunpowder was soaked.

After his bluster about the bullets' charming song, Washington never spoke again of his impressions of combat. He could not have been charmed by what he heard at Fort Necessity. There he heard not only the renewed whistle of bullets but also the sound of projectiles thudding into flesh, the cries of hurt and dying men, firelocks snapping uselessly on guns loaded with sodden powder, voices breathless with panic, and the chilling whoops of the Indians. Worst of all must have been hearing the enemy calling on the Virginians to surrender, for Washington had no choice but to give up. More than one hundred of the men—a full third of his command—were dead or wounded. The demoralized survivors had gotten into the rum stores—soon many soldiers were falling-down drunk. Surrender to the French might be the only way to save the garrison from massacre by Indian fighters. The shooting stopped and negotiations continued through the rainy night.

The Virginians surrendered on July 4, 1754. The

French commander offered surprisingly generous terms— Captain Louis Coulon de Villiers was, after all, brother of the late Lieutenant Jumonville, the unfortunate officer whose brains Tanaghrisson had scattered. He would allow the defeated garrison to leave the fort with all the honors of war, marching away with their arms and their colors flying to return to Virginia unmolested. Colonel Washington had only to sign articles of capitulation written in French and translated for him by an aide working in the rain by the light of a single faltering candle.

Despite the favorable terms, Washington left Fort Necessity profoundly dejected. He became more unhappy still when someone favored him with an accurate translation of the surrender articles. He had signed a paper admitting that he had "assassinated" Jumonville, a diplomatic envoy. He insisted that his own interpreter had rendered the word as "killed." However blame might be assigned, Colonel Washington had handed the French a splendid propaganda victory. They hastened to make the most of it. Governor Duquesne circulated a translation of Washington's captured expedition journal with a scathing commentary. The journal was soon published in Paris as an exhibition of English perfidy. "You will see that he is the most impertinent of all men," wrote the Marquis Duquesne; "he lies very much to justify the assassination of sieur de Jumonville, which he had the stupidity to confess in his capitulation!" Duquesne cheerfully concluded that victory over such incompetents was assured.[35]

No soldier fears the condemnation of his foes, but some closer to home were saying much the same thing.

A London writer called the surrender paper "the most infamous a British subject ever put his hand to."[36] Sir William Johnson, the New York Indian agent, thought that Washington had been "very wrong," rushing headlong into disaster because he was "too ambitious of acquiring all the honor or as much as he could before the rest [of the troops] joined him."[37] Maryland Governor Horatio Sharpe, the newly appointed commander of the war effort in the Ohio, condemned the "unmilitary conduct of Colonel Washington" and called Fort Necessity a "useless little entrenchment between two eminences."[38] A gentleman, of course, should know French, and Washington suffered an additional humiliation when the widely publicized controversy revealed his ignorance of the language of civility.

The frontier warrior who had promised to chase the French all the way back to "damned Montreal" had been driven out of the Ohio himself.[39] If Colonel Washington had not exceeded his orders in ambushing Jumonville, he had certainly demonstrated considerable incompetence. Dinwiddie's instructions had been to fight only if provoked. War may have been inevitable, but it would have been wise to delay its outbreak until a time when Virginia—and Britain—were better prepared. Washington had estranged the Indians who had once favored the English, and the ambassador's death allowed France to label Britain the aggressor. Washington was lucky to survive his decision to make a stand at Fort Necessity. Many of his soldiers were less fortunate. The success of his mission to the French commandant had been eclipsed by a hollow victory followed by a humbling defeat. Although he was never anything but a hero to his fellow Virginians, in Europe Washington was mocked as a bumbling provincial or denounced as an un-principled assassin.[40]

Others could share in the blame. Virginia, Britain's biggest and richest colony, population 300,000, had sent fewer than 350 untrained and ill-equipped militiamen to secure the most strategic point on its western frontier. And it must be remembered that Washington himself had known he was not ready for top command. Six months before his defeat, soliciting a rank "among the chief officers of this expedition," he had said that "the command of the whole forces is what I neither look for, expect, nor desire, for I must be impartial enough to confess, it is a charge too great for my youth and inexperience. . . . I flatter myself that under a skillful commander, or man of sense . . . I shall be able to conduct my steps without censure."[41] But Virginia had no skillful commanders to appoint. Circumstances had thrust the responsibility on Washington. Duty and ambition alike compelled him to accept.

Washington had, in his own words, been "soundly beaten." It must have been with some trepidation that he entered the Governor's Palace again. Dinwiddie had indeed cooled on his colonel, and lack of military success was only one reason. He believed that Washington had returned his patronage with ingratitude. It was true that his attitude toward his superior often deviated from that respectful deference prescribed by the "Rules of Civility." Many of his letters from the field were long, shrill litanies of complaint. He campaigned against the governor with his supporters in the House of Burgesses.

Washington in his twenties was still a man on the make, not a man who had made the pursuit of honorable fame the polestar of his life. During his five years' service in the French and Indian War, Washington's remarkable powers often seemed to be employed most fervently in the cause of his own self-aggrandizement. He waged some of his sharpest battles against the British military establishment and the authorities in Williamsburg. He constantly complained about his rank and pay, lack of supplies and weapons, problems with the regulars and militia of other colonies, his worthless soldiers, and the ignorance, malice, and bad judgment of government officials—even those to whom he addressed his complaints. He threatened to resign half a dozen times.

In October 1754, three months after his defeat at Fort Necessity, Colonel Washington did resign. By then, however, he was no longer a colonel. Governor Dinwiddie had decided to break the Virginia Regiment into ten distinct companies, each commanded by a captain. Although Dinwiddie intended to have the officers commissioned in the regular military establishment, captain would be the highest rank that any Virginian would hold. Washington would have none of it. For military men, rank is intangible honor made solid reality. Washington took as a personal insult —a slur on his honor—George II's order that colonial militia officers, whatever their grade, ranked below British ensigns.[42] Washington resented the difference in pay, but he repeated that his overriding concern was honor—"the Rank of Officers which to me Sir is much Dearer than the Pay."[43]

The solution was obvious—the British must make

Colonel Washington a field officer in the British Army. That would never happen. Washington never understood that his hope for a colonelcy was so extravagant. He did not know that Governor Dinwiddie had appealed unsuccessfully for a colonel's commission for himself. If London was unwilling to make a colonel of the acting governor of Virginia, what chance was there that such a prize be bestowed on a twenty-two-year-old colonial? He certainly had no supporters at court. Earl Albemarle, Britain's ambassador to France and the absentee governor of Virginia, saw Fort Necessity as confirmation of American incompetence. "*Washington* & many *Such*," Albemarle wrote the prime minister, "may have courage & resolution, but they have no Knowledge or Experience in our Profession; consequently there can be no dependence on them! Officers, and good ones must be sent to discipline the militia and lead them on."[44] George Washington probably never suspected that his own mistakes had contributed to British reluctance to promote American officers.

Many have savored the irony of the British establishment denying the future victor of Yorktown a royal commission, and a good deal of ink has been spilled in fruitless speculations on how the course of history might have diverged had the offer been forthcoming. But the familiar story is only half true—a regular commission was in fact offered to Washington in 1754, and he angrily rejected it. The captaincy Dinwiddie proposed was simply not a rank elevated enough to match his expectations. He would settle for nothing less than appointment as a field officer. Throughout his life, Washington pursued lofty goals, and it is testament to his remarkable powers that he almost always succeeded. He failed, however, in his quest for a place in the British Army, and the failure always rankled.

The influence of powerful friends had started Washington on the road to honor, but it was his own abilities that had sped him so rapidly along that road. He had volunteered for the dangerous mission to the Ohio. No titled lord, no royal governor, no king's officer stood beside him as he rafted the icy Allegheny or when the bullets whizzed past his head. He had needed more than delegated authority to compel other men to face death in battle. Nor was it the interest of his patrons that had given him the strength to travel hundreds of miles through the freezing wastelands. His own indomitable will, seconded by his strength and intelligence, was the source of what Washington had achieved in 1753 and 1754. Yet the establishment denied him his reward. George Washington never forgave the British Empire for the deadly insult, and anger fueled his growing sense of identity as an American. As he would put it in 1757: "We cannot conceive that because we are Americans, we shou'd *therefore* be deprived of the Benefits common to British Subjects."[45]

Dinwiddie had been quick to snatch up Washington's resignation. So the survivor turned his back on the Governor's Palace and rode north to Mount Vernon, which he leased from his brother's widow at the end of 1754. He thought that he might as well try tobacco planting like his fathers before him. But something better soon turned up.

≫ 4 ≪

The Rise of George Washington

P EACE STILL OBTAINED between the two European rivals, and their diplomats struggled to preserve it. But news of Washington's defeat at Fort Necessity gave a potent boost to the influence of the war party in the English government. London sent to Virginia two regiments under Major General Edward Braddock, a Coldstream Guards officer of forty-five years' service. Braddock's regulars would succeed where Washington's militiamen had failed. The redcoats would march across the Allegheny Mountains, defeat the French, take Fort Duquesne, establish British hegemony in the Ohio Valley, and then invade Canada.

Washington had wangled himself a spot on General Braddock's personal staff. The bluff, red-faced Englishman was happy to add the Virginian—who had actually seen the disputed Forks and fought the enemy—to his military "family." The ex-colonel would serve as a volunteer aide to the general. He got no pay, but, he explained to his brother, a "little experience will be my chief reward." He was still eager "to push my fortune in a military way."[1]

Edward Braddock had been just fifteen when he joined the army as an ensign in 1710. He had passed from boyhood to a venerable age in the British Army. His ideas on military affairs were as fixed as the Rock of Gibraltar, where he had previously commanded the garrison. He had brought a strong army to Virginia. His faith in its invincibility was stronger still.

That confidence had apparently exempted Braddock from many of the concerns that might have preoccupied another tactician seeking to invest an enemy stronghold deep in hostile territory. While he entertained some fear of an attack on his column, he saw road building and logistics as his greatest problems. Indeed, hauling the mighty army over the mountains seemed to present a greater challenge than taking Fort Duquesne. The garrison of a few hundred regulars and Canadian militias would be helpless against the English thousands. And Braddock had little fear of the threat posed by native American enemies.

Impressed as they were by European soldiers, some Americans were not quite so confident. When Benjamin Franklin suggested that his army, strung out in a miles-long column on narrow forest tracks, might be vulnerable to Indian ambush, Braddock cut him off. "These Savages may indeed be a formidable Enemy to your raw American Militia," he said, "but, upon the King's regular & disciplin'd Troops, Sir, it is impossible they should make any impression."[2]

Braddock esteemed the brave ex-colonel of the Virginia Regiment, but, like most British officers, he had nothing but contempt for American soldiers. He believed the colonials were military incompetents, and most of them cowards to boot. "Very indifferent Men," he called them, "their Officers very little better."[3] Braddock's disdain for the enemy was deeper still. "Regularity and discipline" was indeed the refrain he kept repeating. The tactics that had often prevailed in Europe—massed lines of Britons blasting out volleys of musketry before unleashing their irresistible bayonet charge—would shatter any foe encountered in the wilds of America.

George Washington's charm had worked its usual magic on Edward Braddock. Like his other patrons, General Braddock was about forty years older than the Virginian, and like them he soon came to regard the younger man with fatherly affection. And although one of Braddock's officers described him as a "Virginia planter, simple and young," they also liked Washington, who must have been unable to conceal his admiration for them.[4] They lent the eager student military manuals and talked with him through idle hours that are an inescapable hazard of any campaign.

But it was the general himself who gave Washington the greatest encouragement. Braddock promised that he would help his volunteer aide get a suitable rank in the regular army. Two years later, appealing for a royal commission to Lord Loudoun, the next British commander in chief, Washington said that "had His Excellency General Braddock survived his unfortunate Defeat I should have met with preferment equal to my Wishes; I had his promise to that purpose, and I believe that Gentleman was too sincere and generous to make unmeaning offers."[5] Pre-

ferment equal to Washington's wishes was a field officer's
rank. Like Dinwiddie, General Braddock had the authority to make him a captain in the regulars on the spot. But
Washington had already turned down an offer of a captaincy. He would settle for nothing less than the higher
rank, and that, Washington indicated, was what the general had promised.

With more than a hundred miles to go, the army, pon-
derous with artillery and wagon train, was making only
two or three miles a day. From sunup to dark, six hundred
axmen felled trees while sappers leveled hills and bridged
streams. The Irish recruits suffered through the unaccus-
tomed heat of an American summer. The soldiers were
always hungry and thirsty and tired. Rattlesnakes, bad
water, and fevers killed some of them. Lurking Indians
dispatched a few more. The mutilated bodies of these hapless stragglers confirmed all the ghastly stories of savage
tortures that the Americans delighted in frightening the
redcoats with. By midsummer, they were slowly nearing
the Forks of the Ohio. So slow was progress that, on the
advice of Washington, the general divided his force. He
would push ahead with a fast column of 1,450 picked men,
taking the artillery while leaving most of the wagons.

They left George Washington behind too, prostrate in
his tent. He had been stricken with dysentery and a "severe fever and delirium." The doctors feared for his life.
General Braddock positively ordered him to stay in camp,
but gave his word that, if Washington recovered, he might
come forward to participate in the capture of the French
fort. The patient argued with his doctor every morning,

insisting that he was strong enough to follow the others. Three weeks passed before he was released. Too sick to mount a horse, Washington still insisted on being in at the kill. He had sworn that he would not miss the battle for £500. The sick man painfully jolted ahead in a wagon to rejoin the lead division and witness the capture of Fort Duquesne. Instead he witnessed Braddock's Defeat, one of the most shocking episodes in British military history.

The disaster came on July 9, 1755. The invalid had caught up with the fast division the night before. Washington, so pained by hemorrhoids that he tied pillows to the saddle before mounting his horse for the first time in a month, tried to keep up with the general. Only ten miles now separated them from Fort Duquesne, but one last danger remained before victory could crown the summer's long campaign. The British feared an ambush at the crossing of the Monongahela River. The steep, wooded banks above the confined riverbed favored hidden gunmen.

The French also understood that a strike against the redcoats as they waded the shallow river presented the last chance of inflicting enough punishment to deter the relentless advance. But the fort's little garrison of regulars and Canadian militia could not sally out against the massive enemy column without hundreds of warriors fighting alongside them, and the Indians rightly feared the odds. The day before the battle, the French had cajoled and promised, trying to rally the tribes for a dawn ambush at the Monongahela ford.

Commanding was a remarkable French officer. Captain Daniel Liénard Beaujeu's battle dress was emblematic of contrasting British and French approaches to native American culture. Beaujeu looked like one of his warriors —stripped to the waist, with war paint on his face, tomahawk and musket in his hands. (It hardly needs be said that English officers were as likely to appear at parade in ball gowns as to go into battle bare-chested, though that would change.) Still, nothing that Captain Beaujeu could do or say—not even leading the Indians in one of their own war songs—had persuaded them to risk battle. Beaujeu finally resolved to fight the English with just his 250 French soldiers. "What—would you let your father go alone?" he taunted his Indian friends; "I am certain to defeat them!"[6] This crazy bravado won over the warriors. Chanting war songs and brandishing weapons, more than six hundred native fighters resolved to go out with Beaujeu's troops the next day.

On the day of the battle, the British had approached the Monongahela ford with extreme caution—men deployed for battle, scouts ahead, flankers out, artillery unlimbered. But not an opposing shot was fired. The advance party crossed, and soon Braddock came over with the rest of the troops. The perilous river passage safely behind them, the soldiers hugged each other in joy and stepped out confidently toward Fort Duquesne. It was a glorious moment, a Virginia officer recalled. "A finer sight could not have been beheld—the shining barrels of the muskets, the excellent order of the men, the cleanliness of their appearance, the joy depicted on every face at being so near Fort Duquesne, the highest object of their wishes."[7]

The French and the Indians ran into the stolid grenadiers marching up the road. The redcoats fired first, quickly getting off three crashing volleys. Captain Beaujeu fell dead. The Canadian militia fled, crying "Every man for himself!" The grenadiers shouted "Long live the king!" as they surged forward behind their glittering bayonets. But British jubilation was fleeting. While French regulars made a stand in the road ahead, hundreds of Indians fanned out along the column's flanks, and began firing into the massed redcoats from the cover of trees and ravines. The entire column was trapped in a corridor of lethal firepower. British soldiers fell in bloody heaps under the withering fire poured in from three sides by an invisible foe. The deadly musketry continued for nearly three hours, destroying Braddock's army. Fully fifteen of the eighteen officers and half of the three hundred fifty soldiers in the vanguard were shot down in the first minutes.[8] The redcoats' guns were also doing deadly work—mostly against their own comrades. Washington guessed that two-thirds of the casualties "receiv'd their shot from our own cowardly dogs of Soldier's, who gathered themselves into a body contrary to orders 10 or 12 deep, would then level, Fire, & shoot down the Men before them."[9]

When the general and his aide rode forward, they found, as Washington later recalled, "the front was attacked and by the unusual Hallooing and whooping of the enemy, whom they could not see, were so disconcerted and confused as soon to fall into irretrievable disorder. The rear was forced forward to support them, but seeing no enemy, and themselves falling every moment from the fire, a general panic took place among the Troops from which no exertions of the Officers could recover them."[10] George Washington was reacquainted with the whistle of bullets. This time several projectiles ripped through his coat, one drilled his hat, and two horses were shot from under him. Luck like his was rare that day. Of 1,450 troops engaged, 977 were killed or wounded; 60 of the 80 regular officers were hit. Except for Washington, all of Braddock's staff officers were cut down. The Americans fought more skillfully than the redcoats, but fared no better. It was with grim pride that Washington reported that the "Virginians behaved like Men, and died like Soldiers."[11] Only 30 of more than 150 Virginians escaped.[12] The enemy suffered only forty casualties. They captured all the British artillery as well as Braddock's headquarters papers, documenting the warlike plans of Great Britain, a nation still officially at peace with France.

General Braddock was on his fifth horse when a musket ball through the lungs finally brought him down. Washington was one of the few officers still standing. He helped lug the general a mile back to the river and loaded him into a cart. Then Washington did what he could to direct the retreat of the panicked survivors. Before Braddock lapsed into a coma, he ordered Washington to race back forty miles to the second division for reinforcements. Though almost too weak to stand a few hours earlier, Washington found the strength to ride all night.

Years later, he vividly remembered the "shocking Scenes" of the battle and desperate night march. "The dead, the dying, the groans, the lamentation, and crys along the Road of the wounded for help . . . were enough to pierce a heart of adamant. The gloom and horror of which was not a little increased by the impervious darkness." George Washington was familiar with the conventions of native American warfare. He knew that the fate that awaited those left behind merited all the lamentation of which human utterance is capable. Soldiers whose misfortune it was to be taken unhurt were slowly burned to death outside the walls of the fort, their agonized screams mingling hideously with the shrieks of the torturers. The wounded were simply massacred.

Twenty years later, in the famous month of April 1775, just as a new generation of Americans and Britons were beginning to kill and to die on new battlefields, an English traveler named Nicholas Cresswell passed through "Braddock's Field" on his way to Fort Pitt. The woods were littered with burned wagons and abandoned military gear, the trees hacked by wild British musketry. And the dead lay still unburied. "On the Banks of the Mon-in-ga-ha-ly River," Cresswell reported, "Found great numbers of bones, both men and horses. . . . We could not find one whole skull, all of them broken to pieces in the upper part, some of them had holes broken in them about an inch in diameter, suppose it to be done with a Pipe Tomahawk."[13]

Braddock died three days after the battle. "Who would have thought it?" were his last words. George Washington's hopes for "preferment" in the British Army died with him. Near the ruins of Fort Necessity, Washington and a few exhausted soldiers buried their general and drove wagons over the spot to hide the grave. Washington feared that the Indians might seek out the great man's corpse for some "savage triumph"—scalping, mutilation, even ritual cannibalism. Although the British Army in the trans-Allegheny theater still outnumbered the enemy, Braddock's successor, Colonel Thomas Dunbar, retreated all the way to Philadelphia, leaving the frontier defenseless. Governor Dinwiddie couldn't believe it. "Surely you must Mistake," he told Washington on hearing the news. "Colo. Dunbar will not march to Winter Quarters in the Middle of the Summer & leave the Frontiers of his Majesty's Colonies without proper Fortifications & exposed to the Invasions of the Enemy, no! He is a Better Officer."[14] But it was all too true. Indian raiding parties were free to ravage the frontier. Thousands of settlers fled east. Those who didn't run mostly died, often by gruesome torture. A generation of westward expansion was reversed in a matter of months.

The action on the Monongahela seemed to confirm not only Washington's courage but also the extraordinary good luck he enjoyed when the bullets flew. Young men go into battle sharing an illusion of invulnerability, but it is always young men war devours most greedily. In Washington's case the common illusion of invulnerability was to prove uncommonly durable, even prophetic. He had already survived several dangerous actions. From the general massacre at the Forks, Washington wrote, "the miraculous care of Providence . . . protected me beyond all human expectation."[15] Whether miraculous, providential, or merely lucky, his good fortune would continue through many years to come. In both his wars, he deliberately exposed himself to the "hottest fire." He never received so much as a scratch.

News of the catastrophe stunned Williamsburg. Virginia's western strategy had been reduced to ruins by a few hours of gunfire. Governor Dinwiddie actually wept as he read the reports. But whatever people said of Braddock's arrogance or the panic of the regulars, there was only praise for George Washington. A high-ranking English survivor declared that the colonial officer had displayed "the greatest courage and resolution."[16] A sermon delivered in Virginia a month after the battle (and soon published in Philadelphia and London) even contained a hint of prophecy: "I may point out to the Public that heroic Youth Col. Washington, who I cannot but hope Providence has hitherto preserved in so signal a Manner for some important Service to his Country."[17] Lord Halifax, the minister responsible for colonial affairs, marveled, "I know nothing of Mr. Washington's character, but, that we have it from his own hand, that he loves the whistling of Bullets, and they say he behaved as bravely in Braddock's action, as if he really did."[18] George Washington was winning the military reputation that Americans would remember when they looked among themselves for a champion twenty years later.

Two weeks after laying Edward Braddock in his secret grave, the survivor struggled back to Mount Vernon and collapsed into his sick bed. Virginia's prospects seemed equally gloomy. Though people could hardly believe that the British Army had really gone into winter quarters in July, the redcoats were now securely lodged in Philadelphia, with no intention of venturing out before the spring of 1756. Indian raiders struck the frontiers from New England to the Carolinas.

Virginia lacked soldiers, weapons, money, and leadership. The obvious choice for military leader was a planter convalescing at Mount Vernon. But when word came from Williamsburg that a commission was drawn up in his name, Washington equivocated.[19] He suggested that the job might be beyond his powers. "I am unequal to the Task, and assure you that it requires more experience than I am master of."[20] The disavowal contained its element of sincerity—any officer would be daunted by the assignment of defending the Virginia frontier in the fall of 1755. Yet in the next paragraph, the diffident warrior went on to detail how he planned to carry out the task he had just declared himself unequal to. George Washington wanted the command. Though sobered by his feast of horrors, he remained intensely ambitious. He had learned, however, to avoid the appearance of eagerness.[21] The pattern would continue. He reacted with similar reluctance to proposals that he accept command of the Continental Army and assume the presidency.

Governor Dinwiddie understood as well as Washington himself that the veteran officer was the only real candidate. The hero of the Monongahela was admired by nearly all Virginians. He was the unanimous choice of the Governor's Council. His officers were fiercely loyal to him, and certainly no Virginian had greater experience with the enemy or the frontier. Even the leading men of other colonies pushed Washington's appointment. Franklin said that nothing would bolster American confidence as much as a call to arms from the Virginian.

By the time Washington did agree, his studied reluctance had enhanced the prestige that could help him succeed in his new assignment. Taking power reluctantly was a means of increasing the power taken.²² His hesitation also supplied leverage to pry concessions from Dinwiddie. Colonel Washington had previously headed only the 1st Regiment, the unit raised expressly for the campaign across the mountains. Now he had charge of all Virginia's overall war effort. He could nominate his field officers, and few questioned his demand for a handsome salary and a complement of staff officers. At twenty-three, George Washington was commander in chief of the armed forces of Great Britain's largest and richest colony.

The redcoats' retreat had exposed Virginia's settled frontier in the Shenandoah Valley to Indian attack for the first time in years. The region's scattered forts, garrisoned by a few Maryland and Virginia militiamen, provided no protection to the terrified pioneer families. After the British regiments marched off, most of the militia deserted, convinced that "they were left by the regulars to be destroyed by the barbarous enemy."²³ Refugees fleeing the Shenandoah brought back nightmare stories of a world plunged into darkness. One of Washington's officers told him that the Indian raiders "go about and Commit their Outrages at all hours of the day and nothing is to be seen or heard of but Desolation and murders heightened with all Barbarous Circumstances and unheard of Instances of Cruelty.... The Smoke of the Burning Plantations darkens the day and hides the neighboring mountains from our Sight."²⁴

Not a little of Washington's reluctance to take command had stemmed from the knowledge that he was not likely to enjoy much success. For the next three years, he would struggle to defend the border with scant resources and a few hundred unreliable men. The war on Virginia's frontier became a sideshow as the British high command shifted strategy north. Washington's men hung on grimly in the chain of frontier forts, miserable stockades too strong for the enemy to storm but too weak to protect a countryside now disfigured by burned-out cabins and unburied dead. Patrols tangled with warriors in ugly little skirmishes whose losers could hope only to die quickly.

Braddock's successor, Lieutenant General John Campbell, fourth Earl Loudoun, arrived in July 1756 and made his headquarters at Philadelphia. Naturally the Virginia colonel was eager for a personal interview with the Scottish peer. Though "tantalized," he complained, by the ever-receding prize, Washington could still hope that a royal commission awaited him. He panted for Loudoun's favor. Washington opened his campaign by welcoming His Lordship to America with a high-flown "Address of the Officers of the Virginia Regiment." To this imposing parchment, he affixed an exquisite six-inch signature that still seems to pulse with the young officer's proud spirit. Loudoun did not reply.

Next Washington sent off a fifty-page autograph letter written on a ream of gold-edged paper. Laid out on page after graceful page was the authentic history of George Washington's war against His Britannic Majesty's enemies, foreign and domestic. Other men's blunders had blasted Virginia's prospects. Washington allowed that the future had looked so grim that he had made up his mind to resign —until heartened by word of the heroic earl's appointment. Then, he floundered on, "I drew my hopes, and fondly pronounced your Lordship our patron. Altho' I had not the honor to be known to your Lordship, your Lordship's name was familiar to my ear, on account of the important services performed to his Majesty in other parts of the world. Do not think, my Lord, that I am going to flatter; notwithstanding I have exalted sentiments of your Lordship's character and respect your rank, it is not my intention to adulate. My nature is open and honest and free from guile!"[25] Loudoun did not reply.

Six months passed before Washington could wheedle a meeting. When the day finally came in March 1757, he was not just disappointed again. This time he was humiliated. Loudoun kept Washington hanging around Philadelphia for a week before summoning him to a brief interview. Here was a powerful older man the Virginian could not charm. The baby-faced little aristocrat had been bullying Americans ever since he reached their shores. He detested them for a gang of cowardly scoundrels and was in no mood to listen to a so-called colonel up from Virginia. The noble lord gave the lowborn colonial a few orders and sent him on his way. The next time George Washington would be so resoundingly humbled by British power he would be the commander of a hostile army, not an earnest petitioner.[26]

Loudoun disdained any suggestion that regular commissions be given colonials. Indeed, he planned to organize colonial troops into "Royal American Regiments" and put British officers over them. This was almost more than Washington could bear. It was now that the awakening nationalist entered his protest against the injustice "that being Americans shoud deprive us of the benefits of British subjects."[27]

His Lordship also declined to attack Fort Duquesne, as Washington and other Virginians urged. Despite Washington's effusions, Loudoun owed the command to his fortunate birth. He had crossed the Atlantic as a veteran general without a single victory to his name and would go home again with that record unchanged. He concentrated on the northern theater, with a notable lack of success.

Earl Loudoun had meantime conducted a parallel war against American political institutions, imperiously treading on privileges the colonists had long prized as the birthright of freeborn Englishmen. He forcibly quartered British troops in private homes. His impressment gangs condemned men to virtual slavery aboard Royal Navy warships. He gave orders that violated not only constitutional tradition but the royal charters of several colonies.[28] When the earl of Loudoun sailed away, he left behind many newly suspicious of British power, and many others who, like Washington, had begun to think of themselves as "being Americans." English officers like Loudoun played an unwitting part in the composition of the Declaration of Independence. Most telling of the clauses they might be said to have inserted into that celebrated document was the charge that the king "has Affected to render the Military independent of and superior to Civil power."

The few minutes that George Washington had spent in the presence of Lieutenant General John Campbell, Earl

Loudoun, was the turning point of his early life. Loudoun's dismissal meant the end of all his hopes for royal rank. He was not to be a soldier after all. Washington did not resign. He would serve almost two more years, until the fall of Fort Duquesne, at the end of 1758. But he no longer expected his well-deserved reward. He began to imagine for himself a future that defined honor by a Virginian's traditional measures of land, marriage and family, and that life of opulence purchased by hogsheads of tobacco and the labor of enslaved blacks.

Disappointment forced Washington to question the place that he and his fellow colonials occupied in the British Empire. Britons, it seemed, regarded Americans as distant stepchildren—imperial orphans—more the lackeys than the subjects of the monarch Americans were proud to call the "best of kings." Though that letter to Loudoun might be taken as evidence that he could bow and scrape with the best of them, George Washington was no one's lackey. His ferocious anger against England would burn on until the day he died.

More fateful still was the ideological dimension of his disillusionment. Beyond wounded pride loomed a growing disdain for the old order of government-by-birth. The accident of his own American birth had denied him the interest needed to boost him up. None of his extraordinary gifts could ever supply the lack—the old order did not always reward merit. Washington finally understood that he could never hope to enter imperial ranks as an Englishman's equal. He knew just as surely that he was the equal of any Englishman living.

Washington rode home from Philadelphia in April 1757. If he had no future in the army, he wanted out. But he could not quit until Virginia's frontier was safe again. How that might be achieved, so long as Loudoun directed the war, Washington could not say. He told a correspondent in England, "I have been posted for twenty Months past upon our cold and Barren Frontiers, to perform I think I may say impossibilitys that is, to protect from the cruel Incursions of a Crafty Savage Enemy a line of Inhabitants of more than 350 Miles Extent with a force inadequate to the task."[29] Only the capture of Fort Duquesne would shake the Indians from their alliance with the French. But the bones of Braddock's soldiers still lay where the wolves had scattered them. The British command had no stomach for another Ohio venture.

That summer Washington fell deathly sick. First was a recurrence of the dysentery that had crippled him during the Braddock expedition. This "bloody flux" was no mere distasteful inconvenience but a debilitating disorder of the bowels that often proved fatal. Next came a chronic fever. Then he was seized by "stitches and violent pleuretick pains" accompanied by a wracking cough. The cough terrified him. He feared he had contracted what he called "decay"—the tuberculosis that had destroyed his brother. A doctor bled the patient copiously, but that sovereign remedy failed to bring improvement. The surgeon could only conclude that disease "hath corrupted the whole mass of blood."[30] Colonel Washington had to leave his command and limp back to Mount Vernon. No one was home but servants and slaves—and perhaps the uneasy shade of

Lawrence Washington, who had choked to death in the same house three summers before.

The winter may have been the low point of Washington's life. He would not be so sick again until he was nearly sixty. To cap the dark year's catalogue of woes, William Fairfax died at Belvoir in November 1757.[31] Washington felt the loss keenly. The beloved old gentleman was his last mentor. Indeed, one scholar believes that Washington "never again looked to an older man for continuing guidance and support. . . . He never again betrayed any sign of regarding, or treating, another person as his natural and rightful superior."[32]

In March 1758, still half-convinced that he was dying, the sick man made his way to Williamsburg for medical advice. Perhaps he also aimed to silence rumors circulating in the capital that Colonel Washington had already expired. He was examined by Virginia's most distinguished physician, who gave the patient rare good news. The illness was not mortal—he would recover. The happy prognosis apparently cured Washington on the spot. He rode out of Williamsburg in high spirits, spurred on by visions of a bright future ahead. His destination was the White House on the Pamunkey River, home of the widow Martha Dandridge Custis. At a gallop, he could cover the distance in a couple of hours.

Washington had stopped at the White House on his way down to Williamsburg a few days earlier. Now he wanted to share the doctor's good news with the lady of the house. He had first met her some time before, at Williamsburg functions Martha attended on the arm of her late husband. Daniel Parke Custis, eight months dead by the time Colonel Washington came calling on his widow, had been the browbeaten only son of a colorful planter as famous for his eccentricities as for his great wealth.

Martha had married Daniel in 1749, months before the old man died and the son came into the fortune. By the time his death ended their marriage, eight years later, Martha had brought four little Custises into the world. Two were still living when their father died. John Parke Custis was born in 1754. His sister Martha Parke Custis had followed in 1756. Like her mother, the little girl was called Patsy. They called her brother Jacky.

The departed also left behind a most handsome estate. Its centerpiece was 17,880 acres of prime tobacco land along the York and James rivers. Hundreds of enslaved people worked their way along the rows of plants. Two-thirds of the land and slaves passed straight to the little boy, and the value thereof did not figure in the appraisal. But even with that most valuable portion excluded, the Virginia property was worth a stunning £30,000. The family's agents in London credited the heirs with another £10,000 sterling in cash and Bank of England stock. There was a house in Williamsburg, the plantation house on the Pamunkey, livestock, a coach and a chariot, horses, cash, silver, furniture, and hundreds of enslaved workers. The Custis plantations themselves were among the most productive in Virginia, growing a superior grade of tobacco that always brought top prices on the London market. The estate was completely free of debt, a highly unusual circumstance in the tobacco colonies in the mid-eighteenth century.

Daniel Custis had died without a will, an oversight that worked to the widow's advantage. According to Virginia law, the estate was divided between the wife, the son, and the daughter. Were the widow to remarry, of course, all her wealth would magically fly into the pockets of her new husband, and that man would control the children's fortunes until they came of age. George Washington wasn't the first suitor to come calling. Mrs. Custis was thought to be the richest marriageable woman in Virginia when the illustrious colonel reined up at her door.

She was also pretty. Ideals of feminine beauty shift through the centuries—Martha came close to meeting the model that prevailed in her time. There is only one portrait of her as a young woman. Companion to portraits of Daniel and the two children, the picture of Martha at about twenty-five was painted in the manner formerly called "primitive" but now more charitably denominated "naive." Stiff and formulaic as it may be, the old canvas hints at a woman possessed of no inconsiderable measure of sensuality. She looks out confidently, the flowers poised in the little hand an allusion to her manifold generosities. Her face is beset with enormous hazel eyes above cupid's-bow lips, while her pale neck and shoulders invite the gaze downward to a bosom displayed to advantage by a low-cut gown.

George Washington spent the night on his second visit to the White House. Before riding off in the morning, he lavished extravagant tips on the house servants. The colonel had been away from his regiment for almost half a year— he was eager to get back to the frontier. He would not see

Martha again until June. By then the couple had agreed
to marry. They had spent fewer than twenty-four hours in
each other's company, but both must have understood immediately that they were a near-perfect match. In April,
each was writing to London for new suits, fashionable, but
dignified enough for an important ceremony. Washington
urged that his order be put on the first ship bound for Virginia. Martha even sent a favorite nightgown across the
Atlantic to be altered and returned to her. George ordered
a ring from Philadelphia. It seems likely that they would
have married immediately had the colonel not had scores
to settle with the French soldiers at Fort Duquesne. Soon
he was headed into the Ohio country again.

But a curious thing had happened on Washington's
way to his wedding. Just before setting off for the Ohio
again, the betrothed officer sent a love letter to Sally Fairfax, the wife of his closest friend, George William Fairfax.
Apparently no one but the Fairfaxes themselves saw the
letter for the next 120 years, but its publication in 1877
touched off a commotion that has continued ever since.
This remarkable production was dated September 12, 1758,
four months before he exchanged vows with Martha Custis. "Dear Madam," wrote George Washington from a frontier fort,

> . . . I profess myself a Votary to Love—I acknowledge that
> a Lady is in the Case—and further I confess, that this Lady
> is known to you.—Yes Madam, as well as she is to one, who
> is too sensible of her Charms to deny the Power, whose In-
> fluence he feels and must ever Submit to. I feel the force
> of her amiable beauties in the recollection of a thousand

tender passages that I coud wish to obliterate. . . . You have
drawn me my dear Madam, or rather I have drawn myself,
into the honest confession of a Simple Fact—misconstrue
not my meaning—'tis obvious—doubt it not, nor expose
it,—the World has no business to know the object of my
Love, declard in this manner to—you when I want to conceal it—One thing, above all things in this World I wish to
know, and only one person of your Acquaintance can solve
me that, or guess my meaning.[33]

'Tis obvious indeed. But Mrs. George William Fairfax
never gave Colonel Washington the answer he wanted, or
even the answer that he never wanted to hear. She refused
take up her half of the dialogue. His next letter, in response
to a lost letter from her, complained, "Do we misunder-
stand the true meaning of each other's letters? I would fain
hope the contrary, as I cannot speak plainer."[34] Nothing
else remains. The entire story of George's anguished love
for Sally rests on the two 1758 letters, and on the misinter-
pretation of other letters he sent her many years later in
1785 and 1798.

Certain biographers have embraced the old romance
as the finest gift a beneficent providence ever bestowed on
the field of American historical literature.[35] The story of
George's love for Sally is actually misleading, not because
it is untrue but because it is finally unimportant. The appeal is certainly not hard to understand. A doomed love
affair carrying a whiff of scandal appeals to modern hearts
just as surely as the fables of Washington's tender devotion
to his mother delighted Victorian sensibilities. The revelation seems to warm the glacial hero, to make Washington
a more "likable" person; it reveals something of the long-

sought "man behind the myths." The story of a doomed
love appears to offer a tragic and noble contrast to his
extraordinary success. Perhaps, some have believed, it is
even the key to Washington's abiding mystery. The notion
is mistaken—romantic love is not the key to unlocking
Washington's secret heart. That explanation lies instead in
his extraordinary ambition, his infallible judgment, and
his inflexible honor.

General Loudoun was recalled by London at the end
of 1757. His replacement, James Abercromby, was an officer whose incompetence may have actually surpassed
that of his predecessor. Abercromby suffered a bloody and
demoralizing defeat in his attack on Ticonderoga. But the
corpulent general could do little more harm. The mind
now directing the war was William Pitt, the extraordinary
statesman who had emerged as the dominant figure in the
British ministry. Soon the mighty kingdom bestirred itself
to seize victory no matter what the cost. Pitt took personal
control of the campaigns, raised new armies and promoted
new generals to lead them, launched new fleets, and spent
as no English minister had ever spent before. His grand
strategy reversed the old pattern of seeking advantage in
Europe first. He intended to win the Seven Years' War by
crushing French power in America. The Royal Navy block-
aded Canada and sailed dozens of fresh regiments across
the Atlantic. Pitt planned several offensives for 1758. Powerful Anglo-American armies would attack the French
in Canada and northern New York. Another army would
move against Fort Duquesne. General John Forbes had
command of the Ohio expedition.

Colonel Washington was soon bent over his desk at a familiar task—soliciting a recommendation to a new general. But this time was different. Washington did not see the coming campaign as a path to carry him into the regular army. He asked to be mentioned to General Forbes "not as a person who would depend upon him for further recommendation to military preferment, for I have long since conquered all such expectancies . . . but as a person who would gladly be distinguished in some measure from the *common run* of provincial Officers; as I understand there will be a motley herd of us."[36]

With Secretary Pitt backing him, and an army three times the size of Braddock's, this new general succeeded in driving France from the Ohio Valley forever. The Virginia colonel was honored to act as a brigadier general in the campaign—commanding a brigade composed of two regiments. He again escaped unhurt when gunfire between two American units in a twilit forest killed men all around him. Winter had arrived before the Anglo-Americans neared the enemy fort. Not surprisingly, the regiments moved ahead cautiously, deployed in intricate formations of scouts and flankers that Colonel Washington had devised. But there was no siege, no climactic battle. The naval blockade had cut off Canada from France. Battles in the north had cut off Fort Duquesne from Canada. English victory was in the air as palpably as winter itself, and native American barometers had detected the change. At the Treaty of Easton, the Ohio Indians had switched allegiance from France to England. Spies told General Forbes that the Indian huts that ringed the walls of Fort Duquesne stood

empty. Deprived of native allies, the French were as helpless as Braddock had been three years earlier, unable even
to feed themselves without Indian hunters. One night the
French set fire to the fort. By the light of the blaze, they slid
their canoes into the black Ohio and paddled upstream,
never to return. The place burned all night. A powder
magazine exploded, sending up a tower of sparks.

Next morning scouts reported smoke over the Ohio
confluence. Brigadier Washington reached the ruins with
the advance corps on November 25, 1758. It was five years,
almost to the day, since a much younger officer had first
stood at the Forks of the Ohio and recognized that the
spot was "extreamly well situated for a Fort."[37] There was
no martial glory to reap on the return, but Virginia had
finally gained the great objective of five years of blood and
anguish. The Indians soon came forward to make new
alliances and resume the fur trade. Peace returned to the
frontier, and survivors returned to their ravaged farms.
The riches of the Ohio beckoned again to speculators and
settlers. Colonel Washington could honorably resign his
command and begin his new life. He was out of the army
before the year ended.

Since the renown Washington won in the first war
gained him supreme command in the second, it might seem
reasonable to ask how much he deserved his military reputation from the French and Indian War. A more enlight-
ening exercise is to catalogue the mistakes he made as a
commander in the 1750s and ask how many of them he
would repeat in the 1770s. That catalogue of failures ex-
tends to some length. He had won no victories, unless one

cares to count the Jumonville ambush that earned him infamy as an assassin of diplomats. He blundered in defending Fort Necessity against a superior enemy. He had spent most of his time away from his officers and men, off politicking or enjoying himself in Williamsburg, Philadelphia, and Boston. (In striking contrast, during the whole eight and a half years of the Revolutionary War, General Washington never once left his army unless called away to confer with Congress. It actually appears that he did not take a single day off until victory came.) In the earlier war, Colonel Washington's greatest failings had been in the political, not the military arena. Both of Washington's wars were political endeavors. To be sure, a soldier's career may be punctuated by episodes of violence and disorder so extreme as to fall outside the common range of human experience. These aberrations—which we call battles—are probably not best understood as political events. (Washington was under fire half a dozen times in five years.) But war itself is essentially a political process. And more than most wars, the War of American Independence called for a commander in chief who was a statesman first and a general second.

During the French and Indian War, Colonel Washington's political skills were unformed and his performance was poor. But from 1775 to 1783, General Washington played the role of the soldier-statesman as successfully as any figure in world history ever has. His political genius evoked feelings of awe from his contemporaries. Properly understood, his achievement is still awe inspiring. Key to General Washington's success was his understanding that the army must remain subordinate to civilian government, no matter how weak, inept, or corrupt that government might be. In contrast, Colonel Washington's most serious failing was his inability to work with civilian authorities. A repetition of that failure could have been fatal to the patriot cause in the American Revolution. The battles on the frontiers and in government chambers did give Washington training that would serve his country well in the Revolution. Few officers of his age have exercised so important an independent command. He survived not only the white-hot madness of combat itself but also the tedious routines of military administration. In such matters, the supremely systematic Virginian would one day display mastery. He observed British officers intently and learned much from them. Washington also showed that he possessed those qualities of leadership that are always difficult to define. He was gifted with that rare and inexplicable power to make others trust and obey him. Many discovered that they actually loved him.

Certainly Washington's legendary courage and his splendid person were important ingredients in his power to command. But those qualities alone can hardly account for the sentiments found in a petition signed by the Virginia Regiment's officers on the last day of 1758. They were begging him to withdraw his resignation:

> The happiness we have enjoy'd and the Honor we have acquir'd, together with the mutual Regard that has always subsisted between you and your Officers, have planted so sensible an Affection in the Minds of us all, that we cannot be silent at this critical Occasion. In our earliest

infancy you took us under your Tuition, train'd us up in
the Practice of that Discipline which alone can constitute
good Troops, from the punctual Observance of which you
never suffer'd the least Deviation. *Your steady Adherence
to impartial Justice, your quick Discernment and invar-
iable Regard to Merit, wisely intended to inculcate those
genuine Sentiments, of true Honor and Passion for Glory,
from which the greatest military Achievements have been
deriv'd, first heighten'd our natural Emulation and our
Desire to excel.* . . . Judge then, how sensibly we must be Affected with the loss of such an excellent Commander, such
a sincere Friend, and so affable a Companion. How rare it
is to find these Amiable Qualifications blended together in
one Man? How great the loss of such a Man?[38]

As Washington himself wanted to excel in the eyes
of the world, so he could make his officers long to excel in
his eyes. At the same time, they called the disciplinarian an
amiable, affable friend and companion. The lines on justice
and merit deserve the emphasis added here. The British establishment had not rewarded Washington according to
his merit because the reward of merit was not an operat-
ing principle of that establishment. Colonel Washington
would not make the same mistake. Neither would General
Washington or President Washington. His impartiality
was one of the great pillars of his public character. As Jefferson would say, "His justice [was] the most inflexible I
have ever known, no motives of interest or consanguinity,
of friendship or hatred, being able to bias his decision."[39]

As commander of the Virginia Regiment, Washington
had resisted the urgings of powerful men to give undeserved commissions to their friends. He avoided any hint
of favoritism. He could affectionately urge one officer to

control his heavy drinking while firing another who cheated at cards. Douglas Freeman says Washington's "somewhat deliberate and formal courtesy was brightened by his amiability."[40]

If the French and Indian War was the best school Washington attended, it also provided an education for many others—Britons and Americans alike. The lessons the two peoples believed that they had learned about each other were not happy ones. Some Englishmen came away from the war with a bitterly gained conviction that the colonials were a despicable people—hardly worthy to call themselves the king's subjects. Their cowardice in battle was boundless, their greed and dishonesty no less conspicuous. Americans were so wedded to their own little provinces, so jealous of their neighbors, and so addicted to making money that they were incapable of working for the good of the empire as a whole. The various colonies often seemed more enthusiastic about feuding with rivals than fighting the French. (Many thoughtful Americans might have agreed with Benjamin Franklin's estimation that, without the superintending hand of Britain, the colonies would soon be at war with one another.)

English leaders accepted that Americans were a common, lowborn people. There was no native aristocracy and no true gentlemen to lead the whining, mutinous rabble they called soldiers. They were all a "parcel of scoundrels," Washington's commander General Forbes told Secretary Pitt. "A few of their principal Officers excepted, all the rest are an extream bad Collection of broken Inn-keepers, Horse Jockeys, & Indian traders, and the Men under them,

are a direct copy of their Officers, nor can it well be other-
wise, as they are a gathering of the scum of the worst people
in every Country."[41] General James Wolfe, the martyred victor of Quebec, swore that "there was never a people collected
together so unfit . . . dilatory, ignorant, irresolute and some
grains of a very unmanly quality and very unsoldier-like
and unsailor-like. The Americans are in general the dirt-
iest, the most contemptible, cowardly dogs you can conceive. There is no depending on 'em in action. They fall
down dead in their own dirt and desert by battalions, officers and all."[42] The colonies might be rich and populous,
but a sweeping disdain for all things American gave His
Majesty's ministers and generals a confidence that there
was little risk in bullying them. Franklin remembered a
British general who said "within my hearing" that "with
a Thousand British Grenadiers he would undertake to
go from one end of America to the other and geld all the
Males partly by force and partly by a little Coaxing."[43]

Many Americans reciprocated the animosity. The colonists had not encountered many British soldiers or officials before the war. Now they saw the redcoats acting like
an occupying force in an enemy land. Franklin observed
of Braddock's army that "from their landing till they got
beyond the settlements, they had plundered and stripped
the inhabitants, totally ruining some poor families, besides insulting, abusing, and confining people if they re-
monstrated." Soldiers would never have dared to disregard
so flagrantly the rights of the king's subjects in Britain.[44]

Living among the colonials, the British revealed to
them how rigidly their society was ruled by a caste system

that simply had no counterpart in America. Army discipline was horrifyingly brutal, and the officers were arrogant and abusive. It was not that colonial America was a paradise. The colonies were not republics, far less democracies, and hundreds of thousands of enslaved people were held in ancestral bondage. But white colonial society was freer, more prosperous, and more fluid than the English example. The Americans became conscious of their distinctiveness. They gloried in it. They began to believe in their own moral superiority.

The appalling ineptitude of the British high command had also shocked the Americans. Persisting through the War of Independence, that same military imbecility, usually seconded by governmental incompetence of the highest order, proved a mighty blessing to the patriots. Of course, some of war's supposed lessons turned out to be wrong. While Britons thought that the colonials were too cowardly to fight, a corresponding notion forming in the minds of the Americans held that professional soldiers— mere hirelings who fought for pay instead of principle— could be readily defeated by a citizens' militia of free men fighting for their homes and their liberties. The Americans' stubborn reliance on militias was one of the gravest obstacles Washington struggled with in the early years of the Revolution. He understood, as most of his countrymen did not, that only a standing army of professional veterans, modeled on the British example, could win independence.

But as one glorious English victory followed another, as French power crumbled under the hammer blows that fell on the Ohio, at Quebec, in Asia, and in the Caribbean, the king's subjects on both sides of the ocean joined together in joyous patriotism. Few then would have credited a prediction that these two peoples would soon be killing one another.

George Washington and Martha Dandridge Custis were married on January 6, 1759. The groom was twenty-six, the bride twenty-seven. The marriage was one of the signal triumphs of George Washington's life, comparable to his later military victories and public offices. Wealth had played no inconsiderable part in Washington's enchantment with Mrs. Custis, while the practical widow stood to gain not only a famous husband but also a shrewd steward for her property and a guardian for her young children. But more than expediency had brought the two together, and if pragmatism had overshadowed passion in their speedy courtship, real love soon followed. Man and woman were both young, healthy, and attractive. They shared a common outlook on life. It is unlikely that either harbored more than the customary share of doubts on the wedding day.

With the property he held in his own right, the Custis wealth was enough to carry Washington into the highest ranks of Virginia's elite. Taking his seat in the House of Burgesses for the first time in 1759 confirmed his new status. Had George Washington been a different man altogether, had he sat out the war like most of his peers, he would have become just another little gentry planter—one who could have never hoped to make so advantageous a marriage.

Settling in with Martha, he wrote, "I am now I believe

fixd at this Seat with an agreable Consort for Life and hope to find more happiness in retirement than I ever experiencd amidst a wide and bustling World."[45] The next few years were, in fact, uneventful. He began life with his new family at Mount Vernon, which he had inherited after the deaths of Lawrence Washington's infant daughter and widow.

No children were born to the couple at Mount Vernon. If Washington deeply regretted the lack, he never said so. He devoted his efforts to planting, local politics, and land speculation. His first objective was to gain the honor and riches that came with raising fine tobacco and selling it in London. It was in order to plant more tobacco that he began buying up adjoining lands with his new wealth. He would eventually expand Mount Vernon from twenty-three hundred to nearly eight thousand acres.

He also bought more slaves to work his land. At the time of his marriage Washington owned about twenty slaves. That year he bought another thirteen. By the end of 1760 he owned fifty. A decade later, a Fairfax County tax roll revealed that the number had grown to ninety. Changing agricultural practices meant that Washington bought no more slaves after 1772, but the Mount Vernon population continued to grow rapidly through natural increase.

Success did not attend Washington's attempts to become a great tobacco planter. All his efforts to grow the quality leaf that commanded the best prices in England were frustrated by poor Mount Vernon soils, indifferent markets, British regulations, and bad weather. At the same time he was spending lavishly—on land, slaves, and equipment, on costly imported luxuries and in the enjoyment of the opulence for which Virginia plantation culture is still renowned. Annual tobacco crops consigned for sale to his London agents failed to offset the cost of luxury goods ordered on credit from those same trading houses. He spent the wealth gained by his marriage and began to run into debt, a circumstance he abhorred as both bad business and a slight on his honor and independence. Washington became increasingly embittered by what he saw as the sharp practices of English merchants, and by his growing conviction that the imperial system exploited colonials.

His military experiences had already done much to disabuse this subject of the crown of his youthful devotion to the mother country. His treatment at the hands of the London traders only strengthened this tendency to think of himself as an American. His failure to gain the rewards he thought the British military establishment owed him had soured Washington on a society in which success was based not so much on merit as on interest—the influence of the powerful. Such considerations may well have made him more open to republican ideals, and, one day, to the radical notion of independent American nationhood.

But it was economic, not political, independence that Washington pursued in the 1760s. While many of his Virginia neighbors sank into a pit of tobacco debt from which they would never claw free, George Washington set out, with characteristic energy, to find a replacement for the traditional staple crop. He began the agricultural experimentation that would absorb him for the rest of his life. He experimented with dozens of crops before he settled

on wheat as the main replacement for soil-depleting tobacco. George Washington would gain a reputation as one
of the most progressive large-scale farmers in America. It
was a new infusion of Custis wealth, however, that finally
allowed him to cancel his English debts. When "our Dear
Patcy Custis" died suddenly during an epileptic seizure in
1773, her stepfather inherited £8,000.

Washington would spend fifteen years as a gentleman
farmer at Mount Vernon between his two wars. It was the
longest stretch of private life he would ever enjoy, and certainly the happiest period of his life. In addition to farming, his other preoccupation was speculation in western
land. In 1763 the Seven Years' War had finally come to an
end. Britain had gained an enormous victory. The choicest
portions of the victor's spoils were Canada and the Ohio
Valley. With the French ousted and their Indian allies be-
reft of a European partner, rich visions floated above the
western horizon again.

No one had grander visions than George Washington. In 1754 Washington had built the primitive road that
opened the Ohio Valley to wheeled vehicles for the first
time in history. By the 1770s he had come to believe that the
construction of a system of canals and roads linking the
Potomac and Ohio rivers was feasible. He was convinced
that the Ohio Valley contained the finest agricultural land
on earth. If its harvests could be funneled to the world's
markets on the river that flowed past Mount Vernon, the
value of Washington's western lands was certain to climb
to the skies, while Alexandria, just a few miles from his
door, stood to become the greatest trading port in Amer-

ica. Washington set about his pursuit of western land with the same drive that had carried him through hundreds of miles of hostile terrain and a half dozen deadly battles. That these dreams of empire demanded the violent dispossession of the region's native peoples was a grim concomitant that apparently never gave George Washington much regret, though as president he did try to secure some justice for the Indians.

After Major Washington had returned to Williamsburg with news of the French challenge in January 1754, Governor Dinwiddie had issued a proclamation promising 200,000 acres of western bounty land as reward to soldiers who enlisted in the campaign to drive the enemy from the Forks of the Ohio. Historians have questioned whether commissioned officers, who were not enlisted soldiers, were eligible to share in the original grant. But in 1770 Washington successfully petitioned to have the bounty extended to officers.

Fifteen thousand acres each was the allotment reserved for Washington and his field officers. An enlisted man could expect just 400. With the purchase of other veterans' claims added to his own share, the Virginia Regiment's former commander eventually acquired about 33,000 acres along the Ohio and Great Kanawha rivers in what is now Ohio, Pennsylvania, and West Virginia. When some complained that Washington's portion contained most of the prime bottom lands, he retorted, with some accuracy, that without "my unremitting attention to every circumstance, not a single acre of Land ever would have been obtained."[46]

Again British imperial policy intervened to frustrate Washington's hopes. In 1763, the ministry issued the Proclamation Line closing the Ohio to white settlement. To Washington this was simply absurd; settlers were pouring into the region, and no edicts from London could stop them. He could "never look upon that Proclamation in any other light . . . than as a temporary expedient to quiet the Minds of the Indians and must fall in a few years."[47] Nevertheless, the Proclamation of 1763 called all Washington's land claims into question. The Quebec Act of 1774 further complicated matters by making the Ohio Valley a part of the province of Quebec. Finally, on the eve of the Revolution, striking out against Washington's opposition to British policies, Virginia's royal governor flatly ruled that all Washington's claims were invalid because his surveyor was not qualified. Washington's anger grew.

He also knew that his western land would never be valuable unless the Ohio was settled and joined, politically and economically, to the seaboard colonies. The Virginian had gained a stake in the West that enlarged his hopes for himself and his country to a continental scale. It remained Washington's abiding conviction that America's future lay in the continent's western interior, not across the Atlantic among the kingdoms of Europe.

The great war for empire had brought many changes, large and small. New France was no more. The English-speakers had secured half of North America. The American Revolution had begun, though few, if any, recognized its commencement. One of the smaller consequences of the big war was the rise of George Washington. Probably no other Virginian in the colony's history had risen as far and as fast as he had between 1752 and 1759.[48] The poorly educated younger son of a middling tobacco planter had become one of the richest and most renowned men in America.

❧ 5 ❧

_____

"Because We Are Americans"

O
N MAY 9, 1775, George Washington rode into Philadelphia in his English chariot and stopped at the City Tavern. He was probably wearing the buff and blue uniform he had designed for himself as colonel commanding the Fairfax militia. (Buff and blue would soon be general officers' colors in the American Army.) He had been probably wearing his uniform during much of his trip from Mount Vernon; in Baltimore he had reviewed local militia companies. Many men in America were wearing uniforms in the spring of 1775, as the colonies suddenly found themselves at war with Great Britain.

Washington was in Philadelphia to attend the Second Continental Congress. With some twenty-five thousand inhabitants, Philadelphia was the largest city in North America. On an earlier trip to the great metropolis, in 1757, Colonel Washington had met with the humiliating rejection by Lord Loudoun of his appeal for a royal army commission. By 1775, the mission had changed, and so had George Washington. In the years since the war against the French, Washington had won his most important victory— the feat his fellow revolutionary Gouverneur Morris described as Washington's victory over himself. The jealous, hot-tempered, and self-aggrandizing young officer who had so relentlessly crusaded for his own advancement had become a mature patriot whose private ambitions were now sublimated in his devotion to a higher cause. That cause, Washington and his compatriots sincerely believed, was nothing less the preservation of liberty itself.

The militancy of George Washington's political views have not always been appreciated. Washington had scores to settle with the British Empire. He did not move reluctantly toward rebellion and independence. His ideas were more advanced than those of most colonials. As early as 1768, he had told a friend that he was ready to take his musket on his shoulder whenever his country called.[1] The next year, he predicted that "our lordly Masters in Great Britain will be satisfied with nothing less than the deprivation of American freedom." He declared that "no man shou'd scruple, or hesitate a moment to use a[r]ms in defense of so valuable a blessing."[2] To speak of war with Britain at such an early date was radical indeed. And certainly no man in America better understood how dangerous such a war must be. Moreover, Washington must have understood then that if war did come, he would not march in the ranks with a musket on his shoulder. Rather, he would be an obvious candidate for high command in the military forces of Virginia or of the united colonies. Years before it came to pass, he must have suspected that a general's rank might await him.

The fierce denunciation of "our lordly Masters" was drawn from Washington's pen by taxes levied on the colonies by the British Parliament. When the Seven Years' War ended, England learned that victory had been as costly as it had been glorious. In 1763, British national debt stood at an appalling £122,603,336. The debt had nearly doubled from £75 million in 1756. The cost of the war itself was estimated at £70 million. London concluded that the Americans had profited most from the war and that they could afford some of its cost. A stubborn new monarch had ascended the English throne in 1760. King George III and his government vowed to bring the ungrateful Americans under the control of rightful British authority.

The imperial crisis broke out with Parliament's passage of the first taxes on the colonies with the Stamp Act in 1765. In the minds of colonials, the Stamp Act conjured up frightful visions of dark conspiracy and limitless tyrannies to follow. Property rights were central to the Americans' notions of freedom. They believed that taxation without their consent amounted to the theft of their property, and thus a first step on the road that led inevitably to absolute slavery. Washington was united with other patriots in opposition to what he called "this unconstitutional method of Taxation" that Virginians viewed "as a direful attack upon their Liberties."[3]

Other Americans greeted the Stamp Act not with dignified appeals to tradition but with mob violence, boycotts, and tax evasion. In the face of such defiance, the law proved unenforceable and was repealed in 1766. Repeal was welcomed with universal rejoicing throughout the colonies. But respect for British authority would never be the same, while London's determination to rule the unruly colonials was stronger than ever.

Americans were outraged anew by the passage of the Townshend Acts in 1767. The bill was intended to raise revenues for the crown through the collection of duties on imports. Colonials countered with "nonimportation," the boycott of trade with Britain. Washington had never stood out as a legislator or orator during his years in the House of Burgesses. By 1769, however, he had emerged as a leader of the nonimportation movement in the House and in Fairfax County, the most radical county in Virginia, a colony that was nearly as outspoken as Massachusetts in opposition to British authority.

But Boston remained the crucible of American resistance. Boston was a port built on trade, as well as a hotbed of radical patriotism. Here opposition to import taxes and dishonest tax collectors was often violent. To bring the Bostonians to their knees, British troops occupied the city in 1768. Finding a standing army among them in peacetime only confirmed Americans' worst fears about the insidious conspiracy to rob them of their liberties. Hatred between soldiers and townspeople spilled over in the "Boston Massacre" in 1770, when redcoats fired into a rioting crowd, killing five. Parliament finally repealed most of the Townshend duties, retaining only a three-penny tax on tea. But even this proved too much for angry Bostonians to swallow. On December 16, 1773, a band of patriots unconvincingly disguised as Mohawks destroyed fifty tons of British property while turning Boston harbor into the world's biggest teapot.

The Boston Tea Party infuriated official London. (George Washington himself disapproved.) Many British now agreed that Massachusetts had to be broken before England's American empire was lost forever. To coerce Boston to bow to its will, Parliament quickly passed the laws known in colonies as the "Coercive" or "Intolerable Acts." The Boston Port Bill closed the harbor to all commercial trade, inflicting grave economic hardship. It amounted to the kind of naval blockade warring nations used against their enemies. The Massachusetts Government Act abrogated the colony's 1691 charter. General Thomas Gage, British North American commander, was appointed royal governor of Massachusetts. (Gage and Washington had been comrades at Braddock's Defeat in 1755.) More of the hated redcoats trooped ashore from warships in the harbor. But since Gage's regiments were confined to Boston, British authority ended at city limits. His Majesty's ancient plantation of Massachusetts Bay had edged into open rebellion.

News of the Intolerable Acts reached Williamsburg when Washington was attending the House of Burgesses. On May 26, 1774, the Burgesses passed a resolution calling for a day of fasting and prayer to protest this "heavy Calamity, which threatens Destruction to our civil Rights, and the Evils of Civil War." The governor promptly dissolved the House. Just as promptly, the delegates reassembled in a tavern and continued debate in an extralegal session. They proclaimed solidarity with Massachusetts and called for a

"general congress" of "the several Colonies of British America." This became the First Continental Congress. George
Washington was elected one of the Virginia delegates.

The British plan to divide the colonies by punishing
only Massachusetts had failed. Washington argued that
"the cause of Boston . . . now is and ever will be considerd
as the cause of America," and his sentiments were shared
by all patriots.[4] Earlier than most colonists, Washington,
who had so often fruitlessly appealed to British authorities,
concluded that further petitions to king and Parliament
were futile: neither side would back down, and Americans
could only choose between surrender and resistance. King
George agreed. "The dye is now cast," he told his prime
minister; "the Colonies must either submit or triumph."
The king wanted war: "The New England governments
are in a state of rebellion. . . . Blows must decide whether
they are to be subject to this country or independent."[5]

Convinced by the republican ideology he had absorbed
from his reading and from his mentor George Mason of
Gunston Hall, Washington now saw a malign British conspiracy to reduce the colonials to slavery. "An Innate Spirit
of freedom has told me, that the Measures which Administration hath for sometime been, and are now, most violently pursuing, are repugnant to every principle of natural justice; whilst much abler heads than my own, hath
fully convinced me that it is not only repugnant to natural
Right, but Subversive to the Laws & Constitutions of Great
Britain itself. . . . I could wish, I own, that the Dispute had
been left to Posterity to determine, but the Crisis is arrivd
when we must assert our Rights, or Submit to every Impo-

sition that can be heap'd upon us; till custom and use, will make us as tame, & abject Slaves, as the Blacks we Rule over with such arbitrary Sway."[6]

In July 1774, Washington chaired a mass meeting at the Fairfax County Court House that adopted a series of influential resolutions—the Fairfax Resolves—affirming the Americans' right to govern themselves and organizing a new boycott of British trade. Ominously, the twenty-third resolution warned that if the king continued to ignore their demands for justice, "there can be but one Appeal"— the appeal to arms.

When the delegates to the First Continental Congress met in Philadelphia in September 1774, they were pleased to discover that leaders from such diverse colonies were in agreement on so many issues. They also took one another's measure. Some who had known Washington only by reputation might have been surprised by the forty-two-year-old's youthfulness. They might be excused from assuming that a man who held so high a rank in the "French war" must be a decade or two older. Congress passed a resolution declaring that colonial assemblies, not Parliament, retained "exclusive power of legislation . . . in all cases of taxation and internal polity" in America.

The folly of king and Parliament had at length driven the Americans from a principled denial of Parliament's right to tax them to an outright rejection of any parliamentary authority over the colonies. The British had unwittingly framed the debate as a choice between complete subordination to or complete independence from Parliament's control. Very well, the Americans responded, we

choose independence. Patriot leaders now claimed in effect
a sort of commonwealth status, in which, as members of
the British Empire, they might grant loyalty to the king
but owed no obedience to Parliament. The British, of
course, greeted such interpretations with indignation. The
Americans were in rebellion and they would be crushed by
British power.

Massachusetts had already felt British power by the
time the Second Continental Congress met. Parliament
formally declared Massachusetts to be in a state of rebellion. General Gage was ordered to move against the rebels. Gage sent a raiding party into enemy territory, which
by now comprised most of the thirteen colonies. The objectives were certain patriot leaders and the gunpowder
thought to be stored at Concord, a few miles outside Boston. No gunpowder was confiscated, but both sides managed to explode quantities of it that day—the momentous
"19th of April," 1775. The morning's first volleys swept the
minutemen from Lexington Green, but in the hours that
followed, the redcoats paid the price. Resurgent minutemen poured fire into the regulars' ranks and sent them
reeling back into the arms of the relief column that saved
them from annihilation. Thousands of armed patriots
from throughout New England converged on Boston and
ringed the city, besieging Gage's regiments within.

In June 1775, the king's men had a chance to redeem
themselves. The patriots tightened their grip on the city by
seizing Breed's Hill, a commanding eminence just across
the harbor. The British resolved to drive them off. In certain circumstances, firearms can give untrained men an

edge over regular soldiers. The battle of Bunker Hill produced just such a circumstance for the Americans. For the British, the battle was productive of little but carnage. They finally forced the Americans from the hill, but only after leaving one thousand dead and wounded, nearly half their number, on the bloody slopes leading up to the rebel redoubt. A few more such victories and Britain would have no army left in Boston. In the future, His Majesty's generals would be disinclined to order frontal assaults on fortified rebel positions.

George Washington had impressed his fellow delegates at the first Congress. They admired not only his youthful bearing but also his calm judgment and his unswerving commitment to the American cause. They recognized in him an astute politician and a practiced legislator. The Virginian made an even stronger impression at the second Congress, for Washington attended sessions at the Pennsylvania State House wearing his buff and blue uniform. Towering over six feet, a glittering sword swinging at his side, Washington looked magnificent. The uniform signified both his command of the Virginia militia and his readiness to risk his life as the men of Massachusetts had done. Washington and most of the other delegates knew that all hope of a peaceful resolution had died at Lexington. "Unhappy it is though to reflect," he wrote, "that a Brother's Sword has been sheathed in a Brother's breast, and that, the once happy and peaceful plains of America are either to be drenched with Blood, or Inhabited by Slaves. Sad alternative! But can a virtuous Man hesitate in his choice?"[7]

The uniform, of course, also signaled Washington's

willingness to assume high command in the coming struggle. On June 14, Congress declared that the New England militia companies camped outside Boston now constituted the Continental Army. The next day it named Washington that army's supreme commander, bumping the Virginia colonel up four grades to full general with a minimum of ceremony. Washington accepted the commission. But he told his colleagues, "I feel great distress, from a consciousness that my abilities & Military experience may not be equal to the extensive & important Trust. . . . I do not think myself equal to the Command I am honoured with."[8] He refused any salary, asking only that his expenses be met, a gesture that deeply impressed his countrymen.

Historians have long debated Washington's reasons for accepting the command, apparently against his better judgment. Douglas Southall Freeman, the indefatigable author of a seven-volume biography of Washington, insisted that the Virginian did not want the command, that he unwillingly accepted it "in spite of wish and inclination."[9] Was it concern for his honor that obliged a reluctant Washington to assume a burden he never wanted? This was certainly the reason the new general gave his anxious wife, waiting for him at Mount Vernon: "You may believe me my dear Patcy, when I assure you, in the most solemn manner, that, so far from seeking this appointment, I have used every endeavor in my power to avoid it. . . . But, as it has been a kind of destiny, that has thrown me upon this Service, I shall hope that my undertaking it is designd to answer some good purpose. . . . It was utterly out of my power to refuse this appointment without exposing my Character to such censures as would have reflected dishonour upon myself."[10]

But such explanations do not always conform to the true wishes of those who offer them. George Washington wanted the command. His ambition demanded nothing less, and he was too good a politician not to know that the appointment would probably be his. As we have seen, he had probably suspected for years that a general's rank might be in his future. One simple fact is often overlooked: Washington must have known that no other American was more qualified than he to lead the armies of the united colonies. If he truly wanted to preserve American liberty, he could make but one decision. As he had put it himself, "Can a virtuous Man hesitate in his choice?" Of course, he had to exercise caution—the smallest hint that he sought power would alarm a people so jealous of their liberties, so fearful of tyrants. Congress had picked one of its own, a gentleman of substantial fortune. His fellow delegates knew him well enough to trust that George Washington stood before them in the uniform of a patriot, not a military usurper.

Washington's duty to what he called "the glorious cause" and his hopes for himself had become two sides of the same coin. For he was contending now for the prize that for him surpassed all others—more brilliant than any rank or title, more alluring than a rich wife or an opulent plantation, more enduring than power itself. If he could achieve victory over the might of Great Britain, the general stood to win the kind of fame that outlasts the centuries. Washington's yearning for honor burned as brightly as ever. Only now his highest aspiration was the success of the American cause, for that success would bring George Washington as much of immortality as fame can ever give. As one eulogist would put it about two weeks after Washington's death, "self-love and love of country coincided."[11] Washington and America were merging, coming together until it was hard to understand where one began and the other ended.

At the same time, Washington's fears were unfeigned. "I am now Imbarked on a tempestuous Ocean," he wrote a friend a few days after his appointment, "from whence, perhaps, no friendly harbour is to be found."[12] He reportedly had tears in his eyes when he told Patrick Henry that "from the day I entered upon the command of the American armies, I date my fall, and the ruin of my reputation."[13] A former militia officer who twenty years before had commanded small bodies of men with limited success, Washington was now charged with leading an entire army against the most formidable power on earth. Within a few months, he would bitterly regret that he had ever taken the assignment.

General Washington arrived in Boston on July 2, 1775, ready to assume command. The motley collection of some seventeen thousand New England militiamen he found encamped at Cambridge was an army only in so far as Congress had designated it one. Troops from other colonies were on their way to Boston, but so far the only genuinely continental feature the army could boast was that a Virginian commanded the New England officers and men. Washington's appointment, John Adams told his wife two

days after it took place, would unite the colonies and af-
firm the continental scale of the American cause by giving
the northern army a southern head.[14] And it would ease
fears that a successful New England general at the head
of a New England army might be tempted to conquer the
other colonies after he had defeated the British.[15]

On his way to Boston, Washington engaged in a revealing exchange with the New York Provincial Congress.
Key to Washington's success was how well he understood
and fulfilled his countrymen's expectations. The New York
Congress congratulated and praised the new general, but
went on to caution "that whenever this important Contest
shall be decided . . . You will chearfully resign . . . and reas-
sume the Character of our worthiest citizen."[16] Speaking in
the first person plural for himself and his fellow soldiers,
Washington assured them that "when we assumed the
Soldier, we did not lay aside the Citizen, & we shall most
sincerely rejoice with you in that happy Hour, when the
Establishment of American Liberty . . . shall enable us to
return to our Private stations in the bosom of a free, peaceful, & happy Country."[17]

As Garry Wills put it in *Cincinnatus,* "More than most
men, this man *was* what he meant to his contemporaries.
If he played a necessary role in the birth of the republic, it
is important for us to assess the expectations of his audience, along with his willingness consciously to meet those
expectations. . . . The way Washington conceived his task,
and went about it, was tempered from the outset by the
responses he hoped to elicit from his countrymen."[18]

Washington now wondered how to mold the unruly

mass of minutemen into an effective fighting force while also keeping up the siege. He was shocked to learn that the army had so little gunpowder that he could issue only nine rounds per man. (A soldier customarily went into battle with forty rounds in his cartridge box.) This fact obviously had to be kept from the British and was treated as a profound secret. Lack of American firepower could enable the enemy to overrun the entire army at will. The shortage of gunpowder remained a problem throughout the siege of Boston.

Issuing his first orders on July 4, 1775, he told the men that they were now the army "of the United Provinces of North America; and it is hoped that all Distinctions of Colonies will be laid aside."[19] But the general himself was still sounding like a Virginia grandee when he wrote a friend at home that the New Englanders were "the most indifferent kind of people I ever saw . . . an exceedingly dirty & nasty people."[20] Their "leveling spirit" was far too democratic for his tastes. He was chagrined when such slurs from his private letters were leaked to Congress.

Washington insisted that officers must be gentlemen, men of reputation, and not elected from the rank and file as the militias did. They should not sleep and eat with their enlisted men. Unable to provide uniforms, he ordered officers and men to wear badges of rank. He cashiered many officers he found wanting. The camp stank. He ordered the soldiers again and again to dig proper latrines and use them, instead of resorting to ditches and fields. His efforts bore fruit. An army chaplain observed that "there is a great overturning in camp as to order and regularity. New lords, new laws. The Generals Washington and Lee [Charles Lee, second in command] are upon the lines every day. . . . Great distinction is made between officers and men. Everyone is made to know his place and keep it, or be tied up and receive thirty or forty lashes depending on his crime."[21]

Sometimes the commander in chief took more direct action. The story is told that when a riot broke out between a regiment of Virginia riflemen and some of the New England troops, Washington rode full speed into the center of the thousand-man melee, threw himself from his horse, and grabbed two of the brawlers by their throats. He held them out at arm's length and shook them, all the while filling the air with awesome curses. The fight quickly broke up.[22]

Washington faced a more daunting concern. Terms of enlistment for most of the troops would expire in December 1775.[23] The men would be free to go home. The army would dissolve. The general declared that this would "expose the Country to desolation, and the Cause perhaps to irretrievable Ruin."[24] But he was up against the long-standing New England tradition of contractual military service. The men believed that they had done all they had signed up to do. In November 1775, Washington and the Congress set about to raise a new Continental Army to serve for one year, until the end of 1776. Meanwhile, Massachusetts pledged a militia of 5,000, New Hampshire 2,000, and those men slowly came into camp. The task of training and disciplining would have to start all over again with the new troops. Many of the new soldiers did not even have muskets. Washington was most eager to reenlist the experienced men who had been serving in the siege. He was able to persuade about 3,500 to stay on. He ended up with a new army of about 10,500. "It is not within the pages of History perhaps to furnish a case like ours," he wrote John Hancock, president of the Continental Congress. "To maintain a post within musket shot of the Enemy for six months together, without powder, and at the same time disband one Army and recruit another within that distance of twenty odd British regiments is more than probably ever was attempted."[25]

He warned Congress that "to bring Men well acquainted with the Duties of a Soldier requires time—to bring them under proper discipline & Subordination, not only requires time, but is a Work of great difficulty, and in this Army, where there is so little distinction between Officers and Soldiers, requires an uncommon degree of attention— To expect the same Service from Raw, undisciplined Recruits as from Veteran Soldiers is to expect what never did, and perhaps never will Happen."[26]

From his earliest experiences as an officer, Washington had learned to despise militias—irregular troops with amateur officers drawn from the same locality and contracted to serve for a limited period. During the French and Indian War, Washington had drilled his own Virginia Regiment into an elite force—the equal, he insisted, of any regiment of British regulars. But he had believed that most of the militias at his disposal were worthless. It was a puzzle how men who had not been paid for months could manage to stay perpetually drunk. No doubt intoxication dulled their chronic hunger and helped them forget that they still had no uniforms or tents or cooking kettles. Drunk or sober, the militiamen had robbed civilians, neglected their weapons, and brawled lethally with one another. Colonel Washington built a guardhouse to lock up the worst offenders. The men tore it down. They deserted nonchalantly—singly, in groups, by units. The colonel hopefully recalled the savage punishments he had watched Braddock's officers inflict on the redcoats in their ranks—practices described as "discipline by torture."[27] Flogging was the cornerstone of this brutality. Washington handed out twenty-five lashes with a cat-o'-nine-tails on the bare back for cursing, fifty for faking illness, one hundred for drunkenness, five hundred for brawling, and a round thousand lashes for desertion.[28] Sometimes he treated desertion as a capital crime. He erected a forty foot–high gallows and hanged two habitual deserters from its lofty crossbeam. Then he pardoned the rest of the condemned men. One of the penitents demonstrated his gratitude by running off again. Colonel Washington presently concluded that hanging was as useless as flogging: his militiamen appeared beyond the reach of military discipline. Whole companies vanished. Fifty of the fifty-eight men in one company disappeared, sixty-four of seventy from another.[29] He couldn't hang them all.

Now, twenty years later in this new war, the country wanted him to fight the British Empire with militias. He wrote, "The Dependence which the Congress has placed upon the Militia, has already greatly injured—& I fear will totally ruin, our Cause—Being subject to no control themselves they introduce disorder among the Troops you have attempted to discipline while changes in their living brings on sickness—this makes them Impatient to get home, which spreads universally & introduces abominable Desertions."³⁰

Washington knew that victory required a regular army, a standing army of professional soldiers enlisted for the duration of the war. Yet fear of standing armies was one of the central precepts of republican ideology. Standing armies were the bane of liberty, the tool of tyrants. Militia volunteers were virtuous patriots who owed their first loyalty to the people. Standing armies were loyal to the government that paid them or, worse yet, to their own commanders. All educated people remembered that ambitious generals at the head of victorious legions had overthrown the liberties of classical republics of antiquity. Many Americans were also convinced of the ineluctable superiority of their citizen soldiers to professional troops from Europe. Imbued with virtue, motivated by love of country, fighting for all they held dear, the Americans would surely overcome the mercenaries who fought for pay. The destruction of Braddock's redcoats, as well as the performance of the New England minutemen at Lexington, Concord, and Bunker Hill had also fostered the notion that irregulars could triumph over professional armies. This conviction was an abject fantasy, as one British victory after another would soon demonstrate. Washington argued, "I am persuaded and as fully convinced, as I am of any One fact . . . that our Liberties must of necessity be greatly hazarded, if not entirely lost If their defense is left to any but a permanent, standing Army I mean One to exist during the War."³¹

Washington extolled virtue and patriotism but knew that those qualities alone could not win the war. "Men may speculate as they will—they may talk of patriotism—they may draw a few examples from ancient story of great achievements performed by its influence; but whoever builds upon it, as a sufficient basis for conducting a long and bloody War, will find themselves deceived in the end."[32] Washington was a bedrock realist; he believed humans were primarily motivated by self-interest, which he called "Interest." On September 25, 1776, he lectured the president of Congress:

> When Men are irritated, & the Passions inflamed, they fly hastily, and chearfully to Arms, but after the first emotions are over to expect . . . that they are influenced by any other principles than those of Interest, is to look for what never did, & I fear never will happen. . . . A Soldier reasoned with upon the goodness of the Cause he is engaged in and the inestimable rights he is contending for, hears you with patience and acknowledges the truth of your observations, but adds that it is of no more importance to him than to others—The Officer makes you the same reply, with the further remark, that his pay will not support him. . . . The few therefore, who act on Principles of disinterestedness, are, comparatively speaking no more than a drop in the Ocean. It becomes evidently clear then, that this contest is not likely to be the Work of a day . . . you must have good Officers, there are, in my judgement, no other way to obtain them but by establishing your Army upon a permanent footing; and giving the officers good pay. . . . To place any dependance on Militia, is, assuredly, resting upon a broken staff.[33]

Congress and the states would continue to resist his efforts to establish and support a standing army for a long time to come. But eventually longer terms and enlistments for the duration of the war were put in place.

While the siege of Boston dragged on, two American armies led by heroic commanders invaded Canada, both meeting defeat at Quebec. On Washington's orders, Colonel Benedict Arnold led about twelve hundred men on a grueling march through the Maine wilderness to the Saint Lawrence River. The journey was so arduous that many turned back, and some perished. The troops were reduced to eating bark and shoe leather. Nevertheless, the survivors reached Quebec in November 1775 and besieged the city. From the shores of Lake Champlain, Brigadier General Richard Montgomery led a similarly sized column north and captured Montreal. Then Montgomery moved downriver to join Arnold at Quebec. On the last night of 1775, in a driving snowstorm, Arnold and Montgomery launched simultaneous assaults on opposite sides of the city. Both were driven back with heavy losses. Arnold was badly wounded in the leg. Montgomery was killed, his face shot off. Hundreds of Americans were killed or captured. The survivors kept up a halfhearted siege, then withdrew when smallpox ravaged their encampment. The plan of Congress to bring Canada into the Revolution had ended in failure.

The siege of Boston had become a stalemate, a staring contest. General William Howe had replaced Thomas Gage in October 1775, becoming the second British commander Washington would face. Howe had led the redcoats up Bunker Hill. That battle had given him too much respect for American irregulars fighting behind fortifications to contemplate an assault. Washington, on the other hand, had retained all his aggressive instincts and was more than willing to bring on battle. Three times he proposed an all-out attack on the town. The third time was to have been an assault across the frozen expanse of the bay with the lead elements on ice skates. Three times he was dissuaded by his generals' council of war, a body Congress had suggested that he heed. It is well that no attack was ever made. The American amateurs would probably have been annihilated by the firepower of the British fleet and fortifications. Washington was discouraged. He lamented, "I have often thought, how much happier I should have been, if, instead of accepting a command under such Circumstances, I had taken my Musket upon my Shoulder & enterd the Ranks, or, if I could have justified the Measure to Posterity, & my own Conscience, had retir'd to the back Country, & livd in a Wig-wam."[34]

He continued to worry about his most precious asset, his reputation. Many Americans believed that Washington's army was large and well equipped. Why, then, did he not move aggressively against the British? But he could hardly afford to announce the true condition of his army. "I know, that much is expected of me—I know that without Men, without Arms, without Ammunition, without any thing fit for the accommodation of a soldier that little is to be done—and, which is mortifying; I know that I cannot stand justified to the World without exposing my own Weakness & injuring the cause."[35]

London soon recognized that nothing could be gained in Boston and ordered General Howe to abandon the city. But Howe did not have the ships he needed to bring off all his troops, their equipment, and the loyalists who wanted to leave with the king's men. He would have to stay until the spring of 1776. By spring, the tactical situation had been transformed. In February 1776, in an extraordinary logistical feat, Henry Knox had hauled into camp the artillery from Fort Ticonderoga. In March, Washington placed the guns on Dorchester Heights overlooking the city and its harbor. Now Howe had to attack to take out the artillery on the high ground or evacuate Boston. He chose evacuation, on March 17, 1776. The Continental Army marched into the city. Harvard awarded the commander in chief an honorary degree. Congress voted him a gold medal. But despite American rejoicing, it was an empty victory. The enemy had left Boston only in order to win the war elsewhere. Although British conduct of the war was never distinguished by strategic brilliance, or even by much strategic coherence, the high command did understand that Boston, far to the north, was not a suitable base from which to undertake the subjugation of the colonies. When the fleet carrying England's regiments sailed out of Boston harbor for Halifax both sides knew that New York City would be the next target. And disaster awaited Washington and his untried army at New York.

⁂ 6 ⁂

Winter Soldier

THE BRITISH REACHED NEW YORK in July. Washington had been waiting there since April. From England, Canada, and South Carolina, Great Britain had brought together the greatest expeditionary force ever assembled. The masts of the 430 ships at anchor resembled a forest. The thirty-two thousand soldiers and ten thousand sailors made up the largest assembly of humanity on the continent, their numbers exceeding the population of Philadelphia. The great army encamped on Staten Island.

In command were a pair of brothers. General William Howe was chief of the army in America. His elder brother, Admiral Richard, Lord Howe, one of England's most distinguished seamen, commanded the North American fleet. Each had won celebrated victories in the late war against France. The Howes were also royal cousins of George III. Everyone knew that their mother was an illegitimate child of the king's great grandfather, George I. There had once been three Howe brothers. The eldest, George Augustus, then Lord Howe, had been a hero to the colonials. When he was killed at Ticonderoga in 1758, Massachusetts voted £250 to build his monument at Westminster Abbey, a gesture that deeply touched the younger brothers. Indeed, the Howes had an abiding affection for their colonial American cousins. They would conquer them if they must, but they had really come to bring peace. For the Howes held a dual appointment from their government—they had been appointed peace commissioners as well as military commanders. Their devotion to peace would influence the way they made war, a contingency that worked to Washington's considerable advantage in the coming campaign. The Howes' peacemaking powers, however, were limited. They could negotiate and grant pardons only after the Americans had abandoned their rebellion. And far from backing down, the Americans had now chosen independence.

Not least among advocates of independence had been the commander of the Continental Army. Washington had been pushing independence for months. His actions over the past year had already done much to move his country in that direction. But the British themselves had done far more. The king to whom Americans appealed had harshly condemned his subjects as traitors and rebels. His Majesty's soldiers and sailors had attacked American commerce, destroyed property, even burned whole towns like Norfolk in Virginia and Falmouth in Massachusetts. They had armed Virginia slaves against their masters and sent the tribes surging across the western frontiers. Killing is carried forward by its own inexorable logic. Few were ready to forgive in 1776.

That January, Washington and thousands of others had discovered the intoxicating prose of Thomas Paine's *Common Sense*. "A few more such flaming Arguments as were exhibited at Falmouth and Norfolk, added to the sound Doctrine, and unanswerable reasoning containd (in the pamphlet) Common Sense," Washington predicted, would soon convince Americans to seek independence.[1] Paine urged them to embrace not just independence but a whole new era of history. "We have it in our power to begin the world over again," he insisted.[2]

Paine condemned government-by-birth and sentenced it to death. Monarchy and aristocracy were evils surviving from a savage past. The time had come to destroy hereditary power forever, and that high destiny belonged to the Americans. Paine appealed to their growing conviction that they were a people chosen to lead the world to liberty. "The cause of America," he assured them, "is in a great measure the cause of all mankind."[3] Paine was right. The future that the American Revolution inaugurated would eventually tumble Europe's proud ones into political obscurity. The protracted war that was just beginning in 1776 would transcend the contest for colonial independence to become a mighty revolution waged in the name of human equality.

And so, as the Continental Army awaited battle in New York, the great news came from Philadelphia. Congress had voted independence. Washington ordered the Declaration of Independence read to every unit in the army "with an audible voice." The preamble proclaimed it a self-evident truth "that all men are created equal," but the proposition Washington's soldiers must now argue with their lives was contained in the final paragraph: "That these United Colonies are, and of Right ought to be Free and Independent States; that they are Absolved from all Allegiance to the British Crown, and that all political connection between them and the State of Great Britain, is and ought to be totally dissolved."

Yet Washington had chosen to defend an indefensible city. He was badly outnumbered by superior troops, and New York's geography of rivers, bays, and islands gave overwhelming advantage to an enemy who possessed absolute naval supremacy. It was true that New York was the strategic hub of the war. The British planned to win by splitting the colonies in two, sending one army up the Hudson corridor to meet another army coming down from Canada. Then isolated New England, cradle of the rebellion, would be reduced before the British set about to subdue the mid-Atlantic and southern colonies.

Still, why had Washington elected to fight a campaign he seemed certain to lose, one that he did in fact lose so badly that he nearly lost the war in the bargain? There was the putative victory in the siege of Boston. The evacuation had not shown that Washington was a military genius or established that the Continental Army was a match for the British regulars. Nevertheless, many came away from the siege with exaggerated notions of American prowess. Some of this optimism may have rubbed off on Washington. Most republicans still mistakenly believed that militia, virtuous citizen-soldiers, could overcome regulars. Although Joseph Ellis has written that Washington's experiences in the French and Indian War had given him "immunities against any and all forms of youthful idealism," the commander in chief himself may have also fallen, however briefly, for this fallacy.[4] His orders to the army before the New York battles are hymns of praise to patriotism and republican virtue as the keys to victory. He may also have feared the Revolution would collapse in despair if he failed to defend New York. He dreaded a long war. If there was a chance for a quick victory, he must take it. His sense of honor also compelled him to fight. The Congress itself seemed to assume that America must fight for New York.

With about twenty-three thousand troops, most of them unreliable militia, Washington faced Howe's thirty-two thousand regulars. (Though Washington's force was weak enough, it was, unfortunately, as numerous as any he would ever have at his disposal. He would never again command so large a body of American soldiers as the one assembled at New York before the debacle of 1776.) British numbers included some eight thousand Hessians, tough, brutally disciplined soldiers King George had hired from the German princelings. Washington had divided his army in the face of a superior enemy. Most of the army was in New York City on the southern tip of Manhattan Island, but he also had forces on Long Island, on Governor's Island, and in northern Manhattan.

The enemy regiments landed on southern Long Island on August 22. In the kind of consummately executed amphibious joint operation of which only the British were capable, the army and navy brought ashore thousands of redcoats and Hessians without losing a man. Brushing aside feeble resistance, they moved north toward the main American position. Washington believed the Long Island

landing was a feint to mask the main attack on New York.
He kept most of his army on Manhattan. He was wrong.
Howe had most of his force on Long Island—twenty thousand regulars and Hessians were deployed. The Americans faced them with about ten thousand soldiers.

The American position ran roughly west to east for
about four miles along a ridge of high ground anchored on
the west—the American right flank—by fortified Brooklyn
Heights and the East River. The line continued southeast
along a range of steep, forested hills called the Heights of
Guan. The hills were penetrated by four passes, each with a
road running through it. West to east, the first three passes
were strongly defended by Continental troops. The fourth,
however, Jamaica Pass and Jamaica Road, was guarded by
exactly five men. Jamaica Pass was the eastern extreme of
the American line—the army's left flank. That vital flank
had been left unprotected. It was, in military parlance, "up
in the air."

Washington hoped above all for a British repetition
of the Bunker Hill fight, a costly frontal assault on his en-
trenched army. He had prepared a second line of entrench-
ments to fall back to if the first were overrun. A series of
bloody charges could bleed the enemy to death. Washington assured Congress that "if our Troops behave well,
which I hope will be the case, having everything to contend for that Freemen hold dear, [the British] will have
to wade through much blood & Slaughter before they can
carry any part of our Works, if they carry 'em at all."[5] But
General Howe, who had personally led the attack on Bunker Hill, had no intention of obliging. He would simply

outflank the Americans. It was a maneuver first proposed by Major General Henry Clinton, Howe's second in command. Clinton was intimately familiar with the backroads of Long Island from his boyhood as the son of the provincial governor of New York.

On the night of August 26, Clinton led a column of ten thousand soldiers in a silent march through Jamaica Pass and around west into the rear of the American positions. Howe followed. He had left another ten thousand facing the Continentals' front. The Americans, facing two-to-one odds, were now sandwiched between two armies. The British troops in contact with the American right and center went into action in the predawn darkness of August 27. The redcoats and Hessians had been ordered to bring the Americans to battle, but not to press them too aggressively before the trap was sprung. At about 8 A.M., two signal guns fired. In that moment, the rest of the British surged forward into the American's rear. The enemy already in contact went over to all-out attack. Outgeneraled and outnumbered, surrounded by better-trained, better-equipped opponents, some of the Americans fought bravely, one Maryland regiment futilely charging the British grenadiers six times. Most Americans, however, did not fight at all, running at the first sight of the enemy. It was the first true battle of George Washington's military career, though he was not in command in the field. He could only watch helplessly through his telescope. As he saw one small detachment heroically resisting an overwhelming attack, he exclaimed in dismay, "Good God! What brave fellows I must this day lose!"[6]

Soon it was all over. The Continental regiments collapsed. They ran west to the safety of the fortifications on
Brooklyn Heights. Numbers were killed or captured as they
ran. Many were killed as they tried to surrender. Bayonets
were the weapon of choice for dispatching rebels. Some
were pinned to trees by the long blades. Others drowned
crossing a creek and the salt marshes that bordered it. At
low tide their leg bones could later be seen sticking up out
of the muddy bottoms. A British observer said that in the
battle the Hessians and the redcoats failed "in one thing
only—they could not run as fast as their Foes, many of
whom indeed were ready to run over each other."[7]

With many hours of daylight remaining, Howe could
have could well have continued the offensive—his men
were so excited by victory that he had trouble holding
them back—with a good chance of annihilating the American army and perhaps bagging Washington himself. Howe
chose not to. Was his role as peace commissioner closer to
his heart than his mission as military commander? Did he
hope that his smashing victory had taught the Americans
a lesson that would incline their hearts toward reconciliation? Perhaps he simply thought the Continental Army
was already finished and the war already won. Washington was pushed up against the East River with no apparent way to join the rest of his army in New York City. A
couple of frigates from Admiral Howe's fleet could seal
him in for good. Still unwilling to risk his men in a frontal
attack on Brooklyn Heights, William Howe began a siege,
digging trenches to approach the American lines. A heavy
rainstorm broke out, keeping the fleet away.

Washington knew that he had to evacuate Long Island, but retreat while in contact with the enemy is one of the most perilous of all military undertakings. He gathered in all the boats that could be found on both sides of the half-mile-wide river. Two regiments of Massachusetts watermen from Marblehead and Salem took charge. When darkness fell the army began embarking. The soldiers moved in complete silence—British lines were only 250 yards away. The evacuation took all night and well into daylight the next morning, when a providential fog blinded the British to the departure of the final boats. Washington had brought over ninety-five hundred men as well as most of his artillery, equipment, and horses in one of the most successful retreats in military history. He was the last man to step onto a boat. He had not slept in more than two days.

New York City was a town of less than a mile square located at the southern end of Manhattan Island. The only way off the island by foot was King's Bridge, which crossed the Harlem River at the northern tip. To fatally bottle up the Continental Army, all Howe had to do was land an army in the north. Then he could destroy the Americans at his leisure, which was how the British commander preferred to make war in the first place.

Major General Nathanael Greene, who had started the war as a private, was a complete military amateur. He was, nevertheless, George Washington's most gifted subordinate. Greene now urged an immediate retreat from New York. "A General and speedy Retreat is absolutely necessary and that the honour and interest of America requires it," he argued. "I would burn the City & its suburbs."[8] The other general officers agreed. Greene wanted to save the army, which Washington was willing to risk. Washington would soon come to see that Continental Army *was* the Revolution, its preservation his highest mission. Nathanael Greene seems to have arrived at that realization before his commander: Washington elected to stay on and risk the army to defend New York.

Meanwhile, the Continental Army was already near collapse. The soldiers were undisciplined, exhausted, hungry, and demoralized by their crushing defeat. Many were sick. They had no faith in their ability to stand up to the fearsome redcoats, and they no longer had faith in their commander in chief. Washington had lost about fifteen hundred men in the battle of Long Island. But in the days after withdrawing to New York, he lost many times that number from desertion. The militia was heading home by companies, practically by regiments. Washington informed Congress that "the Militia of Connecticut is reduced from 8000 to less than 2,000."[9] He sent the rest of them home as useless.

Still in no hurry to finish the job, Howe waited two weeks before going on the offensive. On September 15, the British landed at Kip's Bay, midway up the island. With the thunder of a spectacular naval bombardment still ringing in their ears, the redcoats and Hessians came ashore from the East River. They formed up, and presently the well-ordered British columns started for the American trenches, advancing steadily across farmers' fields where today only the towers of midtown grow. Washington's men, some of whom were armed only with spears, sprang up from behind their earthen walls and ran in utter, abject panic. Those who tried to surrender were massacred by the Hessians.

Admiral Howe's secretary watched from the flagship and recorded the British victory in his diary: "The Spirit and Activity of the Troops & Seaman were unequalled: Every man pressed to be foremost. . . . The dastardly Behaviour of the Rebels, on the other Hand; sinks below Remark."[10] The "Poltroons," he wrote, fled without firing a shot. General Washington would not have argued with the Englishman's assessment of his men's performance. He tried to halt their disgraceful retreat, cursing and striking out at the fleeing soldiers. "Good God," he cried, "have I got such troops as these?" "Are these the men with whom I am to defend America?"[11] Dazed by humiliation, Washington rode within eighty yards of the enemy and would have been killed or captured by the advancing Hessians if an aide had not pulled him off the field. The Americans fled New York City, leaving behind their artillery and equipment. The British let them escape. Howe marched triumphantly into the city, rapturously welcomed by the numerous loyalists. The enemy would hold New York for seven years, until the end of 1783. In reward for his victories, Howe's royal cousin King George III made him a Knight of the Bath. He was now Sir William.

Despite the drubbing he had taken, Washington still did not follow the course that strategy obviously dictated— to abandon New York altogether. And Howe did not follow what was obviously his best course—to seal the Americans up on the island. About ten thousand Americans dug in on Manhattan's Harlem Heights, where cliffs made for natural fortifications. The line spanned the island from river to river. The enemy halted a mile or two south. A small American patrol went out to probe the British position. A brisk skirmish broke out and reinforcements were fed in until each side had about two thousand engaged. This time it was the redcoats' turn to run. The Americans fought well and drove them back to their lines. Some of the same men who had retreated so shamefully from Kip's Bay the day before were now cheering wildly as they chased the fleeing British. The Battle of Harlem Heights was of no tactical significance but it did much to raise the drooping spirits of the Continental Army.

After the September 16 battle both the British and the Americans sat still for almost a month. Congress had ordered Washington not to burn New York. Just after midnight on the windy night of September 21, a great fire, origins unknown, broke out and soon destroyed about a third of the city. "Providence, or some good honest fellow," Washington commented, "has done more for us than we were disposed to do for ourselves."[12] The Americans still held two forts on the Hudson, Fort Washington in New York and Fort Lee opposite in New Jersey. The ostensible purpose of these forts, and of the obstructions in the river, was to deny the Royal Navy passage of the Hudson. But warships had already sailed right past the forts. It would seem time to withdraw the garrisons. But Washington ordered the forts held.

On October 12, Howe finally swung into motion. Sailing up the East River, he landed a force in the Bronx, east of King's Bridge, the Americans' only exit from Manhattan Island. At last, Washington abandoned New York, pulling out of the lines on Harlem Heights, crossing the Harlem River off the island, and making a day's march north to the village of White Plains.

The Americans, about fourteen thousand of them, dug in again on some hills along a line centered on White Plains. Howe had missed another chance to hurt the Continental Army when it was strung out in a long, vulnerable column on the retreat from Harlem Heights. It took him another week to confront Washington at White Plains. After driving in some skirmishers, Howe's troops hit the American line. Fighting centered on Chatterton's Hill on the Continentals' right flank. Howe sent regiment after regiment, British and Hessian, as well as cavalry, against the hill before finally driving the defenders off. The American flank was turned, but Howe made no attempt to exploit it. It was another American defeat. The Continental Army continued its northern withdrawal.

Howe did not follow. He turned back to New York to take out Fort Washington. George Washington had wanted to give up Fort Washington. Against his instincts, however, he had let Greene and other officers convince him that the place could be held, retaining an American toehold on Manhattan. It may have been the worst blunder he ever made.

On November 14, Howe sent an overwhelming force against the fort. From across the river, Washington watched through his telescope. He saw the defenders driven back into the fort, the surrender, and finally the slaughter of some of the prisoners by the Hessians. He knew he was responsible for the debacle that had cost three thousand casualties. Washington Irving, the general's Victorian biographer, even claimed that in his despair Washington broke down and wept.[13] While this is hard to credit, given the man's steely self-control, there is no doubt that Fort Washington was the low point of George Washington's war. In Congress, and in the army, even among his top aides, there was talk that he was not up for the task.

What was left of the American army was divided into three forces. Washington commanded about five thousand. General Charles Lee, Washington's second in command, a respected but erratic British officer who had thrown in his lot with the Americans, had about fifty-five hundred effectives in the Hudson Highlands guarding the approach to New England. The third division, under General Edward Heath, numbered about thirty-two hundred effectives. Washington moved his army across the Hudson into New Jersey. It was getting cold. The soldiers had lost almost all their equipage in the long retreat. They lacked tents and blankets and warm clothes. They were dressed in rags. Many had no shoes and marched barefoot or with rags wrapped around their feet. And enlistments were set to expire. New Year's 1777 was approaching, and, at the stroke of midnight, most of Washington's Continentals would resume the character of civilians, free to return to their homes. Many soldiers decided not to wait—the epidemic of desertion continued.

General Clinton had been sent north to occupy Newport, Rhode Island. Howe's new second in command was

General Charles, Earl Cornwallis, a most able thirty-eight-
year-old aristocrat. Howe sent Cornwallis across the Hudson to destroy Washington's disintegrating army. Cornwallis scooped up Fort Lee with its vast store of valuable
supplies. But he failed to trap Washington. The Americans
retreated to Newark. They were now, said one of Washington's aides, "the wretched remains of a broken army."[14]
Cornwallis continued his relentless pursuit. Washington
talked of retreating into the Ohio Valley. In a letter to his
brother he predicted that, unless Congress found a way
to recruit a new army, "the game will be pretty near up."[15]
He said that "£50,000 Should not induce me again to
undergo what I have done."[16] In another private letter he
wrote, "Such is my situation that if I were to wish the bit-
terest curse to an enemy on this side of the grave, I should
put him in my stead with my feelings. . . . I see the impossibility of serving with reputation, or doing any essential
service to the cause by continuing in command, and yet
I am told that if I quit the command inevitable ruin will
follow from the distraction that will ensue. In confidence
I will tell you that I was never in such an unhappy, divided
state since I was born."[17] But concern for his reputation,
injured now by repeated failure, and, above all, his devotion to the glorious cause compelled General Washington
to soldier on.

Cornwallis had one chance to destroy the Continentals
but held back, constrained by orders from Howe to wait for
the arrival of the rest of the British Army. The Americans
reached Trenton on the Delaware River and crossed into
Pennsylvania, collecting all the boats they could find to

prevent Cornwallis from following them over. Still, nothing could long keep the British from crossing. Soon they could cross on the ice. The enemy was now within thirty miles of Philadelphia. Patriots began leaving the city. Congress itself fled to Baltimore. General Washington, who just four months earlier had commanded an army of more than twenty thousand, now counted about three thousand dispirited troops. Howe issued a proclamation offering a pardon to rebels who would swear allegiance to the king. Many in occupied New Jersey came forward to take the oath.

On December 12, a desperate Washington requested and Congress granted him authority to raise a "New Army," voting him for six months "full power to order and direct all things relative to the department and to the operations of war." Some claimed that Congress had made him a dictator. "Happy it is for this Country," the congressional motion continued, "that the General of their Forces can safely be entrusted with the most unlimited Power."[18] Washington himself thought he had been given "powers that are too dangerous to be entrusted. I can only add that desperate diseases require desperate remedies; and with truth declare I have no lust after power."[19] He set about to recruit his New Army, but that would take time. He called the other American armies to join him in Pennsylvania, but they were slow in coming. Meanwhile, the people of New Jersey were learning that not even a loyalty oath could keep them safe from looting, brutality, and rape at the hands of the Hessians, Europeans who had gone to war for plunder and marched with wagons full of stolen goods. Throughout the war, George Washington did everything he could to assure that his troops did not abuse civilians, with some measure of success.

Then, with the destruction of the Americans apparently within his grasp yet again, Howe decided to suspend the campaign in December and take his army into winter quarters in New York. It had turned bitterly cold. (Howe's was not such a strange decision; eighteenth-century armies did not campaign in winter.) He left a chain of garrisons facing the Americans. The most advanced outpost was at Trenton, on the Delaware's Jersey shore. The town was held by three crack Hessian regiments, about fifteen hundred men. Commanding was Colonel Johann Gottlieb Rall, a hard-drinking soldier who had spent thirty-six of his fifty years in the army. His regiments had performed well at White Plains and Fort Washington.

Washington understood that the death of the Revolution was at hand if he did not seize the initiative. Exposing his army to destruction as fearlessly as he exposed his own person to gunfire, Washington decided to recross the Delaware and strike the enemy in a surprise attack. Trenton was to be the target. Three American columns would make the crossing on Christmas night, aiming for predawn attack on the town. The main army, some twenty-four hundred men under Washington himself, would cross the eight hundred–foot–wide Delaware about ten miles upstream from Trenton and march to hit the town from the north and west. This contingent would include a heavy force of artillery, eighteen guns in all. A force of eight hundred militia would cross at Trenton to block the Hessians' escape. A third force of about two thousand would land twelve miles below the town to create a diversion. As it turned out, only Washington's army made it across that stormy night. Ice jams stymied the other two columns.

Contrary to legend, the Hessians in Trenton were not drunk or hung over the day after Christmas. But they were exhausted and sleep-deprived. Incessant raids and ambushes by American militia and guerrillas had made their nights miserable. The German soldiers were ordered to sleep in full uniform with even their cartridge boxes buckled on. Spies and loyalists brought warnings of the impending attack, but Colonel Rall, whose contempt for the American rabble was measureless, only scoffed. Still, the Germans must have felt a sense of relief when a winter storm blew in of such intensity as to preclude any military action that night. Or so it seemed.

The storm caught Washington's soldiers at the crossing on Christmas night. It rapidly increased in violence, the "hurricane" winds driving rain, sleet, hail, and snow into the men's faces. Washington was deeply worried. The operation was seriously behind schedule. That meant his army would attack Trenton in broad daylight, not in predawn darkness. He stood to lose the element of surprise. It was three in the morning on December 26 before the artillery and horses reached the Jersey shore. He had planned to be across by midnight. The soaked and freezing soldiers set out for Trenton. Two fell out in a snowbank and froze to death. The falling snow soon covered the bloody tracks left by the bare feet of some men.

Washington moved along the column on horseback, encouraging the men and urging them forward. "'Soldiers keep by your Officers,'" he said. "'For Gods Sake keep by your officers.' Spoke in a deep & solemn voice."[20]

About halfway to Trenton, the main road divided. Washington split his force and sent a column on each road to hit the Hessians from two directions. It was now after eight A.M., but so intense was the storm that it was almost as dark as night. Fortune favored the Americans. Both columns arrived to attack at the same moment. The Americans charged aggressively, emerging out of the swirling snow. Washington led from the center. The Hessians were completely surprised. The Germans tumbled out of their lodgings and formed up in the streets. Rall commanded on horseback. Now the heavy artillery the Americans had hauled and floated to the battlefield with so much difficulty began to tell, raking the enemy ranks with round shot and canister. The Germans too deployed artillery, but their guns were quickly taken out by cannon and musket fire. A Hessian attempt at a counterattack by two regiments was turned back. Then Rall was hit in the side by two bullets, falling from his horse mortally wounded. Soon the German regiments were grounding their muskets and striking their colors. About five hundred escaped over a bridge at the lower village, but the Americans captured the rest of the garrison, some nine hundred men in all. About one hundred Hessians were killed or wounded. No Americans were killed in the battle and only a few wounded.

Washington and his officers briefly considered the possibility of continuing the offensive against another British post. But the soldiers were frozen and exhausted, the severe weather continued, and they had nine hundred prisoners and a vast store of captured munitions to contend with. The Americans crossed the Delaware back into Pennsylvania.

The year was drawing to its end, and then the enlistments of many of Washington's soldiers would end too. But Washington was still determined to drive the British out of New Jersey altogether. Emboldened by their success, the general and his officers decided to renew the campaign a few days later. On December 29, the reinforced American Army crossed into New Jersey again. On New Year's Day, Washington had more than five thousand troops and forty artillery pieces in Trenton. Sent at a gallop from New York, Cornwallis moved against him with eight thousand regulars and Hessians. (The Hessians were furious over Rall's defeat. Their commander ordered them to take no prisoners. Any soldier who showed mercy to an American captive would receive forty lashes on his bare back.) Cornwallis left three regiments of redcoats, fifteen hundred men, behind in Princeton as a rear guard, with orders to join the main army the next day. On January 2, 1777, the two armies clashed on the approach to Trenton. American resistance slowed Cornwallis's advance. But the Continentals were driven back to a strongly defended position along the creek that ran below the town. Cornwallis attacked, but his troops couldn't fight their way across the bridge that spanned the creek. He had meant to try again that day, confident of overwhelming his foe. He was sure he could turn the Americans' right flank. But the early January twilight gave him pause. His men were exhausted. Should he ask them to assault a strong position in darkness? He decided to hold off. "We have the old fox safe now," he said. "We'll go over and bag him in the morning."[21]

Indeed, Washington seemed to be pinned against the creek with no way out. He considered staying to give battle to Cornwallis the next day, but soon decided on an even bolder plan. The Americans pulled off another skillful night withdrawal on an obscure, unmapped country road. He left behind some men to make noise and feed the campfires to lull the British. When daylight came, Cornwallis was astonished to find his enemy gone.

Washington's twelve-mile night march was not a retreat, but a renewed offensive. The objective was Princeton, garrisoned by Cornwallis's fifteen hundred–man rear guard. Washington outnumbered them four-to-one. Almost as soon as the Americans reached the outskirts of Princeton, they ran into two regiments of redcoats marching to Trenton to join Cornwallis. The British, astonished to find the Americans there, nevertheless attacked aggressively. After an exchange of volleys, the Americans broke under a bayonet charge. Just as the British were getting the upper hand, Washington rode into the fight on his white charger. "Parade with us, my brave fellows," he shouted. "There is but a handful of the enemy, and we will have them directly!"[22] He rode between the lines and within thirty yards of the redcoats. Both the Americans and the regulars fired a volley at the same moment, with Washington between. Smoke obscured the general. When it cleared, he was still on his white horse, unscathed, still urging his soldiers forward. Many of the officers and men were dismayed by their indispensable commander's reckless bravery. An artillery major said that the army had only one quarrel with their beloved general: "the little care he takes of himself in any action. His personal bravery, and the desire he has of animating his troops by example, make him fearless of any danger. This, while it makes him appear great, occasions us much uneasiness."[23]

Presently American numbers began to tell—the British broke and ran. The Americans pursued them with Washington leading the way on his charger, shouting, "It's a fine fox chase, my boys!" Most of the British brigade escaped, but the Americans had killed or captured nearly five hundred. It was a brilliant action that enraged Cornwallis, who marched his army to the sound of the guns at a killing pace but arrived too late to catch the Americans.

With Princeton, the fighting season ended. Washington took his army into winter quarters at Morristown, New Jersey. The British, who had occupied nearly all of the state just ten days earlier, now withdrew from New Jersey almost entirely. They remained in winter quarters in New York City. General Howe enjoyed his season of food, drink, and the charms of his lovely mistress, the wife of a cynical loyalist. Winter quarters for Washington and the Continentals was considerably less comfortable.

Trenton and Princeton had been small affairs, hardly more than skirmishes by European standards. Yet the impact was immense. Back from the dead, the Continental Army marched through Jersey again, this time as victors, and General Washington began issuing pardons to those the British had cajoled into swearing allegiance to the crown. Eager to adhere to the winning side, many came forward. It was a complete reversal of fortune. News of Trenton and Princeton came with a miraculous ring to the ears of a people certain that the speedy extinction of the American cause was at hand: George Washington and his soldiers had saved the Revolution. The once-confident British began to despair that the war might be lost. Sir William Howe, who had seen things going his way, toward American collapse and imperial reconciliation, the soft peace he and his brother so desired, was now confounded. He wrote his superiors in London, "The unfortunate and untimely defeat at Trenton has thrown us further back than was at first apprehended, from the great encouragement it has given the rebels. I do not see a prospect of terminating the war but by a general action, and I am aware of the difficulties in our way to obtain it."[24]

And George Washington had won a measure of the military glory he had craved since he was a boy. He had also redeemed himself from half a year of crushing defeat, despair, and self-doubt. He was again America's hero. "Had he lived in the days of idolatry," reported the *Pennsylvania Journal*, "he had been worshiped as a god."[25]

The commander in chief had also gained a new respect for his soldiers. His general orders to the army the day after Trenton glowed with newfound pride in his army: "The General, with the utmost sincerity and affection, thanks the officers and soldiers for their spirited and gallant behavior at Trenton yesterday. It is with inexpressible pleasure that he can declare, that he did not see a single instance of bad behavior in either officers or privates; and if any fault could be found it proceeded from a too great eagerness to push forward upon the enemy."[26] In the months of defeat, he had expressed real contempt for his feckless soldiers, particularly the lowborn New England men the Virginia aristocrat so disdained. Victory had swept all that away. He was beginning to regard these common people as his own brothers in arms. As Ron Chernow has observed, "Though he still believed in hierarchical distinctions, especially between officers and their men, the war was molding him into a far more egalitarian figure."[27] His affection swelled further when he was able, in a dramatic personal appeal from horseback, to persuade many of the soldiers on their way home to sign up for another enlistment. Many of the reenlistees later said in their Revolutionary War pension applications that they had stayed with the army because of their admiration for their commander.[28]

In winter camp in Morristown, Washington risked putting the entire army through the complicated and dangerous procedure of inoculation against smallpox. The program was successful; there was no mass outbreak. Since a smallpox epidemic raged throughout North America during most of the Revolution, it was one of wisest decisions Washington ever made.[29]

∻ 7 ∾

Brandywine, Germantown, and Monmouth

I**T WAS NOT UNTIL** nine months after Princeton that Washington again faced the British Army in a major engagement. Most of the campaigning season of 1777 had been consumed in fruitless maneuverings, marches and countermarches, as the baffled Washington tried to divine Howe's intentions. The two armies finally collided on the banks of Brandywine Creek, west of Philadelphia, on September 11, 1777. The result was another splendid victory for British arms, another stinging defeat for the Continental Army. Yet that army escaped intact, and most of its regiments had fought creditably. Then, outmaneuvering Washington, the British marched into Philadelphia on September 26.

It was an event the Americans had long dreaded and the Howe brothers had looked to as a signal of victory. Yet taking the American capital city and chasing Congress from its seat never did yield advantages commensurate with European expectations. Indeed, occupying the three largest cit-

ies in America—Boston, New York, and Philadelphia—had
brought the British no closer to winning. Moreover, Howe's
fixation on Philadelphia contributed to an all-important
British defeat at Saratoga, New York, in October 1777.

The ministry in London and the British high command
in America had long believed that the Hudson River was
the strategic key to the war. Holding the river corridor from
Canada down to New York would split the colonies and
cut off radical New England. Howe's capture of New York
in 1776 had secured the southern end. In London in early
1777, General John Burgoyne persuaded King George to
give him an army that would invade the upper Hudson
Valley by way of Lake Champlain, going all the way to Albany. There, presumably, an army under Howe, striking
north out of New York, would join him. But Burgoyne expected little American resistance—he considered Howe's
support unnecessary.

Burgoyne started south from Canada in June with an
army of more than eight thousand regulars, about half of
them German, augmented by hundreds of Canadians, loyalists, and Indians. Soon news came that the British general
had captured the strategic American post of Fort Ticonderoga. Meanwhile, Howe had already cast his eyes toward
Philadelphia. He wanted above all to bring the Americans
to battle and was certain that Washington would fight to
defend his capital. The British general also had great, if
misplaced, faith in the strength of American loyalists in
the Philadelphia area. Meeting Burgoyne in Albany was
low on Howe's list of objectives. Dispatches made their
months-long voyages back and forth across the Atlantic.

London reluctantly acquiesced to Howe's choice but still seemed to think that he would somehow be able to link up with Burgoyne after Philadelphia fell. Strategic incoherence prevailed in the British government and high command.

Howe also had a choice of how to approach Philadelphia. He could march his army overland through New Jersey or use Lord Howe's fleet to go by sea, sailing up the Delaware River directly to the city or landing on Chesapeake Bay. On July 23, 1777, having already spent two weeks onboard, Howe and his eighteen thousand troops sailed out of New York on the 270 ships of the transport fleet. The fleet was headed south, apparently setting out to capture Philadelphia. Still, Washington could not be sure of British intentions. Sound strategy, he was convinced, would certainly compel Howe to support Burgoyne. The southern departure could be a feint to disguise Howe's real plan of taking the army up the Hudson to aid the Canadian invasion. Washington meant to march the Continental Army to Howe's destination, wherever, north or south, that might be.

It presently became clear that Howe's objective was indeed Philadelphia. After seeming ready to go up the Delaware River directly to the city, the fleet withdrew, entered Chesapeake Bay, and, three weeks later, dropped anchor near the mouth of the Elk River, in Maryland. The troops started coming ashore on August 25, after six weeks of punishing confinement aboard the cramped, stifling transports. Most of the horses had died on the voyage, depriving Howe of the advantage he had once possessed in cavalry.

Reinforcements had by now brought American numbers up to sixteen thousand. France, though still neutral, had secretly reequipped the Continental Army, sending thousands of muskets, gunpowder, and military supplies. Washington was as eager for battle as Howe. He put himself between the British and the city. On his way, he marched the Continental Army through Philadelphia. He wanted to impress the populace, patriot and loyalist alike, with its strength and numbers. Washington led on his white charger with his aides; cavalry and the general officers followed, and then came the men, marching twelve abreast through the streets for two hours. Despite their commander's repeated pleas to Congress, most soldiers had no uniforms. Many were dressed in rags, and not a few were without shoes. Their muskets, on the other hand, appeared well burnished and were carried with an air of intimacy with their uses. And every man was wearing in his hat a "green sprig, emblem of hope." Congressional delegate John Adams, no soldier himself, judged the soldierly qualities of the Continental Army: "Much remains to be done. Our soldiers have not yet quite the air of soldiers. They don't step exactly in time. They don't hold up their heads quite erect, nor turn out their toes exactly as they ought. They don't all of them cock their hats; and such as do, don't all wear them the same way."[1]

On September 11, the Americans were in a strong position on the east side of Chad's Ford on the Brandywine. There they awaited Howe's attack. Douglas Freeman wrote that "Washington conducted the Brandywine operation as if he had been in a daze."[2] The resulting battle bore an uncanny resemblance to the disaster on Long Island fourteen months earlier. Again Washington's grasp of local terrain was conspicuously defective. He had few maps, and his mounted scouting detachments were poorly directed. He should have done more reconnoitering himself. He did not know that unguarded fords across the Brandywine upstream and some miles north of Chad's Ford offered the British a way around his right flank. Howe learned of the crossing from a spy and quickly decided to repeat his Long Island success by flanking Washington and attacking his army in the rear. A strong force would hold the American center and left at Chad's Ford.

Unlike Long Island, however, this time Washington suspected that Howe would try to turn his flank. He was confident that he could counter the move or possibly withdraw without fighting. Howe and Cornwallis, leading a force of some eight thousand troops, started their long flanking march at dawn. Another British column, sixty-eight hundred men under Hessian Lieutenant General Baron Wilhelm von Knyphausen, moved east to confront the Americans at Chad's Ford. Washington began skirmishing across the creek with Knyphausen. He was confused by contradictory reports about the approach of Howe's flanking column. Howe and Cornwallis arrived to threaten the American right flank about 2:30 in the afternoon but did not immediately attack. The American regiments on the flank shifted north to meet the British threat, and Washington had enough time to rush in some reserves. The Americans maneuvered frantically to get into position. Howe sent his redcoats and Hessians forward at 4:00. Unlike the Long Island debacle, this time the outflanked Americans fought fiercely, lashing the advancing enemy with musketry and cannon. The crest of a hill that formed one line of battle changed hands five times. Both sides suffered heavy casualties. Gradually, relying as usual on the bayonet, the British gained the upper hand. The Americans began to run. Washington sent Greene's division at a run from Chad's Ford to cover the retreat. He himself rode the scene of the fighting, arriving in time to see the line collapse. At about the same time, Knyphausen's regiments crossed the Brandywine and drove the Americans back from Chad's Ford. The Continental Army's left flank was turned as well. It was now a question of whether the Americans could get off the battlefield without being destroyed. In the end, Greene's hard-fighting division slowed the British advance until darkness fell. The Americans narrowly escaped destruction. The weary men staggered along most of the night, fleeing east from the battleground. Howe did not pursue them. Despite the defeat, American morale remained high. "I saw not a despairing look, nor did I hear a despairing word," one American officer declared. "We had our solacing words already for each other—'Come, boys, we shall do better another time.'"[3] To Congress, Washington confirmed that "notwithstanding the misfortune of the day, I am happy to find the troops in good spirits."[4]

He remained determined to defend Philadelphia. He was preparing for a new battle a few days later when a prodigious downpour intervened, immersing both armies. "It came down so hard," a Hessian officer remembered, "that in a few moments we were drenched and sank in the mud up to our calves."[5] The Americans were in worse shape. The

rain had soaked all the ammunition in their flimsy cartridge boxes. They couldn't fire a shot. Washington had to
withdraw to resupply. Ten days later, Cornwallis marched
into Philadelphia. The Congress had fled to Lancaster.

To the north, Burgoyne was finding that his progress
down the Hudson was not to be the parade of triumph he
had foreseen. The uncontested capture of Ticonderoga on
July 5 was satisfactory enough of course, but after that nothing went according to plan. The Americans took advantage
of terrain by felling trees across the roads, wrecking bridges,
damming up streams, and digging ditches. The British took
twenty days to cover one stretch of twenty-two miles. It
was impossible to keep the large army supplied. Nearly
two hundred miles of hard travel ruled out relief from
Canada, and the region through which they were marching was largely unsettled. Burgoyne sent a Hessian colonel
with about one thousand men on a raid to Bennington,
Vermont. The Hessians were to seize food, horses, cattle,
and wagons. But New England militia decisively routed
them on August 16.

Burgoyne then crossed his army from the west bank of
the Hudson to Saratoga on the eastern side. Horatio Gates
commanded the American Northern Department. He had
six thousand or seven thousand troops and would soon
be heavily reinforced by militia. The Americans dug in at
Bemis Heights, smack in Burgoyne's path to Albany. The
British attacked on September 19. Gates held overall command, but the extraordinarily brave General Benedict Arnold provided the crucial combat leadership. The day was
a draw, though the British took heavy losses they could not

hope to replace. The two armies clashed again on October 7. Again, Arnold led brilliantly until he was wounded. Burgoyne was defeated. Unable to retreat to Canada, surrounded by militia and Continentals, he had no choice but to surrender his entire army, nearly six thousand survivors, on October 17, 1777. The capture of the British army at Saratoga was the turning point of the American War for Independence. American morale soared, and France now concluded that it was time to enter into a military alliance with the rebels.

And Washington was still eager to fight, despite Brandywine and the fall of Philadelphia. Howe had scattered his army around the city. The largest detachment, some nine thousand men, was stationed at Germantown, a village five miles to the northwest. Four roads leading into Germantown seemed to beckon to Washington for a coordinated attack on the enemy garrison. Four columns of infantry—two militia and two Continental—would hit simultaneously at 5:00 A.M. on October 4, 1777. The Continentals would attack straight into the town from the north in parallel columns, while the militia would hook around both flanks to hit the British rear. The scheme, with its dawn surprise attack and its converging columns, bore some resemblance to Trenton. Historian Robert Middlekauff has written, "On the map the plan looked brilliant, and it very nearly worked on the ground."[6] Another night march got the attackers into position, but British scouts alerted Howe to their approach. Washington had ordered "bayonets without firing." Nevertheless, gunfire broke out as soon as the troops came together. The Continentals on the right, commanded by New Hampshire General John Sullivan, came into contact first, and, fighting in a heavy fog, managed to drive the outnumbered British light infantry back into Germantown. Washington again exposed himself to "the hottest" enemy fire until Sullivan begged him to retire. Several companies of redcoats, about a hundred men, barricaded themselves in Cliveden, the Chew family's imposing stone mansion, and began to fire from the windows on the advancing Americans. The Continentals wasted a good deal of time, and as many as seventy-five lives, trying unsuccessfully to drive them out. The delay may have cost them the battle. Gun smoke thickened the fog that confused all movements. Even sounds were distorted. Two Continental brigades exchanged fire when a possibly drunken American general disobeyed orders. Slowly, the Americans began to pull back. When the reinforced British pressed forward, the pullback became a general retreat.

The other column of Continentals reached the town only after Sullivan's men had retreated. Their flanks exposed, they too were overwhelmed and routed. One entire American regiment, the 9th Virginia, was captured. The two columns of militiamen did not manage to join the attack at all.

Germantown was yet another defeat for the Continental Army. Historians have usually faulted Washington for the excessively complicated battle plan, which divided his army. But it was clear that the Americans were fighting with greater skill and resolution. The British were impressed. A Scottish grenadier, Captain John Peebles, called "this attack . . . the most spirited I believe they ever made on the British troops."[7] It was equally clear that George Washington remained an aggressive commander, despite ample evidence that his army could not yet match British performance on the open battlefield. Americans and Europeans alike were impressed that Washington had been bold enough to go on the offensive so soon after his defeat at Brandywine.

Germantown marked the end of the 1777 campaigning season. The main British force would make winter quarters in Philadelphia, while Clinton's army continued to garrison New York City. For the Continental Army's winter camp, Washington chose some barren hills northwest of Philadelphia, a place known as Valley Forge. On October 22, Lieutenant General Sir William Howe resigned his command. General Howe knew that the ministry in London was dissatisfied with him for conducting the American war with too much leniency and for his part in the Saratoga catastrophe. Howe himself was dissatisfied with the ministry. He believed the war could not be won without the massive reinforcements that London would not provide. Because of the time required for dispatches to cross the ocean, Howe was not replaced until May 8, 1778, by Lieutenant General Sir Henry Clinton, the third British commander that Washington had opposed. By that time, Great Britain was at war with France.

The suffering of the Continental Army at Valley Forge is the stuff of legend, but the reality was hardly mythological. Something like a quarter of the army, about twenty-five hundred men, died of starvation, cold, or disease. Washington believed that "Men without Cloat[hes] to cover their nakedness, without Blankets to lay on, without Shoes, by which their Marches might be traced by the Blood from their feet . . . is a mark of Patience and obedience which in my opinion can scarce be parallel'd."[8] Washington said that "in Camp not less than 2898 Men [are] unfit for duty by reason of their being bare foot."[9]

Valley Forge provided a defensible position close enough to Philadelphia to keep an eye on the enemy while far enough from settlements to prevent conflict with civilians. The eleven thousand soldiers (of whom eight thousand were considered fit for duty) marched into Valley Forge on December 21. They had already been living in the open for months. The hills were forested, and the soldiers set to work building crude huts of fourteen by sixteen feet to hold a dozen men each. They lived in tents until the huts were finished in mid-January. Washington himself slept in a tent until the men had huts, then moved into a small farmhouse. (Martha soon joined him in the camp, as she would do every winter of the war.) The soldiers were already half-starved and worn out by hard campaigning. At first, there was nothing in the commissary but twenty-five barrels of flour, which meant that the only food was firecakes, a kind of biscuit of flour and water baked over the campfires. Albigence Waldo, a surgeon with the Connecticut Line, recorded in his diary on December 21 that there was "a general cry thro' the Camp this Evening among the Soldiers, 'No Meat! No Meat!'—the Distant vales Echo'd back the melancholly sound—'No Meat! No Meat!' Immitating the noise of Crows & Owls, also, made a part of the confused Musick. What have you had for your Dinners Boys? 'Nothing but Fire Cakes & Water, Sir.' At Night. 'Gentlemen the Supper is ready.' What is your Supper Lads? 'Fire Cakes & Water, Sir.'"[10] Washington called the hooting and cawing "a dangerous mutiny."[11] He saw only three courses ahead for the army—it must either "Starve, dissolve, or disperse."[12] Foraging parties brought in enough to keep most of the men alive, but there were plenty of days when no rations at all were distributed. Farmers, wherever their sympathies might lie, preferred to sell their goods for British gold rather than take Continental paper or government IOUs. The worst month was February 1778, when rains turned the roads into mires and kept even meager supplies from reaching camp.

Conditions improved slightly as the winter passed. More rations came into the camp and most of the men got new clothes, if not uniforms. And there were some other important changes.

In March, Frederick Wilhelm von Steuben, a forty-seven-year-old captain from the Prussian Army, arrived at Valley Forge. He claimed to be a former lieutenant general and a baron. He spoke no English. Despite not sharing a common language, Washington took to the ebullient Steuben. He put him in charge of drilling the army. The phony baron started with 150 men. He taught them to march and maneuver like professionals, drilling them by platoons, companies, and finally whole regiments. He trained assistants to drill the rest of the army. The process was complete by spring.

Hundreds of officers resigned their commissions or

took long furloughs to escape the grimness and squalor of
Valley Forge. Washington stayed in camp all winter, writing letters, tirelessly lobbying Congress and the states to
come to the aid of his suffering soldiers. He did not really take a day off during the entire war. (And for what it's
worth, there is no reason to believe that George Washington ever prayed on his knees in the snow at Valley Forge,
despite the many cornball depictions—ranging from prints
and paintings to statues and stained glass windows—of his
doing so. He never prayed on his knees, even in church—he
always stood during prayers. Besides, it would have soiled
his uniform, a result he would have abhorred. The story is
another fabrication of Parson "Cherry Tree" Weems, ap-
pearing for the first time in the seventeenth edition of his
enormously popular life of Washington.)

While American soldiers perished at Valley Forge, American negotiators in Paris achieved a signal diplomatic triumph. After three years of watching, France threw its might
into the struggle. French statesmen had been encouraged by
the Declaration of Independence, the victory at Saratoga, and
reports of capable fighting by Washington's Continentals.
They also had confidence in George Washington himself,
whose heroic reputation had reached across the ocean.
Early in 1778, in two treaties signed at Paris, England's old
adversary promised to support the Americans, and, if war
broke out between Britain and France, not to stop fighting until America won its independence. On May 5, 1778,
George Washington announced to the army that "it having
pleased the Almighty ruler of the Universe propitiously to
defend the Cause of the United American-States and finally

by raising us up a powerful Friend among the Princes of the
Earth to establish our liberty and Independence . . . it becomes us to set apart a day for . . . celebrating the important
Event."[13] Every soldier got a shot of rum and chance to fire
his musket in a running fire of the entire army. "Long live
the king of France!" they shouted. The alliance was hardly
a surprise. Rivalry between Britain and France stretched
back for centuries, and France badly wanted revenge for defeat in the Seven Years' War. The European nation had held
back for three years to make sure the Americans would not
collapse or reconcile with Britain. France had a large army,
a powerful navy, and many strategic overseas possessions.
In one stroke, the Revolution had become a world war that
would be fought in Europe and the Caribbean as well as
North America.

Direct French military aid was not initially as decisive as the Americans hoped. France, however, also had
an ample treasury. Throughout the rest of the war, thanks
to the inspired diplomacy of American minister Benjamin
Franklin, France advanced vast loans to the United States,
sustaining the war effort when Congress and the states
consistently failed to provide money. The huge French national debt this created helped to bring about the revolution that eventually cost America's benefactor King Louis
XVI his head.

King George and his government struggled to adjust
to the altered circumstances. France was now the primary
enemy; there were even fears of an invasion of the British
homeland. For a time the British considered withdrawing troops from the colonies altogether to concentrate on

fighting France and Spain, which had followed its fellow Bourbon power into the war. The American rebellion would be suppressed by a naval blockade. Clinton, in command in Philadelphia, was ordered to send five thousand men to the West Indies and three thousand to Florida. He was also told to abandon Philadelphia and pull back to New York.

The British placed some hope in a new peace commission sent by the king to negotiate with the Continental Congress. The Carlisle Commission offered what would once have been thought generous terms, terms that might have proved fully sufficient to resolve the crisis before independence was declared. But since George III adamantly refused to recognize American independence, Congress refused to meet with the commissioners. The peace commissioners even tried unsuccessfully to bribe some of the congressional delegates. King George was convinced that the loss of America would mean the dissolution of the Empire and would plunge his nation into irretrievable ruin, reducing Britain to a second-rate European power. In the face of great opposition, against many in Parliament and long after most of his ministers had given up, the king would cling to his determination to hold on to the colonies. He almost abdicated his throne rather than concede independence. The war would go on another five years, in no small part because of the stubbornness of the king.

Despite the near-reverence with which many patriots regarded George Washington, no one could fail to note the contrast between Horatio Gates's triumph at Saratoga and the string of defeats Washington had suffered at the hands of Sir William Howe. There were subdued murmurings that he might not be up to the task. Historians once considered this to have been a full-scale conspiracy in Congress and the army to bring Washington down—the "Conway Cabal," so named for the Irish-born general Thomas Conway, Washington's chief foe in the army. Scholars now discount the notion of an authentic conspiracy, but Washington and his allies certainly thought there was one. Putative military incompetence was not the detractors' sole concern. They saw Washington's immense prestige as antithetical to republican principles. "The people of America have been guilty of idolatry in making a man their God," charged an anonymous pamphlet, *Thoughts of a Freeman*.[14] John Adams told his wife, Abigail, that it was a good thing Saratoga had not been Washington's victory: "If it had been, idolatry and adulation would have been unbounded, so excessive as to endanger our liberties."[15] Washington and his supporters struck out fiercely against what he believed to be a plot against him, revealing himself as a formidable political infighter. No one really dared to challenge him again after he destroyed Conway.

Clinton pulled out of Philadelphia on June 18, 1778, marching overland through New Jersey to New York City. The Continental Army shadowed him. Clinton's progress was slow. He had a vast twelve mile–long train of some fifteen hundred wagons, most filled with loot plundered from Philadelphia. He was also bringing along thousands of loyalist refugees and camp followers and a herd of cattle to feed the army. His army itself numbered about ten thousand.

The weather that summer was unusually hot, with temperatures approaching one hundred degrees. There was no shade and little water. Both armies suffered intensely. Scores of men on both sides dropped dead from heatstroke. Suffering the most were the Hessians in their heavy woolen uniforms with knee-length boots, cumbersome muskets, and sixty-pound packs. Many died. Even more deserted, leaving the army and making their way back to American-held Philadelphia. (As many as one-quarter of the German soldiers that King George sent to the war chose desertion, staying in the New World and becoming Americans.) Many of Clinton's redcoats also deserted during the overland march.

Washington was eager for a fight—he wanted to attack the British on the march. But almost all his generals were strongly opposed. They urged him to follow the British column without seeking battle, giving Clinton a "golden bridge" to withdraw to New York. No subordinate was more strongly opposed to fighting than the eccentric Major General Charles Lee. Congress had named Lee Washington's second in command in 1775. He had many supporters in Congress and an undeserved reputation for military brilliance. Even Washington deferred to him. Lee was strange looking, slovenly, and uncouth. He went everywhere with a pack of dogs, the only companions he could tolerate. He had done nothing to fulfill the promise some saw in him. In truth, he had long been a thorn in Washington's side. He declined to obey Washington's orders to bring his army to join the Continentals in the grim winter of 1776. Then, in November 1776, he allowed himself to be taken by a British patrol while carelessly sleeping in a tavern away from his army. He was carried away in humiliation, still wearing his nightshirt. Americans were downcast. The British were jubilant—they believed they had captured the most able of all the rebel officers. Lee remained a prisoner until he was exchanged for a captured British general in April 1778. During his captivity, he apparently collaborated with the British, giving them advice on how to win the war and offering to negotiate with Congress on their behalf, an offer Congress declined. Nevertheless, on his release he was restored to his post as Washington's second in command. Now he vehemently opposed any attack on Clinton's retreating army. Still, unwilling to abandon the offensive, Washington decided on a compromise. He would not seek all-out battle but would use part of his army to attack the end of Clinton's column, the wagon train and rear guard. But as planning proceeded, the force assigned to this attack grew to some five thousand men, nearly half of the twelve thousand–man Continental Army. Despite his initial opposition, Lee now insisted that, as second in command, that he deserved leadership of the attack he had argued against. Washington deferred to his wishes, blundering in giving command to an officer who had opposed the operation in the first place.[16]

Lee moved against Clinton at Monmouth Court House on June 28, 1778. The general had no plan, and Washington had erred again in giving his subordinate no clear orders. Lee apparently intended simply to advance until he met the enemy, then play it by ear. Again, American preparations were deficient. Lee had no maps and had sent forward no scouts. He had no idea of enemy dispositions, and he was advancing across unknown terrain. And, as he would soon demonstrate, Lee was also feckless and

indecisive, completely lacking the attributes of a successful commander. The result was a near-debacle that Washington heroically redeemed. One historian has described
Monmouth as an "extraordinarily confused and confusing
battle."[17] Lee came into contact with elements of the enemy
at midmorning. He had no plan and gave no orders. The
American regiments were mixed up, mixed together. The
field officers had no idea what was going on. The heat continued hellish. The thermometer stood at ninety-six in the
shade. Heatstroke killed dozens of soldiers, dropping them
dead in their tracks. Presently, Clinton turned back from
his march to join the rear guard and deployed to attack
the Americans. Washington was meanwhile bringing up
the rest of the Continental Army. It was to be a general
engagement after all. Then one American brigade in contact with the enemy shifted position, pulling back to more
easily defended terrain. Observing this, other American
units thought a retreat had begun and also pulled back.
The movement became a general, disorderly retreat. Lee
gave no orders. Although the withdrawal may have been
tactically justified, Lee had not ordered it. In truth, he had
completely lost control of his army. He sat on his horse,
helplessly watching his soldiers stream past him. He had
lost the confidence and support of his generals. One of
them, Anthony Wayne, refused even to speak to Lee.

Coming forward with the rest of the army, Washington
ran into the retreating mass. He couldn't believe his eyes.
The officers had no idea what was going on. One colonel
said the men were flying from shadows. Then Washington met Lee. There are several versions of what passed be-

tween the two men. Enraged, Washington demanded an explanation for the retreat, the disorder, and the confusion. Reduced to incoherence by his commander's wrath, Lee could only stammer, "sir, sir." Some old stories said that Washington's language was "strongly expletive . . . a terrific eloquence of unprintable scorn," that he cursed out Lee "till the leaves shook on the trees" and "swore like an angel from heaven."[18] But these tales are probably apocryphal. There is no doubt at all, however, that Washington was extremely angry. Lee tried to excuse himself by explaining that he had opposed the attack from the beginning. Washington sternly told him that his doubts did not relieve him from his duty to obey orders.

Turning his back on Lee, Washington rode forward toward the British. It turned out that, properly led, the Continentals were still eager to fight. They rallied to Washington on his white charger. Of Washington at Monmouth, Lafayette said: "His presence stopped the retreat. . . . His fine appearance on horseback, his calm courage . . . gave him the air best calculated to excite enthusiasm." Lafayette remembered that Washington rode "all along the lines amid the shouts of the soldiers, cheering them by his voice and example and restoring to our standards the fortunes of the fight. I thought then, as now, that never had I beheld so superb a man."[19]

Washington grabbed a pair of sturdy regiments—the 13th Pennsylvania and the 3rd Maryland—and arrayed them in a battle line to slow the advancing British. Then he brought forward the main body of the army and put it in strong position behind the temporary line. The Americans were drawn up on high ground with artillery, both flanks securely anchored. From that line, fighting all afternoon and into twilight, the Americans beat back a series of poorly coordinated attacks by the flower of the British Army, including the elite grenadiers and light infantry under the ever-aggressive Cornwallis. Cornwallis even personally led a desperate cavalry attack. The Americans shot the British horsemen to tatters, driving them back in bloody defeat, but Cornwallis was unhurt. Both sides fought with courage and determination, and casualties were heavy.

Night found both exhausted armies sleeping on their arms. Washington planned to renew the fighting in the morning, but Clinton, imitating a tactic Washington had employed, chose to slip his army away in the night, leaving his campfires burning. The battle of Monmouth was over. Clinton completed his march to Sandy Hook, from which the Royal Navy ferried his army and wagon train to New York City. Washington claimed victory, warmly praising and congratulating his troops. In his memoirs, Clinton would declare that the victory had been his. Both claims had some merit. Monmouth was a draw, but never, after the near-debacle of Lee's retreat, had Washington and the Continental Army performed so splendidly.

Lee demanded a court-martial to vindicate his reputation. Washington was happy to oblige. Washington accused Lee of making "an *unnecessary, disorderly,* and shameful retreat."[20] Lee was soon convicted of disobedience and insubordination. The court suspended him from the army for a year. Congress then cashiered him altogether. Another of Washington's rivals in the army had gone up.

No one knew it at the time, but Monmouth marked the end of the war's campaigning in the northern and middle states. Washington would not fight the British in a major engagement again for more than three years—not until the war-winning victory at Yorktown in October 1781. The theater of war shifted to the South, where the British initially achieved considerable success. But in the summer of 1778, British prospects appeared bleak. Despite all their efforts, they held only the two little enclaves at New York City and Newport, Rhode Island. All the rest of America was rebel territory, despite the presence of numerous loyalists. And the Continental Army was growing, fighting more strongly in each successive battle.

The two opposing armies settled into the posts they would occupy for years to come. Clinton was fortified in New York City. Washington's forces were arrayed in an arc to the west, watching the enemy. Clinton had too few men to venture far into the interior. Washington could not attack without the naval superiority that only the timely arrival of a French fleet could provide. That victory-bringing fleet was long in coming. The promise of the French alliance would not be fulfilled until Yorktown.

The armies were nearly back where they had started in 1776. "It is not a little pleasing nor less wonderful to contemplate," Washington reflected, "that after two years Manoeuvering and undergoing the strangest vicissitudes that perhaps ever attended any one contest since the creation, both armies are brought back to the very point they set out from, and, that that, which was the offending party in the beginning is now reduced to the use of the spade and the pickaxe for defense. The hand of Providence has been so conspicuous in all this that he must be worse than an infidel that lacks faith."[21]

In the two years since the antagonists had first concentrated at New York, that portion of the Continental Army under Washington's direct command had fought eight significant battles. He had won only the two little surprise attacks on Trenton and Princeton, battles against outposts, not against the main enemy army. British professionals had beaten Washington at Long Island, Manhattan, White Plains, Brandywine, and Germantown. Monmouth was a draw.

It may not seem at first glance a record likely to enroll Washington's name among the great commanders of history. Yet it was in just such terms that the American chief was now being praised. "The old Generals of this martial Country," Benjamin Franklin reported from Paris, "join in giving you the Character of one of the greatest Captains of the Age."[22] For the tally of battles lost and won greatly understates George Washington's achievement. He had kept his army and the cause alive. By so doing, he had won the war, even though another five years would pass before the celebration of independence in 1783.

Washington's army was the soul of the Revolution. The Continental Congress remained little more than a provisional committee until the Articles of Confederation, adopted in 1777, were finally ratified in 1781. As presidents of Congress came and went, as Congress itself dodged from one temporary capital to another, General Washington was more a head of state than any figure in America. He struggled to maintain a coalition—not only the alliance with France, but the alliance among the thirteen states themselves. To succeed in such a command required a statesman of genius.

Washington had seen firsthand in the 1750s the destruction wrought by stubbornly disunited colonies striving to wage a common war. (Colonel Washington had certainly done his part to contribute to disunity, often fighting for Virginia's interests against the greater good of the empire as a whole.) In the run-up to the Revolution, George Washington had become an American nationalist before there was an American nation. From the day of his appointment, the commander in chief had labored "to discourage all kinds of local attachments, and distinctions of Country, denominating the whole under the greater name of American." He soon became the symbol of national unity, as well as its advocate. The Revolution was fought in the name of noble ideals, but abstract principles do not always provide the most inspiring standard for rallying a people. Noble words must be made flesh, and that substance Washington provided. A few republicans feared his immense popularity, but this general did not hunger for power. Indeed, his devotion to republican principles, particularly the scrupulous obedience he gave popular government, was the quality of Washington's leadership his contemporaries found most heroic. As a French general wonderingly observed in 1782: "This is the seventh year that he has commanded the army, and that he has obeyed the Congress; more need not be said."[23]

The first French fleet arrived in American waters in the summer of 1778, shortly after Monmouth. It was commanded not by an admiral but by a general, Charles, compt d'Estaing. Washington wanted a joint attack on New York City, scene of his 1776 humiliation. The Royal Navy in New York Harbor was outgunned. But it turned out that some of the huge French warships drew too much water to enter the harbor. The allies settled instead on the British garrison at Newport. Presently, however, a joint land-sea operation against Newport under d'Estaing and the less-than-competent American general John Sullivan miscarried because of poor cooperation, sowing mistrust between the new allies. Washington, on the other hand, dealt superbly with the French. The Europeans admired the American commander, deeply impressed by his affability, deference, and civility, and by the grandeur of his person. They were perhaps less enthusiastic about his military abilities.

The British war effort had shifted to the subjugation of the southern states. They captured Savannah, Georgia, in December 1778. An attempt by a joint French and American force to recapture Savannah failed the following year. Then, leaving a garrison to hold New York, Clinton himself entered the southern campaign. He sailed with an army of eighty-five hundred at the end of 1778. He captured Charleston, taking an American army of fifty-five hundred prisoners, the greatest American defeat of the Revolution. Clinton then returned to New York, leaving Cornwallis with an army of eight thousand to continue the conquest of the South.

Leading the Americans in the South was Major General Horatio Gates. Short and bespectacled, plagued by chronic diarrhea, Gates, was as unprepossessing as Washington was impressive. Despite having commanded at Saratoga, the greatest American victory of the entire war, Gates's military talents were limited. The heroic battlefield leadership of Benedict Arnold had actually won the day at Saratoga. Still, Gates had many supporters in Congress. When the time came to appoint a commander for the campaign to oppose the British invasion of the southern states, Washington wanted Nathanael Greene, his most able subordinate. Congress overruled him, giving the assignment to Gates.

Gates came to grief at Camden, South Carolina, in August 1780. Though outnumbered, Cornwallis utterly destroyed Gates's army in one of the greatest American routs of the war. Gates was mocked for running sixty miles from the battlefield in a single day. His army of four thousand was reduced to seven hundred. Congress ordered an investigation. Gates, once a rival spoken of as a possible successor to Washington, was finished. Command of the Southern Department went to Greene, as Washington had always intended. Greene would fulfill all of Washington's expectations, though he never commanded enough power to actually defeat Cornwallis.

While the war in the South continued, Washington and his Continentals suffered through three years of standoff, and three grim winter encampments, outside New York.

8

The Great Man
Yorktown, Newburgh, and Annapolis

ROM THE MOMENT THE GUNS fell silent at Monmouth in June 1778 until the summer of 1781, Washington's army in the North remained locked in a dreary stalemate. Clinton's army was garrisoned in New York City, while Washington's Continentals camped uncomfortably outside the city. British naval superiority gave Washington little hope of invading the island of Manhattan without the arrival of a powerful French fleet. Clinton, his army depleted by the loss of the eight thousand troops he had been ordered to send away, did not care to venture far beyond the reach of the big guns of his forts and the Royal Navy's ships. So the two commanders dueled for control of the Hudson River above the city. British seizure of the great waterway could still yield the potent advantage of cutting American communications. But Clinton's halfhearted attacks on American posts up the river were countered by Washington and came to nothing. The deadlock in the North persisted.

In 1779, Washington sent a strong force, an entire division of the Continental Army under General Sullivan, on a punishing raid against the homeland of Iroquois Six Nations on the New York frontier. The Iroquois, allying themselves with loyalists, had been attacking patriot settlements. The Indians never recovered from the destruction of their farms and villages, but they continued to fight against the Americans.

Benedict Arnold's betrayal of the vital American fortress at West Point on the Hudson in 1780 miscarried when the traitor was detected on the very eve of his treachery. Arnold was a hero, undoubtedly the most effective combat leader in the American armies. George Washington greatly admired him. He had demonstrated his heroism in 1775 on the grueling wilderness march to Quebec and in the bloodily repulsed New Year's Eve attack on the city. Arnold was badly wounded in the attack. He had particularly excelled at Saratoga in 1777, where he had led American forces against the British in two battles, fearlessly exposing himself to enemy fire. In the second battle, the great victory of Saratoga, he was severely wounded in the same leg. For a time, he was a complete cripple, unable to walk without help or to mount a horse. Washington gave him a sedentary post, city commander of Philadelphia. But Arnold was an embittered hero. He had been greatly angered when, because of state regulations, he had not been promoted to major general as quickly as some of his less-deserving peers. Then, in his command of Philadelphia, Arnold followed a dubious course. He lived in the most extravagant luxury, pursued a variety of business enterprises, and behaved arrogantly. He made enemies. The widowed general also took to bride the lovely and much younger daughter of a prominent Tory family. The girl, Peggy Shippen, had been fast friends with many of the redcoat officers during the British occupation of Philadelphia.

Then Arnold was charged with corruption. His enemies in the Pennsylvania government convicted him on a minor charge. Washington was forced to reprimand Arnold, which he did as gently as possible. Now Arnold was enraged: not only were his merits unrewarded, but America was persecuting him. No doubt with the approval of his Tory wife, he decided on treason, if he had not before. Arnold had already been bargaining with Clinton to betray his country for a substantial sum of money and a general's commission in the Royal Army. His opportunity came when Washington gave him command of West Point. Capturing the fort would go a long way toward opening up the Hudson to British power. There was even the possibility that the capture could come during an inspection tour of Washington, thereby bagging the indispensable American commander in chief.

The plot fell through when Washington actually was at West Point, baffled by Arnold's absence. American militiamen had captured Clinton's go-between, Major John André. In his boot, they found papers revealing the conspiracy. Learning of André's capture, Arnold escaped to a British warship in the Hudson. For the rest of the war, Washington remained obsessed with capturing Arnold alive so he could hang him. He concocted several schemes. Arnold, for his part, went everywhere with two pistols in his pockets. He meant to blow his brains out before he could be taken.

His great chance lost, Clinton sunk back into passivity. But British inactivity did not spell the end of Washington's perils. At times, the Revolution seemed in danger of collapsing in on itself. The states were not contributing to the war effort and the Congress had no effective way of raising money. Continental currency had depreciated so much that Washington complained that it took a wagon full of money to buy a wagon load of provisions. (Congress printed $160 million of unbacked currency.) Hoarders and speculators grew rich while the army suffered. When the soldiers were paid at all, which was most infrequently, they were paid in the worthless paper money. One new batch of currency was canceled because Congress couldn't afford to buy the paper to print it on. The money wasn't even worth printing anymore, and printing indeed stopped. At one point, the Continental Army dwindled to four thousand troops, little more than Washington had commanded at the time of Trenton. Unpaid, hungry, lacking decent uniforms and footwear, battered by the coldest winter in memory, their enlistments extended without their consent, some of Washington's soldiers were on the edge of revolt. A few units crossed the line.

The Continental Army had spent the winter of 1778–79 in Middlebrook, New Jersey. The next winter, which they spent in Morristown, New Jersey, was the coldest in living memory. It was sixteen below zero in New York City. The harbor froze solid; sleighs could cross from Manhattan to Staten Island on the ice. The soldiers probably suffered that winter more intensely than even at Valley Forge. They were cold and frequently starving. Many of the Continentals had enlisted for three years or the duration of the war. No one had said whether release was triggered by the first or the second to occur, an ambiguity that now led to discord. Many believed they had served out their time and should be free to return home.

What Washington had so long dreaded—mutiny—presently came to pass. On New Year's Day, 1781, the Pennsylvania Line revolted. The Pennsylvanians were encamped near Morristown, away from the main army with Washington at New Windsor. They paraded fully armed at night. They seized cannon and defied all their officers' attempts to restore order. One captain was killed, other officers wounded. At 11 P.M., the mutineers, dragging along artillery, set out for Philadelphia. They meant to take their complaints directly to Congress. Congress considered fleeing the city, but decided instead on sending a committee of Pennsylvania state government officials to meet with the mutineers in Princeton. Washington stayed out of it. He was afraid the mutiny might spread and wanted to stay with the main army. He also knew there was little he could do personally. As Freeman put it, "Orders that could not be enforced should not be given."[1]

The committee negotiated with the mutineers' leaders and made many concessions. Satisfied, the troops agreed to return to duty. Though it had ended in a stand-down, the mutiny might be said to have paid off handsomely for the mutineers. Most of them got discharges based on three years' service. Others got three-month furloughs to visit home.

Congress had listened respectfully to their complaints. All were pardoned. They got back pay. There had been little bloodshed. The example of this success may have influenced the men who launched the second major mutiny.

On January 21, 1781, the New Jersey Line at Pompton revolted. This was again at one of the smaller Continental Army cantonments, away from Washington and the main army. This time Washington intended no concessions, lest the mutiny become general throughout the army. He determined to suppress the revolt by force. He gathered five hundred troops he could rely on and sent them marching to Pompton. These troops surrounded the rebellious regiments with artillery and musketmen. The mutineers were ordered out their huts, unarmed. Assembled on the parade ground, they were still surrounded by armed soldiers. Fifteen ringleaders were identified and pulled from the ranks. Two were summarily condemned to death—immediately, on the spot. The remaining thirteen ringleaders were condemned to serve as their friends' executioners. They were weeping as they pulled their triggers. Six bullets per man, three in the head, three in the heart. The condemned were shot down at so close a range that the muzzle flash of the muskets set alight their blindfolds. The rest of the mutineers abandoned their revolt and begged for mercy. As Washington put it, without a trace of irony, "the principle Actors were immediately executed on the Spot, and the remainder exhibiting genuine signs of contrition, were pardoned."[2]

The first mutiny was greeted by leniency and concessions and was followed, perhaps because of its success, with the second mutiny. The second mutiny was ruthlessly put down. There was no third mutiny.

Washington still hoped above all for a concerted attack by the allied armies, supported by the French fleet, on Clinton in New York City. New York, however, was strongly held. The French had little faith in Washington's plan. The French pretended to be completely under Washington's command—they made a great show of deference and respect. But Washington knew better. The French admirals and generals would never act against their nation's interests to accommodate the Americans. Nor would they go against their own military instincts on Washington's urgings. The French favored taking the war to the Chesapeake.

Another who favored moving the seat of war to the Chesapeake was Lieutenant General Charles, Earl Cornwallis, Clinton's second in command and head of all British forces in the southern theater. Cornwallis had come south in 1780 with Clinton's campaign that succeeded in capturing Charleston. When Clinton returned to New York, Cornwallis was left in command in the South. Cornwallis had hoped to supplant Clinton as commander in chief for North America. He held a "dormant commission," giving him the post should anything happen to Clinton. (Clinton himself, seeing little hope of a successful outcome, had tendered his resignation to London, but the offer had been refused.) Cornwallis, who disagreed with Clinton's passive approach, began to ignore, even disobey, his superior's orders. He began to communicate directly with the ministry in London and take his orders from there. Strategic confusion naturally ensued.

Cornwallis completed the conquest of Georgia. Royal government had already been restored in the former colony. Most of South Carolina also fell under his control. Then Cornwallis destroyed Horatio Gates's larger army at Camden. North Carolina now was the only battleground on which the Americans could continue to offer resistance, but in fact the patriots no longer had an army in the South. They did have a general, though—the able Nathanael Greene, who began to gather a new army about him. Greene did not have the strength to confront Cornwallis in a set-piece battle yet, but he did lead him on a merry chase throughout North Carolina, frustrating British plans and wearing the redcoats down to exhaustion. At the same time, British detachments not under Cornwallis's command were soundly defeated at King's Mountain and Cowpens by American militia and regulars. Greene continued to raid British garrisons in the Carolinas.

Benedict Arnold, in the uniform of a British brigadier general, had been walking to and fro in the earth. In December 1780, he invaded Virginia with sixteen hundred regulars. He went up the James River, raiding and burning settlements, and captured Richmond, Virginia's capital, torching much of the city. Then, disobeying Clinton's direct orders, Cornwallis also invaded Virginia in April 1781. He had recently fought Greene at Guilford Court House, winning a costly, futile victory over the Americans. He had lost a quarter of his army.

With Cornwallis's invasion of Virginia, the theater of war had shifted decisively to the Chesapeake, contrary to the wishes and expectations of both Washington and Clinton.

Washington followed the enemy's steady progress through his native state with alarm. Many Virginians, including the new governor, Thomas Jefferson, implored Washington to come south and defend his state. Virginia even offered to make him dictator, military ruler of the state. Washington declined. He had to stay within striking distance of the main enemy army in New York. Instead, Washington sent a small detachment of Continentals under Lafayette to counter the invasion of Virginia. But the outnumbered Frenchman's force was too weak to deter Cornwallis.

Fortunately for the allies, the British seemed completely bewildered. Clinton sent contradictory orders that Cornwallis ignored. What next? Perhaps Cornwallis's army should be reinforced? Perhaps the Virginia campaign should be abandoned altogether and Cornwallis evacuated by sea? Perhaps part of Cornwallis's army should sail to New York to reinforce Clinton? The element the competing plans shared was the need for a deepwater base on Chesapeake Bay. Cornwallis occupied Yorktown, a little port on the York River. His Lordship was now in a tight spot. Surrounded by water, his whole army could be fatally bottled up. Safety depended on British naval superiority.

The allied armies were still considering an attack on New York in August 1781 when news came that a powerful French fleet was on its way from the West Indies to the Chesapeake. George Washington saw at once that the distant warships might be bringing what he had longed for since 1775—the chance to land a crushing blow. Reluctantly abandoning his long-held plans to take New York, he ordered an immediate march on Virginia.

For six years, the commander of the Continental Army had waged a war for which he was temperamentally unsuited. Washington was an aggressive gambler. He yearned for the glory only a decisive victory could bring. He knew that only victory would return him to his beloved Mount Vernon. But the shocking defeats at New York in 1776 had taught the general the lessons that would allow him to win the war. Both the imperfect instrument he wielded in the Continental Army and the emerging republican society of which he was the faithful servant required that Washington pursue a conservative strategy calculated to keep the army intact. He was never actually the "Fabian" commander that some historians have claimed—a general who consistently avoided battle with a superior foe. But although he often struck out boldly, Washington had fought a defensive war. It was one measure of his extraordinary self-control that this combative, fearless man allowed himself to be governed by prudence and his devotion to the republican ideal of the subordination of military to civilian authority.

British confusion contributed not a little to the triumph at Yorktown, but the two allied armies, the French navy, and the commander in chief performed brilliantly. Washington directed the logistical feat of rapidly moving seven thousand men from New York to Williamsburg, just up the peninsula from Yorktown. When the Royal Navy squadron sent to break the siege was repulsed at the battle of the Chesapeake Capes on September 5, 1781, Cornwallis was doomed.

Washington was commander in chief of the entire army, nine thousand American and seventy-eight hundred French soldiers, but the French officers, supremely skilled in the arcane arts of siege craft and heavy artillery bombardment, directed all the operations. Washington could only watch in awe. The men dug trenches approaching British lines and placed the big siege guns. Washington had the symbolic honors of opening the first entrenchment with a few blows of a pickax and of touching off the first cannon in the massive bombardment that soon reduced Yorktown's fortifications and dwellings to ruins. The bombardment also killed many British officers and men and not a few civilians. Cornwallis hid in an underground "grotto." Washington, as usual, recklessly exposed himself to danger. Observing a British cannonade from an embankment, he looked through his telescope as impacting cannon balls threw dirt over him. When an aide begged him to retire, Washington coolly advised the man to take cover if he was afraid. Meanwhile, the siege trenches came closer and closer to British lines. The outcome was as certain as sunrise.

By October 17, 1781, Lord Cornwallis, squirming with "mortification," had no choice but to write Washington, "I propose a Cessation of Hostilities for Twenty four hours . . . to settle terms for the surrender." Washington gave him just two hours. Two days later, His Lordship found himself too indisposed to attend the surrender ceremony. He sent a subordinate in his place. When that officer tried first to present Cornwallis's sword to the French commander and only then to the American commander in chief, Washington waved him aside, declining to take the sword from a subordinate, and directed the British brigadier to make the surrender to the American second in command. Then the whole army of 7,250 marched out between lines of natty French and ragged American soldiers and threw down their muskets. It was the largest surrender of the war.

In no way disgraced by his defeat, Cornwallis went on to enjoy a most distinguished career, including a term as governor general of India. The biggest losers of the battle of Yorktown were the fugitive slaves, thousands of men, women, and children who had fled to Cornwallis's army, hoping to secure their freedom. As the siege progressed, the British could no longer feed or house these refugees. They were driven out of British lines, into the no-man's-land between the two armies. There, squatting miserably in swamps and thickets, hundreds died of hunger and small-pox. Soon hard-eyed slaveholders were stalking through the refugee camps, looking for their property. Washington recaptured here two of his slaves that had escaped Mount Vernon aboard a British warship.

"Oh God! It is all over!" groaned Lord North, the English prime minister, when the news of Yorktown reached London. Indeed it was. Though the Continental Army would remain in the field two more years, the military phase of American Revolution had ended.

But Washington's troubles were still not over. Peace negotiations dragged on in Paris while the unpaid Continental Army waited in camp at Newburgh, New York. A long war for short rewards had at length brought the American officer corps to a state of near-rebellion. Private soldiers had mutinied before, but the general had always had his officers on his side. By late 1782 it was the officers themselves who threatened civilian authority. A foreign-born Continental colonel had already advised Washington to overthrow Congress and set himself up as king. Washington had angrily rebuked the thickheaded officer. The Americans had not been fighting for monarchy. It was as certain that Washington would have refused a kingly crown as it was certain that the people would never have offered him one.

But military revolt might have been an outcome more plausible than the crowning of an American king. Many officers insisted that, before disbanding, they would have their back pay and their promised pensions. The army could march on Philadelphia to threaten Congress, which, the officers might argue, had betrayed the republican ideals of virtuous patriotism that had guided the Revolution. If the American army had turned against its government, the result would hardly have been astonishing. Popular revolutions that end in such a way are not unknown to history. The prospect was certainly credible enough to horrify George Washington. He wrote that "the patience, the fortitude, the long and great sufferings of this Army is unexampled in History; but there is an end to all things, & I fear we are very near one to this."[3]

The plotting actually began in Philadelphia. Certain politicians and holders of government debt eager to promote stronger national government and pay national debts were conspiring with the discontented officers. The threat of military revolt might succeed in frightening the states into paying taxes and giving Congress new powers. This was an exceedingly dangerous game to play at. "The army have swords in their hands," one statesman wrote another. "You know enough of the history of mankind to know much more than I have said."[4] Many in Philadelphia, both in and out of Congress, held government financial certificates, often purchased at deep discount to face value. It was obviously in the interest of these investors that the government redeem the certificates at full value. But Congress had no funds with which to do this and no power to collect taxes from the states. Both the officers and the investors faced the prospect that they would never be paid by the bankrupt Congress. As James Flexner has observed, "The fact that the army and the ablest, most prosperous businessmen were being similarly defrauded opened a promising field for common action."[5] The two groups could work together—the officers for their back pay and pensions, the businessmen for the investments. The conspirators probably intended to use the army to reform civil government, not overthrow it. And it is unlikely that any unlawful military regime could have ruled the huge territory and diverse population of the thirteen loosely confederated American states. But civil war might have been the result. Such an attempt might have made Americans too fearful of strong government to ever embrace the bold federal experiment represented by the Constitution of 1787.

The great question that now confronted the plotters was George Washington's intentions. Their position would be much stronger if they could persuade the commander to go along. They knew that he had always deferred to Congress. At the same time, he had strongly supported more vigorous national government and justice for the army. Washington's former aide, Colonel Alexander Hamilton, now a New York congressional delegate, offered to sound out the general. Hamilton wrote Washington on February 13, 1783. Come peace or continued war, Hamilton insisted, the army must be paid. The officers particularly feared that if Britain declared peace, Congress would have no remaining motive to do them justice. And "if they once lay down their arms, they part with the means of obtaining justice." Hamilton urged Washington "to guide the torrent." He warned the general that he was losing his influence with the officers, who thought he was practicing "a delicacy carried to an extreme" in not confronting Congress.[6] Washington replied, "The predicament in which I stand as Citizen & Soldier, is as critical and delicate as can well be conceived."[7] But he said the army "was a dangerous instrument to play with."[8] He resolutely rejected the suggestion that he take a leading role in the plot, believing that his officers were "wavering on a tremendous precipice" above "a gulph of Civil horror" that threatened to "deluge our rising Empire in Blood."[9]

The Continental Army had passed another hard winter at Newburgh. In March 1783, papers written by an anonymous "fellow officer" circulated at the encampment. The author argued that when peace came, the officers must never lay down their arms until they had wrested from their ungrateful country the reward their years of sacrifice had earned. He called for unlawful mass meeting of the officer corps. Washington countered by calling an official meeting in the officers' assembly hall known as "the Temple of Virtue."

Washington used his twenty-minute speech and a bit of inspired stagecraft to remind the skeptical, even hostile, officers of the true meaning of their Revolution. The

Continental Army had fought not only to preserve American liberties from a perceived threat of tyranny. They had fought a revolution to create a republican society. A republic's vital spark was the virtue of its people. The survival of a republic required that those citizens with ambition and talent sacrifice their own interests to the greater good of their country. This the army had done for eight years. For the officers to repudiate their selflessness in the final passage of the great struggle would betray virtue and tarnish the glorious fame that promised to ennoble them to posterity. Washington pleaded for political heroism to match their battlefield courage. Congress would do them justice. They must be patient a little longer.

However convincing the speech may have been, the emblematic flourish that followed won the day for Washington. He began to read a letter from a congressman. But something was wrong. His Excellency faltered, was unable to read, and finally drew from his pocket a pair of spectacles. None of the officers had ever seen him wear them. Putting the glasses on, Washington said, "Gentlemen, you must pardon me. I have grown gray in the service of my country and now find myself going blind." He finished the letter and left the hall without another word. The gesture, conveying both Washington's humanity and his unswerving dedication to the cause, pierced the hearts of his men. Many a once-rebellious officer was moved to tears. They immediately passed a resolution declaring their loyalty to civilian government. George Washington had saved the Revolution again.

Three days later, on March 18, 1783, word reached

Newburgh that peace had been concluded in Paris: Great Britain had at last recognized the independence of the United States. Negotiations had begun in earnest in September 1782, almost a year after Yorktown. By November, even the obstinate King George was ready to give up. In a letter precisely dated "Windsor Nov. 19th. 1782 23 min[utes] p[as]t 10 PM," His Royal Highness directed the home secretary to go ahead with the treaty. But only, the king lamented, because "Parliament having to my astonishment come into the ideas of granting ~~Independence~~ a Separation to North America, has disabled Me from longer defending the just rights of this Kingdom."[10] The treaty was signed ten days later.

All that remained was for the principal actor to make his exit. This he did with the greatest of care. He embarked on a series of farewell addresses. Washington first drafted a farewell in the form of a letter to the governors of the states. In the "Circular Letter to the States," sometimes called "Washington's Legacy," he advanced certain propositions: The United States could become a great and powerful and happy nation. By its example America could lead the world into a new era of freedom. Like Thomas Paine, George Washington was suggesting that the American experiment could recast the future: "With our fate will the destiny of unborn Millions be involved."[11]

America was uniquely favored:

> The Citizen of America, placed in the most enviable condition, as sole Lords and Proprietors of a vast Tract of Continent . . . are, from this period, to be considered as the Actors on a most conspicuous Theatre, designated by

Providence for the display of human greatness and felicity; Here, they are not only surrounded with every thing
which can contribute to the completion of private and domestic enjoyment, but Heaven has crowned all its other
blessings, by giving a fairer oppertunity for political happiness, than any other Nation has ever been favored with. . . .
The foundation of our Empire was not laid in the gloomy
age of Superstition and Ignorance, but at an Epocha when
the rights of mankind were better understood and more
clearly defined.[12]

But the experiment could as easily fail if the American people did not meet the test. ("If their Citizens should
not be completely free and happy, the fault will be intirely
their own.")[13] Washington insisted that a vigorous national
government—"An indissoluble Union of the States under
one Federal Head"—was "essential to the well being, I may
even venture to say, to the existence of the United States
as an Independent Power."[14] His ideas carried a greater
moral authority since they were those of a man leaving
the stage of public life forever. He could pledge that "no
sinister views" influenced him—if a stronger government
were created, George Washington would take no part and
would gain no high office.

After addressing a farewell to "Armies of the United
States," Washington personally signed the discharge cer-
tificates of all the thousands of men in the Continental
Army, so that, he said, each soldier would know that the
commander in chief had seen his name and known that
he had done his duty. He entered New York the day the
British evacuated the city. Riding alongside him was New
York Governor George Clinton, Washington's nod to the

primacy of civilian government. At Fraunces Tavern, he said good-bye to his remaining officers and generals with tearful embraces. He soon left for Annapolis, then the seat of Congress. There, on December 23, 1783, Washington ceremoniously handed back to the president of Congress the parchment commission he had received in Philadelphia on June 15, 1775. Since then Congress had seen eight presidents, the British Army four commanding generals, the Continental Army a single Washington. The delegates greeted him wearing their hats indoors—this was their way of demonstrating that they were not receiving a king. (Parliament received the British monarch bareheaded.) When the commander in chief greeted them, the delegates quickly doffed their hats and returned them to their heads. Deep emotion informed the ceremony that all the participants recognized as being of the highest symbolic importance. They showed their feelings, as Washington's aide James McHenry remembered: "The spectators all wept, and there was hardly a member of Congress who did not drop tears."[15] Washington made a brief farewell address, resigning "with satisfaction the Appointment I accepted with diffidence," and taking his "leave of all the employments of public life."[16] His voice shook, his eyes teared, and he trembled so much that he had to hold the speech with both hands. At one point, when urging justice for his officers, he nearly lost his composure altogether. The president of Congress responded with a speech written by delegate Thomas Jefferson, a statesman who apprehended the dimensions of Washington's achievement. "You have conducted the great military contest with wisdom and fortitude, invariably regarding the rights of the civil power through all disasters and changes. . . . Having defended the standard of liberty in this new world: having taught a lesson useful to those who inflict and to those who feel oppression, you retire from the great theatre of action, with the blessings of your fellow-citizens, but the glory of your virtues will not terminate with your military command, it will continue to animate the remotest ages."[17] The younger Virginian would later tell Washington privately that "the moderation and virtue of a single character has probably prevented this revolution from being closed as most others have been, by a subversion of that liberty it was intended to establish."[18]

The new civilian mounted his horse and rode hard to reach Mount Vernon on Christmas Eve, 1783. Giving up power was more glorious than winning the war. By stepping down, Washington had raised himself up to a pinnacle of fame as the embodiment of republican heroism. It was the most exalted moment of an exalted life. According to one story, George III asked the American painter Benjamin West what General Washington was likely to do when peace came. Would he stay with the army, would he become head of state? West replied that Washington would probably return to his farm. The king was astounded. "If he does that," His Majesty declared, "he will be the greatest man in the world!"[19] The story may be apocryphal, but most Americans, and not a few Europeans, now considered George Washington the most distinguished figure of the age.

9

"The Destiny of Unborn Millions"

AMERICA'S FIRST CITIZEN returned home after an absence of eight and a half years to find his private affairs in disarray. Mount Vernon was run down. A major renovation of the mansion house Washington had begun a full decade earlier remained unfinished. The roof leaked. The farms were unproductive. Eighteen Mount Vernon slaves had escaped to seek freedom when a British warship had put in at the plantation. Many debtors had paid Washington off in vastly depreciated Continental currency. Others had not bothered to pay at all. Years of rent on his western lands remained uncollected. The republican commander had refused any salary for his military service. He promptly submitted his wartime expense account for reimbursement. It came to $64,335.30, or about $7,500 a year. (This actually amounted to more than he would have gotten if he accepted Congress's proposed $500 a month salary.) But the government paid him off in devalued certificates,

some of which he was forced to sell at one-twentieth of
their face value. Family and friends soon came with their
hands out. Washington often had to tell them he had no
cash to spare.

Despite it all, he was overjoyed to be home. "I feel now,"
Washington wrote one of his generals, as "a wearied Travel-
ler must do, who, after treading many a painful step, with
a heavy burden on his shoulders, is eased of the latter, having reached the Goal to which all the former were directed,
and from his House top is looking back, and tracing with
a grateful eye the Meanders by which he has escaped the
quicksands and Mires which lay in his way."[1]

He took up again the agricultural experimentation
that had so fascinated him before the war. He particularly
admired the new scientific agriculture then practiced in
England. He read English farming journals and books and
copied out long passages. He devised elaborate crop rotation schemes. He tried new crops. He spread Potomac
mud and even fish on his fields to enrich the soil. He tink-
ered with farm machinery. In designing a seed drill—a device that opened a furrow, dropped in seeds, and covered
them in one pass—he needed to calculate the number of
individual grains in a bushel of timothy. (13,410,000.)

Meanwhile, hundreds of uninvited guests were turning up at Mount Vernon, eager to see with their own eyes
the most famous man in the world. Some came with letters
of introduction. Some were Continental Army veterans.
Others were complete strangers. Washington felt that Virginia tradition obliged him to entertain them, give them
dinner, put them up for the night, and take care of their

horses. (The nearest inn was miles away.) Washington complained. He was spending himself poor, and his slaves and servants were run ragged. The strain on the whole family was considerable. At the same time, a procession of artists arrived to paint and sculpt the hero.

Martha Washington's rich and feckless twenty-six-year-old son, John Parke Custis, after sitting out the war, had elected to visit his stepfather's headquarters at Yorktown to be in at the kill.[2] Unexposed to army diseases, he had come down with camp fever and soon died. Martha had now lost all four of her children. She was sunk in grief. Jacky Custis himself left behind four young children. Martha and George took in the two youngest grandchildren, George Washington Parke Custis ("Wash") and Eleanor Parke Custis ("Nelly"), to be raised at Mount Vernon. The couple effectively adopted the grandchildren, who regarded the Washingtons as their true parents. It was the second set of Custis children to be raised at Mount Vernon. George Washington was devoted to the little people.

Washington's efforts to bring scientific agricultural methods to his lands, even his efforts to make Mount Vernon a paying proposition, met with failure, a failure that can only have deepened his growing disenchantment with agrarianism. The farms were no longer self-sufficient—after one bad harvest, he had to buy eight hundred barrels of corn to feed his slaves. He was more than ever frustrated by the inefficiency of slave labor. He had many more slaves than he needed to run the farms. George Washington took pride in being regarded as one of the richest men in America, and he spent lavishly, both to keep up appearances and because he and his family had long been accustomed to a life of opulence. He was also supporting a legion of family and friends. Luck was against him too. After his return from the war, he faced a series of failed corn and wheat harvests. The crops were destroyed in the fields by an infestation of the dreaded chinch bug, by drought followed by flooding rains, and by a series of hard winters.

Almost no one knew how broke he really was. He had vast assets but could realize no ready cash from them. His slaves were valuable, but he "principled ag[ains]t selling Negroes." His western lands were presumably valuable, but when he advertised them for sale, no buyers came forward. The only offers came from scheming developers who could pay only after their far-fetched plans had been realized. They would take the land now, try to rent it to tenants, and perhaps pay later, at some point in the indefinite future. And he couldn't collect the rents and debts owed him. Patriotism had compelled him to take in a lot of government paper, both currency and certificates, but those notes were so depreciated there was little point in cashing them in. He couldn't pay several years of taxes owed on his western lands. One county threatened him with foreclosure. He even owed back taxes on Mount Vernon. He confided to an intimate friend who had asked for a loan, "I never felt the want of money so sensibly since I was a boy of 15."[3]

Cash-poor though he may have been, George Washington was still a mighty rich man. As we have seen, most considerable of his assets were his western lands. Although the native inhabitants had not been consulted, the 1783

Treaty of Paris had established that the Ohio Valley—the Northwest Territory—was United States soil. Washington's particular concern was his own land in the Ohio country, tracts embracing, he calculated, some thirty-three thousand acres. "There is no richer, or more valuable land in all that Region," he boasted.[4] But he could find few buyers.

Still, his main source of income was now rent from those who had settled on his western lands. And most of his tenants had defaulted on their rents. He decided to visit his Ohio holdings. He hoped to collect rents and to survey the route of his visionary project—the system of canals and roads linking the Potomac and Ohio rivers. He set out in September 1784. The 680-mile journey was his last visit to the Ohio country, the land that had played so great a part in his destiny. He was a denied the chance to visit the crown jewel of his Ohio properties, the square miles of prime bottom lands on the Ohio and Kanawha rivers. The native peoples did not recognize Washington's title, nor indeed the claims of the United States. When reports reached him that war parties were killing white settlers in the region, Washington abandoned his plans to go down the Ohio.

If he had hoped he would return with saddlebags stuffed with cash from back rents, he was to be disappointed. His tenants declined to cooperate. Washington tussled acrimoniously with one squatter who had carved a little farm out of some of Washington's land. Apparently not overawed by "the greatest man in the world," the frontiersman was defiant—he refused to vacate, buy the land, or pay rent. Washington loved the West but he had little but contempt for western frontiersmen. Washington dangled a red silk hand-kerchief. "I will have this land," he said, "just as surely as I now have this handkerchief."⁵ He took the case to court, where, two years later, he prevailed. At the same time, par-adoxically, the disgruntled landlord had to recognize that these despised pioneers were on the cutting edge of the development he believed to be the central mission of the new nation—the settlement of the West.

Washington knew that the land's promise was over-shadowed by the lack of a practical means to bring its pro-duce to market. Moving bulk goods overland would never pay. The long trip down the Mississippi to Spanish New Orleans was strewn with dangers, and presently the Spanish closed New Orleans to American trade altogether. Washing-ton saw a growing threat not only to his private fortune but to the integrity of the new nation itself. He believed that, without an alliance of mutual interest based on trade, the Ohio Valley settlers might turn from the United States to align themselves with Spain or Britain.

As he wrote on October 4, 1784, in the diary he kept of his western trip, "No well informed Mind need be told, that the flanks and rear of the United territory are pos-sessed by other powers, and formidable ones too—nor how necessary it is to apply the cement of interest to bind all parts of it together, by one indissolvable band. . . . For what ties let me ask, should we have with these people; [the Ohio Valley settlers] and how entirely unconnected sho[ul]d we be with them if the Spaniard on their right, or Great Britain on their left . . . should envite their trade and seek alliances with them? . . . The Western Settlers—from my own observation—stand as it were on a pivot—the touch of a feather would almost incline them any way."[6]

Again, Washington's hopes for his nation and for his own private interests coincided in an almost uncanny fashion. Not only would the detachment of the Ohio Valley from the eastern states diminish the success of the revolution he had led, but it would jeopardize the huge profits he hoped to win from his western land speculations. Washington soon brought out of retirement his scheme to link the Potomac and Ohio. He was elected president of the Potomac Navigation Company. He had already surveyed the route on his western trip in 1784. Before long, labor gangs of Irish immigrants and enslaved blacks were hacking and blasting the canal out of the bedrock over which the Potomac flowed. Potomac navigation became for a time one of the most important causes Washington pursued, second only to his advocacy of a stronger national government. He endlessly bored his guests by expounding on the wonders of the new canal.

Such a mammoth engineering project required cooperation between the states. Unfortunately, little such cooperation was evident. Under the Articles of Confederation, the states had consented only to join in a "firm league of friendship," in which each state retained "its sovereignty, freedom and independence." Americans had always feared centralized power. They had fought a war against it. By design, the Articles furnished a feeble central government.

George Washington and other nationalists, imbued with a "continental vision" by their experiences in the Revolution, were convinced that the republican experiment would fail unless popular government was supported by a strong union of the states. "I can foresee no evil greater, than disunion," Washington wrote in August 1785.[7] Without an effective national government, he was certain that America "never shall establish a National character, or be considered on a respectable footing by the Powers of Europe. . . . We are either a United people under one head, & for Federal purposes, or, we are thirteen independent Sovereignties, eternally counteracting each other."[8]

Foreign powers did continue to treat the United States with the contempt its impotence invited. Britain refused to give up its posts like Detroit in the Northwest Territory, despite the stipulations of the treaty of 1783. From these forts, the British Army supplied the Ohio Indians with weapons and encouraged them to war against the Americans. Britain also banned American merchants from the long-established and lucrative trade with the British West Indies. The Confederation was as weak at home, unable to collect taxes, pay down the war debt, or regulate trade.

But certain outbursts of popular discontent were even more alarming to Washington than the frailties of the Confederation. Many feared an "excess of democracy" as much as they had feared British tyranny a decade earlier. As conceived by men like Washington, theirs was a revolution that would not bring revolutionary social change. The equality they had fought for was an equality of rights, not of social station. Distinctions would remain in the new, republican America. Lesser folk would still defer to their betters, and the management of public affairs would always be entrusted to gentlemen. Men of sufficient talent and ambition, whatever their birth, had a chance to enter the ranks of the gentry, but none but gentlemen should govern. History would soon demonstrate that Washington and many of his contemporaries were mistaken in their apprehension of the American future. Before long, egalitarianism would prevail, while the traditional society of deference would be swept away. Popular democracy would supplant classical republicanism. Common men would decide the elections and hold the high offices.

In the time of the Confederation, however, it seemed to many that the preservation of the culture of deference not only was possible but was necessary for the survival of republican government. Anarchy followed by despotism seemed the only alternative. So Washington was shocked in 1786 by the outbreak of lawlessness by debt-burdened Massachusetts farmers known as Shays' Rebellion. These rebels might be "levelers" intent on rooting out all social distinction. They threatened rights of property. It was a nightmare that Washington called "a formidable rebellion against the laws & constitutions of our own making."[9] He dashed off an anxious letter to a Massachusetts friend, Benjamin Lincoln, his former Revolutionary War general: "Are your people getting mad?—Are we to have the goodly fabric that eight years were spent in rearing pulled over our heads?"[10] Washington now feared that the entire enterprise to which he had devoted so much of his life teetered again on the brink of ruin. "Our Affairs, generally," he wrote in February 1787, "seem really, to be approaching to some awful crisis."[11]

By 1787, however, new hope approached in the shape

of the convention set to meet in Philadelphia in May. The convention had been organized by the leading American nationalists and had been somewhat grudgingly endorsed by the Confederation Congress. Its delegates would try "to devise such further provisions as shall appear to them necessary to render the constitution of the Federal Government adequate to the exigencies of the Union." This they were to do only by amending the Articles of Confederation. In the event, the delegates would radically exceed their instructions, scrapping the Articles altogether and creating a strong central government under the United States Constitution. Not only could such a union establish the United States among the nations of the earth, but it might serve to shift the political high ground from the local to the national level, undercutting the influence of supposed social revolutionaries such as those who had emerged in Massachusetts. State legislatures would pick the delegates to the coming convention.

Naturally, Virginia named George Washington one of its delegates. He declined. Had he not solemnly promised the American people in 1783 that he was forever taking "leave of all the employments of public life?" Had he not achieved his most brilliant success by relinquishing power? His reputation was secure; reentering the political sphere could only put it at risk. It took months of agonizing on Washington's part, as well as the earnest appeals of leading nationalists, to convince the great man that his presence at the convention was indispensable. Certain twentieth-century historians have taken Washington to task for his vacillation, ascribing it to an unseemly preoccupation with his honor.[12] But chances are that George Washington understood the stakes better than the historians.

Washington had long supported strong national government. He had stated that support many times since 1775. He knew that he might be required to play a role if such a government was created. He also understood that the trust he had earned was one of the most precious assets the new nation possessed. That prestige must not be squandered on any attempt that might fail to establish a stronger government. And his ability to lead might be damaged if the people believed he had broken his word. But Washington also recognized that his reputation might suffer if he sat out the convention while other men struggled with the "awful crisis." He feared that his "non-attendance in this Convention [would] be considered as a dereliction to republicanism."[13] His fame could hardly be expected to light the coming ages if the revolution he had directed ended in failure. Speculative notions were also floated. Some warned Washington that if he skipped the convention, people would take it to mean he really did want to be king after all. America seemed to be trending toward anarchy. In republican formulations of history, anarchy was inevitably followed by despotism. By not working for stronger government, they warned, Washington would be seen as pushing the nation into the anarchy that would allow him to seize the crown he secretly lusted for.

In about 1784, Washington began a new friendship with the thirty-three-year-old Virginian James Madison, a recent graduate of Princeton who would emerge as one of the most gifted of all American political theorists. Guided

by his close friend Thomas Jefferson, Madison had read
everything there was to read on the history of republics,
ancient and modern. He was committed to republican liberty. He was also an ardent nationalist who would soon
win his well-deserved reputation as the Father of the Constitution. Despite the differences in age and leadership experience, Madison became not only a friend but a mentor
to Washington, guiding his political thinking during several critical years. (Eventually the party strife of the presidency would tear the two friends apart forever.) Madison
now told Washington that his attendance at the convention was absolutely essential to its success. Washington's
Continental Army comrade Henry Knox enticed him with
the promise that his participation "would be a circumstance highly honourable to your fame . . . and doubly
entitle you to the glorious republican epithet 'The Father
of Your Country.'"[14] The nationalists finally persuaded the
reluctant general.

It was not until March 1787, just two months before the
convention's May meeting, that Washington accepted the in-
terruption of his happy retirement. He returned to the stage
with sincere reluctance and considerable apprehension. His
business affairs, like Mount Vernon's several thousand acres,
demanded constant attention. He was the fifty-five-year-old
heir of a line of men who seldom attained fifty. Age was finally overtaking him, he believed, diminishing his powers.
Rheumatism forced him to keep one arm in a sling.[15] He
had lost most of his teeth, which can only have deepened
his dread of public speaking. He feared that his memory
too was increasingly faulty. He was going deaf, perhaps

from exposure to gunfire. He mistrusted his abilities as a statesman. And he must have shuddered at the future that the creation of a new national government promised to bring. It did not require the gift of prophecy to see that America was likely to call on him at least one more time. It would have, Washington said, "a tendency to sweep me back into the tide of Public affairs when retirement and ease is so essentially necessary for, and is so much desired by me."[16]

Nevertheless, Washington, squirming with ambivalence, left Mount Vernon again, arriving in Philadelphia on May 13, 1787, well ahead of most of the other delegates to the Constitutional Convention. On his journey, he had been greeted by crowds and ceremonies in every town and village he passed through. (Fame was not without its travails. For the rest of his life, whenever he traveled, Washington would be met everywhere by ceremonious welcomes— cheering crowds, booming cannon, speeches, parades, and dinners with endless toasts. Then his departure would become the occasion for elaborate farewells. He regarded the whole business as a waste of time that kept him from the road. He often begged officials to skip the ceremonies, usually to no avail. He sometimes resorted to slipping away unnoticed at an early morning hour.) The convention reached a quorum and met for the first time on May 25.

Of all the issues that threatened to wreck accord among the states at the convention, none seemed more dangerous than slavery. On a gloomy day in February 1786, Washington had ridden across his farms counting certain of the people who lived and worked at Mount Vernon. He counted only those who were black. These people were slaves—what Washington once called "a certain species of property." A careful proprietor accounts for his property—the slaves were inventoried by age, gender, and occupation. When he had completed the task, Washington recorded the result in a little pocket diary: a list of 216 men, women, and children. A few weeks earlier, he had counted his livestock, noting in the same diary the numbers of horses, cattle, sheep, and oxen that grazed Mount Vernon's fields.

But this chilling juxtaposition of two exercises in farm management does not fairly reflect Washington's growing repugnance for slavery. The lavish life Washington and his family enjoyed had always been earned by the labor of enslaved people. Still, by 1786, Washington believed that slavery should be abolished, although he would never say so publicly. "I never mean," he wrote, "to possess another slave by purchase; it being among my first wishes to see some plan adopted, by which slavery in this Country may be abolished by slow, sure, & imperceptible degrees."[17] About this time, Washington told a confidant, "The unfortunate condition of the persons, whose labour in part I employed, has been the only unavoidable subject of regret. To make the Adults among them as easy & as comfortable in their circumstances as their actual state of ignorance & improvidence would admit; & to lay a foundation to prepare the rising generation for a destiny different from that in which they were born; afforded some satisfaction to my mind, & could not I hoped be displeasing to the justice of the Creator."[18]

Washington had been influenced by republican ideology and by his fear that slavery might permanently sunder South from North. The master of Mount Vernon had decided, even before the Revolution, to buy no more slaves. The shift from planting tobacco to farming grain crops had reduced the number of laborers needed to operate Mount Vernon. Still, he could not simply sell off those he did not need. "To sell the overplus I cannot," he would write near the end of his life, "because I am principled against this kind of traffic in the human species. To hire them out, is almost as bad, because they could not be disposed of in families to any advantage, and to disperse the families I have an aversion. What then is to be done?"[19]

Neither Washington nor, during his lifetime, his country ever discovered a satisfactory answer to that question. In the 1790s, while serving as president in Philadelphia, Washington attempted a reorganization of his estates that would, he hoped, allow him to set his slaves free, while providing him with a steady income and the freed people with a way of making a living. He intended to lease the Mount Vernon farms to capable (preferably English) agriculturists. The tenants would shoulder the burden of managing the eight thousand–acre estate. But Washington's foremost objective was to disentangle himself from slavery: "I have another motive which makes me earnestly wish for the accomplishment of these things, it is indeed more powerful than all the rest. namely to liberate a certain species of property which I possess, very repugnantly to my own feelings; but which imperious necessity compels."[20] The sturdy English farmers would operate Mount Vernon so efficiently that the slaves could be freed to stay

on as paid agricultural laborers. But the scheme failed
when no suitable tenants appeared. In the end, Washington elected to free his slaves after his death. It was a radical
decision, known to the world only after his will was published. All Washington's fears would be confirmed by the
debates at the Constitutional Convention: No union of the
states could survive an effort to restrict slavery. Certainly
no such effort was made at the convention.

George Washington, it might be said, played only a
small role in the creation of the United States Constitution. One might as easily argue that Washington was one
of the principal players in the drama of the Grand Federal Convention of 1787. He took almost no part in the debates. For all Madison's tutelage, Washington was largely
unacquainted with theories of constitutionalism. Yet his
majestic presence steadied and gave legitimacy to the Constitutional Convention, the very legality of which many
questioned. Later, ratification of the Constitution would
probably have been impossible without Washington's support. ("Be assured," said one observer of the contentious
Virginia ratification convention, "his influence carried this
government.")[21] As many have remarked, ratification of
the Constitution was a sort of ratification of George Washington himself. Certainly the powerful office of the presidency, one of the most remarkable features of the new government, was crafted to conform to the flawless character
of George Washington. For everyone knew that he would
be first to wield its substantial powers.

The delegates—fifty-five men representing every state
but Rhode Island would attend at one time or another—

convened at the Pennsylvania State House, the same place where the Continental Congress had commissioned Washington general twelve years earlier. From Paris, Thomas Jefferson called it "an assembly of demigods."[22] The new assembly elected Washington its president. It was a role he welcomed. Not only did the appointment recognize his exalted standing, but the office exempted him from speaking during debates.

The Virginia delegation dominated the meeting from the start. If Washington furnished his massive grandeur, short, shy James Madison brought political genius and an encyclopedic knowledge of constitutional republicanism. Madison's leadership assured that a well-rehearsed Virginia delegation appeared at the first session with an altogether radical proposal. On May 29, 1787, it offered the fifteen resolutions known as the Virginia Plan. Though he spoke not a word, all the delegates understood that George Washington supported the plan.

The resolutions mapped out a supreme national government. This republican polity would derive its powers from the consent of the people. It would be composed of executive, legislative, and judicial branches, like the governments of the individual states. The national government would possess sweeping powers to act directly on its citizens. As proposed, the new government would much overshadow the states and go a long way toward ending state sovereignty. The national government would even be given a veto over state laws. Representation would be proportional, probably based on population. Proportional representation seemed most consistent with republican principles. Yet it would depart from the one-state-one-vote formula that had prevailed since the first Congress of 1774.

The Virginia Plan was truly radical. The call for the creation of a supreme national government was a call for a second American Revolution. And no one could doubt that such a scheme went far beyond the directive of the Confederation Congress that the convention meet for "the sole and express purpose of revising the Articles of Confederation." Some delegates were aghast at the Virginia Plan's boldness. Yet the next day, the whole convention voted for a resolution "that a *national* Government ought to be established consisting of a *supreme* Legislative, Executive, and Judiciary." The delegates seemed to agree that the American experiment could be preserved only by such a revolutionary expedient.

But the treacherous question of state representation soon brought the convention to a near-fatal deadlock. The large-state nationalists and other proponents of vigorous government supported the Virginia Plan and proportional representation. Many small-state delegates, along with others who feared powerful government, favored a federal union in which the central authority was endowed with powers less sweeping. They put forward their ideas in the New Jersey Plan. Most of the New Jersey Plan was eventually rejected. The real sticking point that remained was the small states' insistence on the one-state-one-vote formula. They feared being buried by the larger states. But Madison and his allies insisted as vehemently that a republican nation—founded, after all, on the bedrock principle that all people were created equal—must give its citizens an equal voice. As one of the nationalists put it, 150 Pennsylvanians should not be required to equal 50 citizens of New Jersey. As the impasse dragged on, tempers inside the State House grew as heated as the summer weather outside. By the middle of June, the convention appeared to be hopelessly deadlocked.

The delegates could not go home without achieving something. Debate had already suggested one way out. The Virginia Plan called for a national legislature composed of an upper and a lower house. The small states would agree to popular representation in the lower house if given an equal vote in the upper. James Madison and some of the other nationalists bitterly opposed sacrificing republican principles to appease the small states. Supporters of the bargain never convinced Madison, but they did just manage to outvote him. The "Great Compromise" of July 16 broke the deadlock by giving the small states equality in the upper house and cleared the way for agreement on the other issues. (Of course, it was hardly a "compromise," but rather a disastrous defeat for Madison and his allies, who had lost their foremost principle of proportional representation.) State equality would prevail in the upper house (later named the Senate). Population would determine membership in the lower body—the House of Representatives. Slaves would be reckoned as equaling three-fifths of free inhabitants in determining population, a formula already arrived at by the Confederation Congress.

Many questions about the executive remained. Suspicion of power, and most particularly of power concen-

trated in the hands of a single figure, was a central feature
of republican ideology. It would hardly have been surpris-
ing if the convention had severely restricted the powers of
the executive. Various proposals to do just that had been
floated in the debates: Two men or a committee might
compose the executive. The president could be appointed
by the legislature or by the judiciary, and subject to recall.
Veto power could be withheld. The states might be vested
with impeachment powers. An appointed advisory council
might hedge presidential autonomy. The president might
not be named commander in chief of the nation's military,
nor be accorded a major role in setting foreign policy. Service could be limited to a single term.

Instead, the convention created a single, strong, independent executive officer, chosen by the electoral college
and eligible for unlimited reelection. In his silence, Washington had shaped that decision. Delegate Pierce Butler
of South Carolina thought that the president's powers
were "full great, and greater than I was disposed to make
them. Nor (entre nous) do I believe they would have been
so great had not many of the members cast their eyes to-
wards General Washington as President; and shaped their
ideas of the Powers to be given a President, by their opinions of his Virtue."[23]

By the end of July, the convention had made enough
progress to call a ten-day recess while a small committee
worked out a draft of a proposed constitution. Washington
sought diversion. He visited Charles Willson Peale's mu-
seum and William Bartram's botanical gardens. Always
happy to oblige artists, he sat patiently as the Peales, fa-

ther and son, labored to translate his likeness to canvas. The flesh-and-blood Washington found fishing an amusing pastime. He and a fellow delegate rode out to "Valley-forge to get Trout." But, he recorded in his diary, "Whilst Mr. Morris was fishing I rid over the old Cantonment of the American [army] in the Winter of 1777, & 8. Visited all the Works, wch. were in Ruins."[24] Characteristically, Washington wrote nothing of the feelings the scenes of Valley Forge must have stirred in him.

When the Convention met again, on August 6, the result of the committee's work was distributed to the delegates. A few copies of this "Report of the Committee of Detail" had been secretly printed on seven tall folio sheets, provided with wide margins wherein members could record changes made during the coming debates. The report was the first draft of the U.S. Constitution. Within its articles, the lineaments of Madison's Virginia plan were clearly discernible.

As the gentlemen in Philadelphia charted the boundaries of the political freedom accruing to future generations of white Americans, as many as 600,000 black inhabitants of America, nearly one-fifth of the whole population, were held in perpetual slavery. Though slavery was still legal in many of the northern states, nearly all the enslaved people were concentrated in the South. Indeed, in many southern districts black population equaled or exceeded white. The new Constitution offered nothing to these captive people or their posterity. Slavery had already divided the country into the two antagonistic sections that would struggle for dominance until the cataclysm of the 1860s.

Everyone knew that the South—particularly powerful South Carolina, along with North Carolina and Georgia— would never agree to a constitution that gave the federal government any substantial powers over the institution of slavery. The southern states would come into the Union with their slaves or not at all. They also insisted on guarantees that their hold on the enslaved people would remain secure long into the future.

Only a few southern statesmen defended the morality of slavery in 1787, but fewer still hoped for its abolition. Few could doubt that the institution was an open and pernicious violation of the principle of human equality that had driven the American Revolution—the same principle of equality upon which the convention was now constructing a republican government. But politics triumphed over ideology. The delegates chose national unity over natural rights and so postponed the day of reckoning. Madison later judged that "great as the evil is, a dismemberment of the union would be worse."[25] George Washington agreed. The framers bequeathed to the unborn millions a contradictory legacy of freedom and slavery.

Whenever possible, the delegates tried to sidestep the issue altogether. The words "slave" and "slavery" appear nowhere in the Constitution. The preferred code phrases—"person held to service or labor," "all other persons," and "such persons"—of course puzzled no one. Most far-reaching of the concessions made to slave power was the three-fifths rule of counting population. New slaves born or imported would increase slave state representation in Congress and the electoral college, giving those states inordinate power in the federal government. At first, the Deep South slaveholders wanted no tax or time limits on the slave trade, on their rights to import new slaves. Virginian George Mason, himself owner of hundreds of slaves, spoke out against the slave trade in providential terms: The "infernal traffic" would "bring the judgment of Heaven on a Country. As Nations cannot be rewarded or punished in the next world they must be in this. By a national chain of causes and effects providence punishes national sins, by national calamities."[26] At the same time, Mason was no abolitionist; he wanted protection for the existing institution. And the Carolinians accused Mason of wanting to restrict the slave trade only to keep the supply down so that Virginians could profitably sell their own slaves south.

A compromise was reached: The tax the federal government could impose on newly imported slaves was limited to ten dollars, and the government was forbidden to regulate the transatlantic slave trade for twenty years, until 1808. The Constitution also included the fugitive slave clause introduced by Pierce Butler.

The U.S. Constitution need not be viewed as a proslavery document, though the conduct of the federal government over the next sixty years would be decidedly proslavery. Nevertheless, South Carolina delegate Charles C. Pinckney could endorse the new Constitution to the citizens of his state: "By this settlement we have secured an unlimited importation of negroes for twenty years. Nor is it declared that the importation shall be then stopped; it may continue. We have a security that the general government can never emancipate them, for no such authority is granted. . . . We have obtained a right to recover our slaves in whatever part of America they may take refuge, which is a right we had not before. In short, considering all the circumstances, we have made the best terms for this security of this species of property that it was in our power to make. We would have made better if we could; but, on the whole I do not think them bad."[27] So George Washington, for the rest of his life, whatever antislavery notions he might care to entertain, always had to remember that the slaveholders' position in law was strong. Though the Constitution itself was by no means the biggest reason he never spoke out publicly against slavery.

The Constitution, consisting of a preamble and seven articles of about forty-five hundred words, was signed by thirty-nine delegates on September 17, 1787. A glance at the first lines hinted at the summer's progress. The preamble to the first draft of early August had opened "We the People of the States of . . . ," listing all thirteen states by name, in geographical order from north to south. The Constitution began "We the People of the United States." But harmony did not entirely prevail. Three influential delegates, including George Mason, had refused to sign. And all the framers recognized that it would not be easy to persuade the states to accept the proposed charter in their ratifying conventions.

The Federalists (as the Constitution's supporters called themselves) had improved their chances by providing that ratification by only nine of the thirteen states would be sufficient to establish the Union "between the States so ratifying." They had also stipulated ratification by special conventions, neatly bypassing the troublesome state legislatures, bodies that could be expected to resist surrendering much of their authority to a new federal government.

The convention had conducted its business in strict secrecy. People greeted the publication of the Constitution with intense interest. Many were horrified by what they read. These Americans saw in the revolution of 1787 a repudiation of the ideals of 1776. The proposed government seemed too strong, too removed from local concerns, and too likely to be dominated by the rich and powerful. The federal government would "consolidate" the states out of existence. The presidency resembled a "foetus of monarchy." Unlike most state constitutions, the federal Constitution contained no bill of rights protecting civil liberties.

These Antifederalists also found a potent objection in republican theory. Republicanism had first appeared in the little city states of the ancient world. Republican government, philosophers maintained and history seemed to confirm, could flourish only within a small and homogeneous sphere. Only a tyrannical government could exercise authority over a nation as large and diverse as the United States. Such doubts had been expressed on the floor of the convention itself. James Madison refuted this objection with his brilliant insight, most fully developed in *The Federalist No. 10*, that the very size and diversity of the United States would work to counteract the excess of majoritarian power that threatened the anarchy that would be followed by despotism. In a country the size of the United States, Madison maintained, the many competing factions and interest groups would make it impossible for any one party to use its majority status to oppress the minority. Republicanism would flourish in an extended republic.

In the end, nationalist momentum proved irresistible. Four states, including Pennsylvania, ratified before 1787 ended. The Federalists had energy and organization, and the best writers and debaters. They had Great Washington's support, and Ben Franklin's too. Massachusetts, one of the crucial big states, ratified in February 1788. Maryland ratified in April, South Carolina in May. New Hampshire ratified on June 21—the ninth state, thereby making the Constitution effective. It was essential that this nine-state ratification be strengthened by the addition of two of the most important states—Virginia and New York. Then the biggest state of all—Virginia—ratified four days after New Hampshire, following much rancorous debate. New York came in on a close vote in July.

And so the world learned in 1788 that a new nation had appeared on history's stage. How long that nation might endure, none could say.

❧ **10** ❧

"On Untrodden Ground"
The First Term

OME MERIT MAY BE ACCORDED the proposition
that George Washington had become a virtual
head of state in 1775, that taking the oath as first
president in 1789 was but a constitutional confirmation of the preeminence he had achieved long before.
For almost fifteen years, Washington had been the most
influential man in America. He had repeatedly displayed
political skills of the highest order. Commanding the Continental Army, he had performed brilliantly as a statesman and diplomat, his talent here surpassing his military
achievement. The Continental Congress had been only a
provisional government, and an ineffective one at that,
until the Articles of Confederation were ratified in 1781. It
remained largely impotent even then, unable to levy taxes
or regulate trade. General Washington had been guided
by no national executive, and, for most of the war, no minister of war or secretary of state. Those duties had often
devolved on him, though he was always punctilious in de-

ferring to Congress. In 1775, the colonists were deeply suspicious of standing armies, and they remained intensely
jealous of one another. The Continental Army had to remain in the field as long as the war lasted. To command such
an army, made up of thousands of men from the various
colonies, had required an extraordinary leader. Though the
tribulations of the presidency would quickly mount, Washington's acceptance of the office in 1789 probably presented
a less daunting challenge than the one he had taken on in
1775. Yet the presidency would prove a bitter ordeal that
brought him none of the satisfactions of a victorious war.

The Constitution provided that an electoral college se-
lect the president. The electors, chosen in different ways
in various states, would possess two votes, each vote to be
given to a different man. The man getting the most votes
would be president, the runner-up vice president. The first
electoral college was chosen in January 1789 and its votes
were counted the following month. Of course, George
Washington was elected, and by unanimous vote. That is,
every elector cast one of his two votes for Washington. John
Adams of Massachusetts was elected vice president, becoming first occupant of what he called "the most insignificant
Office that ever the Invention of Man contrived."[1] Politicians who had supported ratification won big majorities in
the First Federal Congress—fifty of fifty-nine House seats
and eighteen of twenty-two places in the Senate.

The national capital was New York City, seat of the ex-
piring Confederation Congress. Washington was so broke
that he had to borrow £600 to pay his way to his inauguration. He left Mount Vernon on April 14, 1789. Two

weeks earlier, the president-elect had written a friend, "My movements to the chair of Government will be accompanied by feelings not unlike those of a culprit who is going to the place of his execution; so unwilling am I, in the evening of a life nearly consumed in public cares, to quit a peaceful Abode for an Ocean of difficulties, without that competency of political skill—abilities & inclination which is necessary to manage the helm."[2] He insisted, "Nothing in this world can ever draw me from [retirement], unless it be a *conviction* that the partiality of my Countrymen had made my services absolutely necessary, joined to a *fear* that my refusal might induce a belief that I preferred the conservation of my own reputation & private ease to the good of my Country. After all, if I should conceive my self in a manner constrained to accept, I call Heaven to witness, that this very act would be the greatest sacrafice of my personal feelings & wishes that ever I have been called upon to make."[3]

His reservations were quite sincere, as they had been at similar junctures in the past, but Washington accepted the inevitability of the new assignment. His prestige was again indispensably needed. George Washington's hopes for the new nation, and the preservation of his own fame, left him no other choice. He had resigned himself, nevertheless, to a season of discontent. "When I judged," he told a friend, "it was my duty to embark again on the tempestuous & uncertain Ocean of public life, I gave up all expectations of private happiness."[4] Washington planned to serve as short a time as possible, less, he hoped, than one full four-year term. He might never have taken the assignment if he had known it would mean eight years in office.

Pageantry attended his progress all the way to New York. Nearly the entire population of Philadelphia turned out to welcome him. Balls, banquets, mass meetings, speeches, fireworks, and parades were held in his honor. Soldiers marched, guns fired, choirs sang, poets declaimed, and churchmen prayed. An elaborate device contrived to drop a victor's laurel crown on Washington's head as white-robed maidens threw rose petals beneath his horse's hooves. A boy poked a pin into a tethered eagle to make it scream when Washington appeared. Historian Don Higginbottam said it was "an outpouring of tribute and affection that must have been unparalleled in the western world of that time."[5] But the triumphal procession alarmed Washington as much as it gratified him. All his life he had pursued fame and hungered for acclaim. He had won more than any American. But sensible people can be discomfited by effusive praise and the wise understand that fame is treacherous. This renewed adulation frightened him, for it seemed to carry with it the expectation of ever-greater successes. Despite all he had achieved, Washington could never escape his morbid fear of failure.

The diary he kept then contains some of the most self-revealing passages that ever came from his pen: "I bade adieu to Mount Vernon, to private life, and to domestic felicity; and with a mind oppressed by more anxious and painful sensations than I have words to express, set out to New York . . . with the best dispositions to render service to my country in obedience to its call, but with less hope of answering its expectations."[6] After crossing the Hudson to Manhattan in an elaborate barge rowed by thirteen sailors, he wrote: "The display of boats which attended and joined us on this occasion, some with vocal and some with instrumental music on board; the roar of cannon, and the loud acclamations of the people which rent the skies, as I passed along the wharves, filled my mind with sensations as painful (considering the reverse of the scene, which may be the case after all my labors to do good) as they are pleasing."[7] Washington's fears were prophetic. The presidency would cost him enormous anguish.

He took the oath of office on the balcony of Federal Hall, overlooking Wall and Broad streets, on April 30, 1789. All of New York, it seemed, had turned out. A huge crowd of onlookers, standing shoulder to shoulder, filled the streets below. They cheered when Washington appeared on the balcony. When the ovation died down, the ceremony proceeded. Washington repeated the simple oath required by the Constitution: "I solemnly swear that I will faithfully execute the office of President of the United States and will, to the best of my ability, preserve, protect, and defend the Constitution of the United States." Washington certainly did not conclude the oath with the impromptu exclamation "So help me God!" as has so often been claimed. This is a Victorian fable, a product of that far more pious era. The legend depends on a child's supposed recollections of an event he claimed to have witnessed sixty years earlier. None of the contemporary witnesses, who carefully recorded every detail of the inauguration, mentioned such an addition to the oath. And Washington was, as historian Edward Lengel has noted, a "literalist," unlikely to depart from the script prescribed by the Constitution.[8]

The crowd couldn't hear anything, so an official had to shout, "It is done!" He then cried, "Long live George Washington, President of the United States!" The crowd cheered and the cheering was long continued. Cannon boomed and church bells rang. Then the new president bowed to his admirers and went inside from the balcony to deliver his inaugural address to the House and Senate. Washington was a nervous public speaker. One senator recorded in his diary that "this great Man was agitated and embarrassed more than ever he was by the levelled Cannon or pointed musket. He trembled, and several times could scarce make out to read, tho it must be supposed he had often read it before. . . . I felt hurt, that he was not the first in every thing."[9] In the address, drafted by James Madison, Washington repeated what he had often said before, that "the sacred fire of liberty and the destiny of the Republican model of Government . . . [is] staked, on the experiment entrusted to the hands of the American people."[10] Along with all the praise, many made the same observation: "Well, he deserves it all."[11]

The Washington presidency was almost stillborn. He nearly died (or so his doctors thought) in 1789 and again in 1790. Washington's health had always been strikingly robust. He had not been seriously ill since 1758. But in June 1789, a large, painful tumor appeared on Washington's thigh. The doctors called it a "carbuncle"; it may have been a form of anthrax.[12] It rapidly became larger and more painful and was accompanied by high fevers. The doctors decided on surgery. Two physicians, father and son, carried out the operation. The son performed the surgery, cutting deeply into Washington's thigh to excise the tumor. Washington endured the intense pain stoically. "Cut away— deeper—deeper still," said father to son. "Don't be afraid. You see how well he bears it."[13] The crisis passed, but full recovery did not come for more than three months.

Then, in April 1790, Washington came down with influenza that progressed to full-blown pneumonia. Again his life was despaired of. One doctor declared that the president was "in the act of death."[14] He lingered for a month, then in May staged an unexpected recovery. Never, however, did he regain his former strength. These illnesses made Washington all the more eager to relinquish the presidency. He was sure he didn't have much time left and he wanted to spend as much of it as possible at Mount Vernon. He told a friend that "I already had within less than a year, two *severe* attacks—the last worse than the first—a third more than probable will put me to sleep with my fathers."[15]

At first, with only Congress and the president himself in office, there was little work for the chief executive. Still, Washington was concerned about his every action. "I walk on untrodden ground," he said. "There is scarcely any part of my conduct wch may not hereafter be drawn into precedent."[16] Kings people understood—presidents were another matter altogether. In all the world, no elected head of state exercised substantial powers in a large nation. Washington must now bridge the shift from kingship to an executive authority derived from the people. As the only model available, monarchy loomed large. "You are now a King, under a different name," one of his former Revolutionary War aides had assured the general.[17] But most Americans now hated and feared kings, and Washington himself had already demonstrated that he did not want a crown. Many, however—particularly the opponents of a strong central government under the new Constitution—would never be able to put aside their dread of an American monarch.

Fortunately for the new president, Congress had already settled the awkward matter of an official title, spurning the royal "His Highness the President of the United States of America and Protector of Their Liberties" proposed by the Senate for the republican simplicity of "the President of the United States." Washington had favored the more modest title, rightly believing that grand honorifics would engender fear of the new government.[18] But he would never be able to escape accusations of harboring monarchical ambitions. From the beginnings of his presidency, but ever more often as the numbers of his detractors grew, Washington would be charged with taking on regal airs. George Washington was extraordinarily sensitive to criticism, and for some time his stature had largely protected him. But he soon realized that the presidency would draw attacks upon him as surely as Dr. Franklin's lightning rod pulled bolts from the sky.

The cold face Washington turned to the world was both an expression of his self-doubt and a constructed public persona that had enabled him to exercise power for decades. His enemies, however, would equate aloofness with regal pretensions. The lavish life the president and his family enjoyed in their rented New York mansion was no more opulent than that they had been accustomed to at Mount Vernon, but luxury provided fuel for critics. The weekly receptions (the so-called levees) that Washington staged to guard his working hours from a stream of unannounced callers were painfully stiff affairs, offensive to the republican sensibilities of many.

At first the president's house, as the property of the people (the government, after all, paid the rent), was open to all who wished to visit. The place was crowded with throngs of curiosity-seeking strangers. This predictably proved unworkable. Washington was swamped with visitors. He said, "I should have been unable to have attended to any sort of business unless I had applied the hours allotted to rest and refreshment for this purpose."[19] No one knew how a president should interact with his constituents. Seeking advice from a wide range of people, Washington came up with a system he hoped would be republican, dignified, and practicable. He would make no calls or accept any invitations to private homes. He would hold weekly receptions, his levees, at three o'clock Tuesday afternoons. Any respectable gentleman could attend. The name of each arriving guest was called out by a secretary. Washington was there waiting, standing with his back to the fireplace. He was impeccably dressed. His hair was powdered. A sword hung at his side. In his hand, he held a hat to show that he didn't mean to shake hands. Each new arrival would approach the president, exchange bows, and withdraw into the semicircle of other gentlemen. The president then went around the circle, exchanging a few words with each man before returning to his post before the fireplace. After precisely sixty minutes, each guest would approach the president, exchange bows, and leave.

The arrangement invited derision. When Jefferson complained about the monarchical character of the levees—he had not yet joined the administration when the protocol was set—Washington countered that he had had no precedents to guide him and had taken the best advice he could find. The president also hosted frequent dinner parties for members of Congress, diplomats, and other officials. These too were described as pretty dismal affairs, with Washington lapsing into long silences while impatiently drumming on the table with a fork. Everyone was glad when the party ended. (Jefferson said of Washington, "His colloquial talents were not above mediocrity, possessing neither copiousness of ideas, nor fluency of words.")[20] It is hard to say what might have worked, given Washington's personality. He was by nature aloof and silent, uncomfortable around strangers, unwilling to talk about himself, and his increasing deafness made conversation difficult. For her part, Martha Washington hated being imprisoned in the presidency. Nevertheless, her weekly tea parties, to which women were invited, were more lively affairs. The president always attended, and he was much more warm and open in female company, conversing freely with the ladies, even cracking the occasional joke.

One observer thought that the only feature of the new government that really captured the imagination of the people was George Washington as president. The president meant to use that prestige in his long-continued campaign for national unification. He would bring the new government, in the form of his own person, to as many Americans as possible. He made two arduous road tours of the country—a northern and a southern tour—with visits to all the eleven states that then made up the Union. (North Carolina and Rhode Island had yet to ratify the Constitution. When those two wayward states presently fell into line, Washington made a point of visiting them as well.)[21]

First came the northern or New England tour. He set out for Boston from New York in October 1789, half a year after his inauguration. The aging statesman now preferred to travel by carriage. Just behind the vehicle, however, came a servant riding Prescott, Washington's magnificent white charger. Before entering a town, the president mounted up to become the hero on horseback the people longed to see. He was greeted everywhere with rapturous enthusiasm. There were parades, speeches, and elaborate balls at which he enjoyed dancing late into the night with the local wives and maidens. Next morning saw a ceremonious departure as Washington pushed off for the next stop. Roads were bad, accommodations lacking, and the crowds troublesome, but Washington managed to stick to his schedule, returning to New York a little more than a month after leaving. The southern tour followed in spring 1791. This 1,887-mile journey opened up new territory for Washington: he'd never before been south of Virginia's southern border. He soon found that his popularity in the South was as great as in New England. Southerners seemed generally satisfied with the new federal government. Washington thought the tours a great success. Most seemed to agree. One newspaper reported that "every individual thought he beheld a friend and a patron; a father or a brother after a long absence; and, on his part, the President seemed to feel the joy of a father."[22]

The Philadelphia convention had outlined a skeletal government. It was up to the First Federal Congress to put flesh on the bare bones. The Constitution's reticence and ambiguities may well be a source of its success, but in 1789, the document left many baffled. Article I, with its ten sections outlining the powers of Congress, is more than twice as long as Article II, dealing with the presidency. In republican theory and American practice, the legislature, where the people were most directly represented, was the predominate branch of government. This was certainly the case in the existing state governments. Everywhere, the executive branches tended to be weak, denied substantial powers.

Perhaps legislative predominance would obtain in the new federal government as well. Despite the powers given to the president, it was certainly possible to read the Constitution that way. Such an outcome would comport with the wishes of those Americans who feared a strong government and a powerful presidency. Yet during Washington's terms, a series of enactments enhanced the power of the presidency at the expense of Congress. The president was given authority not explicitly granted by the Constitution. This is not to say that these decisions were unconstitutional. It was all a matter of interpretation. Campaigning openly and working behind the scenes, Washington consistently pushed for a more powerful presidency. His greatest asset in this campaign was the abiding trust he had earned. In Congress itself, James Madison was the most effective advocate of a strong presidency, a position he would before long repudiate.

The Constitution contained only a single reference to "the principal Officer in each of the executive Departments." The Constitution implicitly gave the president authority to appoint those officers, but did not say who would control those departments. Under the Confederation, the executive departments had been directed by Congress. But now Congress voted to put the departments under the president. Secretaries of the departments were to be nominated by the president and confirmed by the Senate. Then came the question of who would have the authority to fire the cabinet secretaries, the president or Congress. Many argued that since the Senate had the power to confirm, it should have the power to remove from office. The vote in Congress was close. The House voted to give the right to the president, while the Senate was tied. For the first time, Vice President Adams exercised his office's prerogative of breaking a Senate tie, voting for the presidency. It was a most significant augmentation of executive authority. A government in which cabinet secretaries served at the pleasure of the Senate, not the president, would be radically different from the system we have. It would have been an arrangement actually parliamentary in nature.

Early in the first session of Congress, Madison pushed through the amendments to the Constitution, eventually numbering ten, known as the Bill of Rights. The states duly ratified them in December 1791. Congress voted the president a salary of $25,000 a year, greatly exceeding the vice president's $5,000 and the department secretaries' $3,500. As he had in the Revolution, Washington declined the salary, asking only that his expenses be met. But this time Congress insisted—the president would be paid. Congress created the departments of Foreign Affairs (soon to be called State), War, and the Treasury. Washington appointed Alexander Hamilton secretary of the treasury, Henry Knox secretary of war, and Thomas Jefferson secretary of state. (Jefferson was still serving as minister to France and did not take office until March 1790, almost a year after Washington's inauguration.) The president named Edmund Randolph attorney general even though there was not as yet a justice department. He made John Jay chief justice of the Supreme Court. The Senate confirmed them. Within this first presidential cabinet were the seeds of the discord that would soon rend the administration and the nation itself.

There was more untrodden ground to cross. The Constitution gave the president power "by and with the Advice and Consent of the Senate, to make Treaties, provided two-thirds of the Senators present concur." But what form should this advice and consent take? Should the president work out the terms of pending treaties with the Senate? The Constitution did not say. The test case proved to be a treaty with the southern Creek tribe in August 1789. (Indian tribes were treated as foreign nations.) Washington had asked Madison how to proceed: "Would an Oral or written communication be best? If the first what mode is to be adopted to effect it?"[23] Washington and a committee of senators soon decided that "in all matters respecting Treaties, oral communications seem indispensably necessary."

The Senate wanted an active role in the making of treaties and foreign policy. President Washington concurred.

But the collaboration did not go smoothly when the president visited the Senate chamber on Saturday, August 22, 1789. After a lengthy document had been read aloud—a list of seven questions about the proposed treaty—some of the senators said that they had not been able to follow the reading because of the clatter of the wheels of carriages on cobblestones outside the open windows. The questions were read again, this time with the windows closed. Then Vice President Adams reread the first question a third time and asked the senators "Do you advise and consent?" No answer. Instead, the senators asked for a postponement until they could consider the questions before them. They wanted to form a committee. Washington became angry. One senator recalled that "the President of the U.S. started up in a Violent fret. *'This defeats every purpose of my coming here,'* were the first words he said."[24] Washington agreed to return two days later. But for the last time— the arrangement was unworkable. Leaving the second session, according to one story, the president was heard to mutter that he'd "be damned if he ever went there again!" In the more than two hundred years since, neither George Washington nor any of his presidential successors has ever returned to negotiate a treaty with the Senate. The senators would "consent" but not "advise." The Senate's role has been confined to ratification of treaties drafted by the president. The episode set a precedent that helped establish foreign policy as the president's domain. It was another important, though perhaps unplanned, enhancement of presidential power.²⁵ But Washington had demonstrated again that he respected the Constitution and the powers of Congress.

George Washington and his contemporaries were convinced that political parties—"factions"—were a corrupting evil, perhaps the gravest threat the new nation faced. The first president believed that leaders must be elected on their reputations for disinterested public service. A republican statesman's only aim should be the good of the nation as a whole. He must pursue no partisan program. Factions were merely crooked alliances to pursue selfish ends. It is ironic, then, that the 1790s emerged as "the Age of Passion"—the most fervently partisan decade in American history. At the heart of the conflict was the ideological clash of two fundamentally opposed conceptions of the American experiment.

The human poles around which the two protoparties began to coalesce were Secretary of the Treasury Alexander Hamilton and Secretary of State Thomas Jefferson. Both were men of rare genius. They were the two ranking officials in the president's administration. Rivalry quickly moved beyond ideology to burning personal animosity— the most consequential and enduring of all American political feuds. Jefferson's political nostrils were exquisitely sensitive to the scent of approaching monarchy. He saw crowns and scepters wherever he looked. Jefferson was also unwilling to acknowledge, even to himself, the extent of his ambition or his passionate political factionalism. Warfare in the bosom of his official family would drive Washington to despair.

The Hamiltonian party came to be called Federalist, the Jeffersonian Republican (or Democratic-Republican—the direct ancestor of today's Democratic Party). It was no accident that the Hamiltonians took up the name used by supporters of the Constitution. The Federalists saw themselves as extending the nationalist movement to build a strong government. Like Washington, they favored a deferential society in which gentlemen would govern. Federalists looked toward a consolidated nation in which a vigorous federal government would overshadow the states. The Hamiltonians supported banking and investment, trade and commerce, and solid national credit. The big cities of the North were their natural realm. They intended that the United States become a great nation, a power among the powers of earth. Federalists openly admired Great Britain for the stability of its government, its military prowess, and the soundness of its financial system. Did they also favor the British monarchical model for the United States?

Jefferson and his Republican followers certainly thought so. The Republicans found their spiritual home among the fields of rural America, especially the plantations of the slaveholding South. Jefferson named those who turned the soil "the chosen people of God."[26] His vision of the American future took in an agrarian utopia in which generation after generation of sturdy farmers passed honest, independent lives, far from cities and scheming moneymen. Jefferson favored states' rights over federal authority. Government should be limited and local. Tyranny was to be feared more than anarchy. His faith in the common people was unbounded. The well-born author of the Declaration of Independence loved republican equality as much as the self-made treasury secretary admired hierarchy. Despite his high-flown denunciations of slavery, some of which would one day be carved into the stone of the Jefferson Memorial, the Virginian's core beliefs favored slavery's continuance. He attached such conditions to emancipation that it could never come about, and he feared a central government strong enough to restrict or abolish slavery. Hamilton for his part was an abolitionist. He would lead the fight to end slavery in New York. Washington too longed for emancipation, though he would never say so publicly. By this time, Washington had also begun to favor the commercial North over the agrarian South. From the outset, then, it was unlikely that George Washington would ever embrace Jefferson's Republican program. By temperament, outlook, and experience, Washington was of the Federalist persuasion, though he struggled desperately to remain above factions. He never admitted that he was a Federalist. In his Farewell Address, he expanded on the evils of parties.

Washington had grown disillusioned with the agrarianism Jefferson so admired. Mount Vernon, with its surplus of slaves, had been hemorrhaging money for years. War and government had given him broad experience in the northern states. Though the North too was still overwhelmingly agricultural, Washington recognized the northern cities as the vital centers of commerce and government in the modern world. He favored energetic government and strong national credit. His experience with the impotence of the Confederation during the Revolution had made him an advocate of powerful government. Washington would not be pleased when his fellow Virginians presently emerged as the most consistent opponents of the measures he deemed vital to national success. As W. W. Abbot has observed, Washington "was the least Virginian of the great Virginians."[27] Indeed, Washington declared that if he had to choose, and if it were remotely possible, he would sell his Virginia property and go to live in the North. According to Edmund Randolph, his attorney general and a fellow Virginia aristocrat, Washington, "on the hypothesis of the separation of the Union into Northern and Southern said he had made up his mind to remove and be of the Northern."[28] Jefferson must have been appalled when Randolph repeated this statement to him.

The Republicans believed that the Hamiltonians aimed at nothing less than the creation of an American monarchy. They called the Federalists "monocrats" and "Anglomen." Some of Washington's conduct that seemed to smack of monarchical pretensions now appeared all the more alarming in the eyes of fearful Republicans. They pondered the president's magisterial aloofness, the very grandeur of his person, the stateliness of the presidential household with its twenty servants, his grand carriage pulled by four matching horses, and the awesome formality of his weekly levees. They wondered whether this was evidence that Washington secretly supported Hamilton's schemes, or at the least, that the president was Hamilton's unwitting tool.

Alexander Hamilton had done little to ease such fears. Many remembered his daylong speech extolling constitutional monarchy at the Philadelphia convention in 1787. He had not hesitated to declare the British constitution the "most perfect in the world." There was a rumor that he had proposed a toast to George III. He had even told Jefferson, perhaps in jest, that Julius Caesar was the greatest man who ever lived. (Or so Jefferson said.) Jefferson believed that Hamilton and his allies regarded the new government as a mere "stepping stone" to a state in which the influence of the powerful would again overshadow human equality. If republican government faltered, as many expected, Hamilton was sure to gain converts. Jefferson had a sunny view of human nature. He believed in the goodness of the common people and their capacity for self-government. Hamilton did not share this optimism. He was convinced that humans were ineluctably corrupt and power-hungry, that they needed the superintending hand of authority to curb their impulses. Distinctions of rank between people, though probably not hereditary distinctions, were part of Hamilton's formula.

Jefferson probably envied Hamilton's military record as well as his influence over Washington. He had expected more solidarity from Washington, a fellow Virginia gentleman and an old friend, against the illegitimate, foreign-born upstart Hamilton. Despite his youth, Hamilton had served as an officer throughout the Revolution. He had risked his life in deadly combat. Jefferson had written his influential *A Summary View of the Rights of British America* in 1774. But his contributions to the Revolution itself, beyond his role in drafting the Declaration of Independence, were rather modest. He certainly never heard a shot fired in anger. His two-year term as wartime governor of Virginia ended in humiliation when he was unable to defend his state and had to flee ignominiously from a British raiding party. He declined diplomatic posts offered him by Congress, preferring to stay home at Monticello. Jefferson, nonetheless, saw fit to question Hamilton's military record, implying that his heroism had been exaggerated.[29] At the same time, one should never lose sight of the most essential distinction: Jefferson's vision took in the empowerment of the common people, the many, while Hamilton looked to a state in which an elite, the few, would set policy. Hamilton's vision of the United States as a great nation, his hopes for a vigorous federal government, and his financial plans have all come to pass. His genius would enduringly benefit the American future. But his embrace of an elitist hierarchy was out of step with history, a repudiation of the highest ideals of the American Revolution. The question then becomes, where does this leave Hamilton's president? Can Hamilton's errors be justly ascribed to George Washington? The most satisfactory answer would seem to be that while Washington shared Hamilton's preference for a hierarchical society, he remained a steadfast republican and an adamantine foe of hereditary power. While Hamilton's policies eventually prevailed, America's evolving political culture would soon pass him by, going in a decidedly Jeffersonian direction. Democracy would eclipse hierarchy, leaving Hamilton to lament, "This American world was not made for me."[30] Nevertheless, history seems to have accorded Hamilton the final victory. His United States as a continental empire of financial, industrial, and military might is a reality, while Jefferson's dream of a simple republic of virtuous farmers has been utterly discarded.

American colonials had always taken pride in their heritage of British liberty. At the same time, among the politically sophisticated, there was a fear that the nation that had been liberty's cradle had become its grave. A hundred-year-old school of Anglo-American oppositional theory spoke of the conflict between "Court and Country." Key to British liberty was the balanced government of crown, Lords, and Commons, the strength of each assuring that no other would gain too much power. But Robert Walpole, considered the first British prime minister and the longest-serving holder of that office (from 1721 to 1742), had put in place a system that allowed the "Court"— that is the king and the ministry—to control Parliament. The king had vast wealth and powers of appointment. By handing out bribes, pensions, corporate charters, handsomely paid offices, and titles of nobility, the Court succeeded in turning many parliamentarians into its creatures, placeholders who could be counted on to vote on the ministry's orders. This perceived corruption of Parliament had ended balanced government and destroyed true liberty. By this time, Great Britain had funded a permanent national debt and set up the Bank of England. Many grew rich from speculation in government securities. Holders of public debt were also seen as creatures of the Court, bound to the ministry's will by their own self-interest. The rich and powerful thrived at the expense of the common people and the honest country gentry. Extremes of wealth and poverty—deadly to freedom—could only increase.

This oppositional ideology held even greater resonance among American republicans than it did in Britain. Country party thought had fueled the drive toward independence. It is hard to imagine anything more alarming to the Democratic-Republicans than Alexander Hamilton's financial proposals. His program seemed expressly calculated to bloat the power of the federal government—particularly the executive branch—at the expense of Congress, the states, and the people themselves. It could give the Federalists a way to consolidate the states out of existence. In a time of rampant political paranoia, the outlines of this dire conspiracy seemed frighteningly clear to the Republican opposition. The ultimate goal of Hamilton and the Federalist "Anglomen," the opposition sincerely believed, was the creation of an American monarchy.

The great schism really began to open in January 1790, when Hamilton submitted the plan for his financial program, Report of the Secretary of the Treasury to the House of Representatives, Relative to a Provision for the Support of the Public Credit of the United States. Everyone knew that money was the greatest problem confronting the new nation. The United States and the governments of the individual states owed many millions of dollars— no one knew how many—to an array of creditors: the French government and Dutch bankers; the still-unpaid officers and men of the Continental Army; farmers and merchants who had been given IOUs for produce, livestock, and goods seized by the army; and the holders of government securities. It also included years of interest owed on all those debts, for the Confederation Congress had been unable to pay. Hamilton possessed an almost superhuman capacity for hard work. It took weeks of collating disparate records, but he succeeded in calculating that the federal debt stood at $54 million, while the states owed another $25 million, a total of $79 million. This was a staggering amount, far beyond the nation's ability to pay under the existing system. The entire federal budget could not even begin to cover the interest on the debt, far less attack the principal. (During Washington's first term, the federal budget rose from $639,000 in 1789 to $1,059,222 in 1792.)[31] There was now, however, an assured source of revenue, the Tariff of 1789, which imposed a 5 percent duty on goods imported from abroad.

Hamilton conceived and presented his financial program as a single seamless system. Opposition soon reduced it to a constellation of contested issues, each of which would be fought over in turn. First was funding, the government's refinancing of the national debt. Linked to funding was discrimination—the controversy over whether to repay original holders of the debt as opposed to the speculators who had later bought it up. The next was assumption, the taking on of the states' war debts. Another issue was residence, the location of the permanent national capital. The creation of the Bank of the United States was another source of conflict, as were Hamilton's excise taxes, and his effort to establish government support for American manufacturing.

Hamilton proposed that the government fund, or refinance, the debt. The government would redeem with new securities those issued by the Continental Congress. Redemption would be at face value, even though the certificates were now selling at well below that on the open market. Refinancing would create a standing national debt, interest on which could be paid by taxes. The national debt, in the form of circulating public securities, would itself become a source of substantial liquid capital and a form of currency in the cash-poor economy. A funded national debt, Hamilton understood, was behind the unprecedented success of the British financial system.[32] In addition, the treasury secretary proposed that the federal government assume the states' war debts. A sinking fund from the post office revenues would retire part of the principal each year. The whole plan, of course, rested on the 5 percent federal duty on imports from abroad passed by Congress in 1789. Since more than three-quarters of foreign trade was with Britain, Hamilton was most anxious that that commerce be in no way deranged. Hamilton favored friendship with, and emulation of, the British nation. Virginians Jefferson and Madison, on the other hand, hated England and its whole system of finance, manufacturing, and commerce.[33] Not only were the Virginia slaveholding agrarians opposed by temperament and upbringing to commercial life, but their state had suffered more than most from British invasion during the Revolution. Most of the debts still due to British merchants, repayment of which was required by the Treaty of Paris of 1783, were owed by Virginia planters. The "Court-Country" theories of republicanism had always regarded sophisticated financial policies as inimical to liberty. The plan also seemed to benefit the East and North—where the holders of government debt were concentrated—at the expense of the South.

The first real sticking point was discrimination, the controversy over rendering justice to the original holders of government debt. In many cases, these were veterans of the Continental Army. They had been paid for their service in government paper. Desperate for ready cash, most of them had sold their paper at deep discounts, as little as ten cents on the dollar. The price of the paper had begun to rise as soon as ratification of the Constitution promised that the national debt would be addressed. Now Hamilton proposed ignoring the original holders, instead paying full face value to the speculators who had gathered in their debt. In February 1790, Congressman James Madison rose in the House to denounce the apparent injustice. "There must be something wrong," Madison insisted, "radically & morally & politically wrong, in a system that transfers the reward from those who paid the most valuable of all considerations to those who scarcely paid any consideration at all."[34] He sought a way to split the payment between the original holders and the speculators. This may well have been an unworkable notion. Madison was voted down, 36 to 13. Most of Madison's support came from the South.

Assumption, the funding of state war debts by the national government, a central element of Hamilton's plan, was the next source of conflict. The whole Hamiltonian program was anathema to Virginia Republicans. This time, James Madison and his allies were able to block assumption in Congress. The Virginians also argued that, since their state had already paid off its war debt, assumption would unfairly favor the states that had not paid. On April 12, 1790, the vote was 31 to 29 against assumption. So just a year into the first term, opposition to administration policies had arisen from a source that might have appeared unlikely. Not only was James Madison the president's most influential adviser and his champion in Congress, he had also been the steady ally of his friend Alexander Hamilton. The pair had worked together to promote vigorous government since they had first met as delegates to the Confederation Congress in 1782. They had done as much as anyone to bring about the Constitutional Convention. Together, and writing over a single byline, they had composed most of *The Federalist*. They had both fought effectively for ratification in their respective states. Now, in his response to Hamilton's financial program, the archnationalist Madison seemed to be reverting into a Virginia localist. Madison had argued at the Constitutional Convention for an all-powerful central government, a government that even had the authority to veto state laws. Now he seemed to favor states' rights and a small, puny federal government, with Congress overshadowing the executive. Madison had come to believe that a powerful government would promote the interests of the commercial North and violate the spirit of the Constitution. He opposed the Hamiltonian programs that were both the objectives and the instruments of government power. At first Hamilton was baffled, but he soon realized that ideology had ended the alliance forever.

Madison's ideological shift, however, may have been more apparent than real. Historian Lance Banning has advanced compelling arguments that Madison's opposition was fully consistent with the ideas he had held during the Confederacy and Constitution periods.[35] In any case, Washington and Hamilton certainly thought Madison had receded from his support for strong government.

Despite the strictures of the opposition, Hamilton eventually succeeded in persuading Congress to pass most of his sweeping fiscal program. He failed, however, to win support for a government initiative to promote American manufacturing. Washington kept out of the debate, believing the Constitution prohibited the executive from interfering in legislative matters. Many observers understood that the president supported Hamilton. Washington had been thoroughly convinced of the dangers of weak government and financial imbecility by his experiences in the Revolution. Hamilton was soon vindicated: his program was comprehensively successful. American credit was restored, the Revolutionary War debt was steadily paid down, and the economy boomed.

A way to revisit the deadlock over assumption had emerged not long after Congress rejected it in 1790. The Constitution had provided for a new national capital, giving Congress authority to "exercise exclusive legislation in all cases whatsoever, over such district (not exceeding ten miles square) as may, by cession of particular States, and the acceptance of Congress, become the seat of the government of the United States." Congress agreed on a federal city, but could not agree where. "Residence" was another divisive issue facing the new nation. Eight cities and towns had been the seat of government since the Continental Congress first met in 1774. All these places and many others—fifty by one count—had been proposed for the permanent capital. Many of them existed only in the imaginations of their promoters. Most compelling to promoters was the promise that the federal city would become the golden goose of whatever spot government chose for its nest. Some guessed that the amount poured from national into local coffers could run as high as $1 million a year.[36] Local property values would climb as well.

Among existing cities the two strongest contenders were Philadelphia, the largest city on the continent, and New York, America's second city and home of Congress since 1784. But a site somewhere along a stretch of the Potomac between Maryland and Virginia emerged as a rival. North of that river, most thought choosing an existing city more sensible than building a whole new one on the Potomac's malarial mudflats. Maps, however, showed that the Potomac lay at the geographic center of American territory, and in 1790 the first federal census indicated that the center of population also fell there. This was also considered the "western" site—the area with the closest ties to the Ohio Valley. Political motives, however, overshadowed all the geographical data. The South wanted a Potomac capital. What better way to protect slavery than to site the city within the slave states of Maryland and Virginia? And the Republicans desired an agrarian setting rather than a commercial northern city.

By June 1790, Congress was stuck in the deadlock that some thought actually threatened the survival of the Union. The great issues in contention remained residence and assumption. So bitter was the quarrel that people predicted the rupture of the year-old Union into northern and southern republics. They whispered about civil war, a second revolution.

Instead of war the politicians achieved the Compromise of 1790. Jefferson invited Hamilton to dine with Madison.

The two made a deal: Madison would allow assumption to pass Congress, and Hamilton would persuade the northerners to agree to the federal city on the Potomac. So it came to pass. (To attribute the compromise solely to Jefferson's dinner party would be an oversimplification. The two sides were already near agreement; there were parallel negotiations going on. But certainly these three— Jefferson, Madison, and Hamilton—had to be in accord for any deal to go forward. Jefferson for his part was later to say that this bargain was the greatest political error of his life.)[37]

By August the president was able to write a French friend: "The two great questions of funding the debt and fixing the seat of government have been agitated, as was natural, with a good deal of warmth as well as ability. . . . They were more in danger of having convulsed the government itself than any other points. I hope they are now settled in as satisfactory a manner as could have been expected; and that we have a prospect of enjoying peace abroad, with tranquility at home."[38]

Washington always put the best face on American affairs when writing to European correspondents, but the president, his cabinet, and Congress had good reason to be pleased with the summer's work. They had engineered the first of the great compromises between North and South, one that, like the bargains future statesmen were to make in 1820 and 1850, would hold the Union together until the guns of '61 moved the contest beyond the remedy of reasoned debate.

President Washington signed the Residence Act of 1790

that July. He had kept quiet during the controversy, but he was mightily pleased with the outcome. The act gave him complete authority to plan the capital. He would personally chose the site from within a broad region specified by Congress. Nothing suggests that Washington objected to the idea of naming the new city after him. The capital would first move from New York to Philadelphia for ten years while the new city was building. Government would transfer to its permanent seat in 1800. (Washington was the only president not to govern from the city that bears his name.) In January 1791, he announced that he would locate the federal district about ten miles north of Mount Vernon. The district was a ten-by-ten-mile square balanced diamondlike on its southernmost corner. Washington had poised that lower corner on Hunting Creek so that his hometown, Alexandria, was included. Of course the capital itself would occupy only a fraction of the hundred-square mile district. The next step was to lay out the city.

Few episodes in Washington's career are so emblematic of his hope to foster an American "national character" as his efforts to create an imposing federal capital on the Potomac. Just as the Washington Monument towers above Washington, D.C., so the monumental figure of George Washington, and his hopes for the new United States, dominate the story of the city's conception. Washington saw the creation of the federal city as an instrument of nation building.

Another powerful bias drove his tireless campaign to site a grand federal capital on the Potomac. At an early age, George Washington had succumbed to the infirmity that historian Kenneth Bowling calls "Potomac Fever."[39] He was

convinced that the Potomac was the river of American destiny, the one true passage to the West, and the inexhaust-
ible fountainhead of future national wealth and prestige.
That those same waters flowed so majestically beneath
Mount Vernon's own high-columned piazza only served to
confirm that this was indeed the finest river in America.
Potomac water had flowed through Washington veins for
four generations. They had flourished on the river's banks
since 1657. When George was still a boy, surveyors working
the parallel ranges of the Allegheny Mountains had noted
the proximity of two tiny streams. They placed a marker
stone at the head of a spring of pure water issuing from
one green mountainside. Flowing north before turning
east, the little stream was the source of the Potomac. A few
miles away, on a reverse slope, was a streamlet that fell away
to the west. Its waters eventually reached the Ohio. Men
began to imagine that these two mighty rivers might one
day be joined by human agency. Then the Potomac would
become the highway bearing the riches of the American interior. Washington made this vision of Potomac navigation
his own. When he became president, his hopes for national
unity and Potomac navigation converged in the campaign
for a new capital city. That he had extensive landholding
on the Ohio and on the Potomac only served to convince
Washington that once again his private interests had come
to coincide perfectly with those of the nation.

Presently the author of the plan for the "Grand Co-
lumbian Federal City" stepped forward. In Major Pierre
Charles L'Enfant, President Washington encountered a
visionary whose dreams matched and often surpassed his

own. The thirty-six-year-old Frenchman was no stranger to the general. The French military engineer had joined the Americans in 1777, serving with distinction in the Continental Army throughout the Revolution. When the war ended, he stayed in America and began to take on architectural commissions. Most significant was his conversion of New York's old city hall into "Federal Hall." Federal Hall became the first home of the U.S. government, its balcony the site of Washington's first inauguration, and the building itself was an element in New York's own bid to keep the permanent national capital on Manhattan Island.

Government had used architecture for political ends since the time of the Pharaohs. A new language of republican symbolism could help bring together a diverse people and unify a country so young that it lacked the traditional emblems of nationhood. L'Enfant's neoclassical designs abounded with iconographic tributes to the rising glory of America—stars and sunbursts, columns in rows of thirteen, flourishes of eagles, allegorical figures of virtue and liberty. L'Enfant saw himself as an artist of the grand scale. The design of a whole city promised to give him the canvas his genius demanded. Before him lay the prospect of celebrating the ideals of popular government in stone and noble vistas that seemed to open out on a boundless future. Fired with enthusiasm, he wrote to the new president in September 1789. Prompted, he said, by the "determination of Congress to lay the Foundation of a City which is to become the Capital of this vast Empire," and desirous of "acquiring reputation," L'Enfant asked for the job of laying it out.[40]

The proposal had been a trifle premature, but in 1790

Washington brought out the letter he gotten from Major L'Enfant a year earlier. One phrase had surely captured his notice. L'Enfant had argued that "the Plan Should be drawn on such a scale as to leave room for that aggrandizement & embellishment which the increase of the wealth of the Nation will permit."[41] Washington was hooked: L'Enfant was the only designer he would consider. The president would endorse nearly every element of the stunningly ambitious plan L'Enfant proposed.

But despite Washington's patronage, L'Enfant would never have a free hand. Thomas Jefferson thought he also had a role to play, both as secretary of state and as a gifted architect in his own right. Jefferson's influence as a shadow leader of the emerging opposition faction was even more important than his architectural gifts. The design of the national city soon became the source of ideological conflict. For the two rival visions of the American future battling for the soul of the new nation now manifested themselves in the planning of the federal city.

George Washington wanted an imposing city for the national capital, one that could give prestige to the government, impress foreign nations, and signify America's continental destiny. Jefferson and Madison had wanted the capital on the Potomac as much as Washington, but they had in mind a different city. The Republicans favored limited government. They hated big cities. So efforts to augment governmental power and prestige with a grand metropolis alarmed them. The creation of a magnificent capital—a city worthy of monarchical Europe—looked like another step on the path to tyranny.

The secretary of state had already given the president his own plan. Jefferson's rough sketch laid out a sensible little village of 650 acres with streets intersecting at predictable right angles. Another thousand acres was reserved for future expansion. Jefferson's plan bore more than passing resemblance to the little "academical village" he would later design for his University of Virginia at Charlottesville. L'Enfant tactlessly described Jefferson's rendition as "tiresome and insipid." The rectilinear street plan he thought "but a mean continuance of some cool imagination wanting a sense of the real grand and beautiful."[42] Washington ignored Jefferson's proposal and took no notice of his fears.

The president and the newly appointed architect toured the district together in March 1791, when Washington himself picked out the site for the "Presidential Palace." Inspired by the rolling landscape and the sweeping vistas its heights afforded, L'Enfant lost no time in composing his plan for the national metropolis. He was finished by June. On a grid of perpendicular streets, he had overlaid a bold pattern of broad diagonal avenues joining those high points on which the temples of popular government would rise. The city was further embellished with malls, cascading fountains, and circles awaiting monuments to the republic's unborn heroes. The Frenchman had laid out a city the size of Paris, sixty-five hundred acres in extent, ten times the size of Thomas Jefferson's modest proposal. The scheme seemed reminiscent of Versailles, the epitome of kingly ostentation. Predictably, Republicans were horrified by Major L'Enfant's grand design. But George Washington approved.

Washington's endorsement meant that the designer's genius would live on, but L'Enfant's lack of political skill made his tenure as chief architect a short one. A kind of heedless grandiosity informed his character as well as his artistic visions. He proved impossible to work with—stubborn, secretive, and insubordinate. His downfall, White House historian William Seale has written, was "as inevitable as rain."[43] The president was forced to fire him after less than a year on the job. The work would go forward without him.

To say that the work went forward slowly is a prodigious understatement. History would prove L'Enfant's detractors right in one of their objections—the fulfillment of the grand design was beyond the powers of the new nation. It may be ungenerous to observe that predictions of the rapidly approaching glory of the federal city were inaccurate enough to approach the borders of hallucination. Washington City did not surpass London in a decade. It did not become the "Metropolis of America." The Potomac Canal disappointed its stockholders—the tidewater would never "groan beneath the weight of western commerce." Alexandria on the Potomac never became as a great a city as ancient Alexandria on the Nile. No American Athens arose there, and the world would have to wait almost two centuries for the coming of an American Rome. For a long time, the capital of the United States was a hardship post for foreign diplomats and the butt of numberless jokes. The harshest judgment of the L'Enfant-Washington design proceeds from the premise that "any plan which takes a hundred years to implement is by definition a bad plan."[44] Washington, however, had again increased presi-

dential power: The Constitution had given the president
no role in establishing the national capital, assigning Congress "exclusive legislation in all cases whatsoever, over such
district." Congress had simply deferred to the president.

In December 1791, the federal government moved
from New York to Philadelphia, as provided for in the legislation establishing the new capital. Washington, Martha and her grandchildren, the president's secretaries, his
servants and slaves, and assorted family members moved
into another rented mansion, the grand home of financier
Robert Morris.

Hamilton had stirred up a new fight in December 1790
with his proposal for a national bank—the Bank of the
United States. Modeled directly on the Bank of England
and funded by the government and private investors,
the new bank would issue paper money backed by hard
reserves, lend money to the government, and serve as the
depository for tax receipts. Southern Republicans were predictably outraged. The bank was yet another wicked British
perversion of republicanism. They said it was one more
element in Hamilton's settled plan to enable the executive,
through the treasury department, to control Congress with
incentives to self-interested legislators, just as the British
crown had long controlled Parliament through patronage.
The bank would extend Hamilton's financial empire and
would again favor the commercial North over the agrarian
South. Virginians Madison, Randolph, and Jefferson composed memoranda urging Washington to veto the bank bill,
insisting that the Constitution gave no sanction to such an
innovation.

Hamilton quickly countered with a long, well-reasoned rebuttal. Each side's argument hinged on the meaning of a single clause in the Constitution. Following its enumeration of the powers of Congress in Article I, in Section 8 the Constitution added that Congress shall "make all laws which shall be necessary and proper for carrying into execution the foregoing powers." Insisting on a strict construction of the Constitution, the Virginians said that "necessary and proper" meant absolutely indispensable, not merely convenient or desirable. Yet during the successful fight to pass the bank bill in Congress, its supporters had already raised the idea of the "implied powers" of the Constitution. Certainly some of the enactments of the federal government in its first two years of existence had pointed to such a broad construction of the Constitution. Hamilton made implied powers the centerpiece for his case for the bank bill. On February 25, 1791, two days after getting Hamilton's masterful paper, the president signed the bank bill into law.

It was at this moment that Jefferson and Madison truly passed over into opposition. For a long time, the two Virginians would continue to think that they were struggling only against Hamilton and not against Washington himself. Later, they convinced themselves that Washington did not understand what Hamilton was trying to do. Finally, they decided that Washington had become senile and easy to manipulate. Jefferson clung to this comforting fiction long into old age. For a long time, Jefferson and Madison refused to accept that Hamilton's policies were Washington's policies. And George Washington himself took an inordinately long time before he could allow himself to see that Jefferson and Madison had become his enemies.

Washington had tried to reconcile his two secretaries, in no small part because he knew that their feud could force him to take a second term. Hamilton was willing to seek accommodation. Jefferson, on the other hand, would brook no compromise with his rival, whom he savagely condemned. In a meeting with Jefferson in October 1792, the president tried to convince his secretary of state that his fears of monarchy were unfounded: "That as to the idea of transforming this govt into a monarchy he did not believe there were ten men in the U.S. whose opinions were worth attention who entertained such a thought. [Jefferson] told him there were many more than he imagined. . . . That the Secy of the Treasury was one of these. That I had heard him say that this constitution was a shilly shally thing of mere milk & water, which could not last, & was only good as a step to something better."[45] In saying there were not "ten men" in the country who favored monarchy, Washington was not only dismissive of Jefferson's fears but almost contemptuous, as though implying that Jefferson had succumbed to delusion.

Jefferson lied to the president when he claimed that he took no part in the Republican opposition. In an interview on July 10, 1792, Washington told Jefferson that the Republican opposition's newspapers "seemed to have in view the exciting opposition to the govmt. . . . He considered those papers as attacking him directly, for he must be a fool indeed to swallow the little sugar plumbs here & there thrown out to him. That in condemning the admn of the govmt they condemned him, for if they thought these measures pursued contrary to his sentiment, they must consider him too careless to attend them or too stupid to understand them."[46] Jefferson actually said that "without knowing the views of what is called the Republican party, here, or having any communication with them," he could not speak for the opposition.[47] This from the leader of the Republicans! "I kept myself aloof from all cabal & correspondence on the subject of the govmt & saw & spoke with as few as I could," he had the audacity to tell Washington on February 7, 1793.[48]

A year before, a speculative run-up in the price of government securities had followed the unveiling of Hamilton's funding plan. Although Virginians loved to gamble on cards and horses, they regarded financial speculation with horror. This earlier bubble was utterly dwarfed by that occurring in stock of the Bank of the United States in the summer of 1791. Bank script, certificates to be used later to buy bank stock, had been offered at $25 on July 4. By August, the hysteria of "scrippomania" had driven the price up to $300. Then the bubble burst and prices dropped as fast as they had risen. Early in 1792, there was a similar run on bank stock, with vast paper fortunes made and lost overnight.

The Virginia Republicans saw another betrayal of the Revolution. In a private meeting with the president, Jefferson told him that the treasury department had "contrived" a "system . . . for deluging the states with paper money instead of gold & silver, for withdrawing our citizens from the pursuits of . . . useful industry, to occupy themselves &

their capitals in a species of gambling destructive of morality, & which had introduced it's poison into government
itself . . . that particular members of the legislature . . .
had feathered their nests with paper, had then voted for
the laws, and constantly since had lent all their talents, &
instrumentality of their office to the establishment & en-
largement of this system."[49] In doing so, the treasury had
subverted the Constitution. Through its power to bestow
wealth, the executive would control Congress by mimick-
ing the venal practices of the British monarchs.

The Republicans were determined to fight. During the
first year or so of the first term, the shadowy opposition had
treated Washington with kid gloves. They had made every
effort not to let their criticisms of the Hamiltonian program
spill over onto the president. But that course now proved
impossible. With decision after decision, George Washington showed that he supported Hamilton's plans. So, about
midway through the first term, the gloves came off.

Hamilton already had a house paper—the *Gazette of
the United States*. This paper had long been a virtual treasury department organ. Jefferson and Madison countered
by recruiting as their house editor Philip Freneau, a college friend of Madison's and a poet and essayist with a talent for satire. Jefferson gave Freneau a paid government
post ($250 a year) as a state department translator. In Oc-
tober 1791, Freneau started the *National Gazette*, a radical
Republican newspaper. It seems incredible that Thomas
Jefferson, a member of the cabinet, and James Madison,
Washington's most important adviser, should secretly set
up a newspaper to attack the president's policies. And they

had been bold enough to give their editor a government stipend. Twenty-first-century sensibilities would judge that Jefferson's only honorable course would have been an immediate resignation. (Hamilton himself said Jefferson should resign.) But in eighteenth-century America, representative government was new and untried and uncertain, especially the notion of a loyal opposition. To foster opposition while still serving in the cabinet was not to Jefferson disloyalty, but rather a greater loyalty to the republican ideals of the American Revolution.

Freneau had no inhibitions about attacking George Washington. The president was notoriously thin-skinned. The attacks infuriated and deeply wounded him, all the more so when he considered how reluctant he had been to assume the presidency in the first place. Jefferson said that Washington "is also extremely affected by the attacks made & kept up on him in the public papers. I think he feels those things more than any person I have ever yet met with. I am sincerely sorry to see them."[50] (Jefferson said this sympathetically, as though he were not the one chiefly responsible.) Another Republican newspaper soon appeared—the *Aurora*, edited by Benjamin Franklin Bache, grandson of the great patriot. Bache was even more intemperate in his attacks.

Jefferson described Washington's reaction to press criticism in a memorandum preserved in the "Anas," the self-serving collection of anecdotes and rumors that was published after Jefferson's death. He recounted a cabinet meeting that took place on October 1, 1792. "The Presidt. was much inflamed, got into one of those passions when he cannot command himself. Run on much on the personal abuse which had been bestowed on him. Defied any man on earth to produce one single act of his which was not done on the purest motives." Washington swore that "by god he had rather be in his grave than in his present situation; he had rather be on his farm than be made Emperor of the world; and yet they were charging him with wanting to be a King."[51]

Washington wanted out. He had originally taken office hoping not to serve even a full term of four years, cheered by the hope that he might be permitted to return to Mount Vernon after just a year or two, as soon as the new government was running smoothly. When such a happy terminus failed to appear on the political horizon, he still intended to resign when his first term ended in 1793. He was feeling his age. If he took a second term, he would be sixty-five when it ended. He told Jefferson that "he really felt himself growing old, his bodily health less firm, his memory, always bad, becoming worse, and perhaps the other faculties of his mind showing a decay to others of which he was insensible himself, that this apprehension particularly oppressed him, that he found moreover his activity lessened, business therefore more irksome, and tranquility & retirement become an irresistible passion."[52] In May 1792, Washington asked Madison to help him prepare a farewell address. Those who may suspect that George Washington's great state papers were the work of other minds would do well to examine this letter. President Washington told Madison what he wanted to say. He was enlisting the services of an editor, not a ghostwriter.

Madison reluctantly drafted the address, but told Washington that his resignation would be a national catastrophe. Others gave the same advice. By 1792 Alexander Hamilton and Thomas Jefferson concurred in little but their antipathy for one another, but they did agree that the fragile Union could never survive the bitterly contested presidential election Washington's retirement was sure to bring. "North & South will hang together, if they have you to hang on," Jefferson promised.[53] Hamilton agreed: "Your declining would be deplored as the greatest evil, that could befall the country at the present juncture and as critically hazardous to your own reputation."[54] (Hamilton knew that, to Washington, the most persuasive argument of all was the preservation of his cherished reputation.) Washington had assured Madison that he would not step down if it seemed that his "deriliction of the Chair of Government . . . involve the Country in serious disputes . . . & disagreeable consequences."[55] The unhappy Washington was finally persuaded ("after a long and painful conflict in my own breast") that he must stay on to save the experiment.[56] He was elected unanimously once again.

Just before his second inauguration, the president spoke of "the extreme wretchedness of [my] existence while in office."[57] A few months later, Washington angrily told his cabinet that he regretted "but once" having agreed to serve a second term. Unfortunately, that "once," Washington continued, was "every moment since."[58]

≫ 11 ≪

The Age of Passion
The Second Term

ASHINGTON'S SECOND INAUGURATION in 1793 did not much resemble the joyous coronation of 1789. He was far too sensitive to accusations of monarchical ceremony to repeat that performance. He bitterly resented being forced to take a second term. It was not for him an occasion for celebration. The opposition was now openly attacking him. Many Americans had grown disillusioned with his leadership. Washington's second inaugural address bespoke resignation and regret. At just 135 words it remains the shortest inaugural on record. He simply said that he was honored that his country had called on him again and that those who were present that day to hear him take the oath would know if he ever violated it.

War between England and France made the second term much more difficult than the first. Not only was the Republican opposition more fully formed, but their confidence was bolstered by the knowledge that most of the

American people supported them over the Hamiltonian Federalists. The war in Europe had raised political passions in America to intolerable levels. In February 1793, the newly proclaimed French Republic, having beheaded the deposed King Louis XVI, declared war on a coalition of monarchies led by Great Britain. It seemed that liberty battled reaction. Word reached the president shortly after he had begun his second term. Washington recognized at once that it would be disastrous for the United States to become involved in this European war. In principle, he still favored his Revolutionary War ally over monarchical England. It was ironic that his enemies continued to brand him a tool of the British with monarchical ambitions. The bitter hatred Washington had long felt toward Britain would burn on until the day he died. But war with England now would probably mean the end of the Union.

On April 22, 1793, Washington issued a proclamation declaring American neutrality in the ongoing struggle. The Federalist and Republican factions were anything but impartial. The Hamiltonians, of course, supported England, the Jeffersonians France. Even Thomas Jefferson and Alexander Hamilton, however, recognized the necessity of avoiding war.

Washington had embraced neutrality to preserve the United States. Though they supported the president, Jefferson and Hamilton were too caught up in their ideologies to fully understand. Washington's grasp of the realities of power in international affairs greatly exceeded that of the younger men.[1] Neutrality was not a tactic the Federalists might use to align America with Britain, or a weapon for the Republicans to employ on behalf of France. Neutrality was strategy for buying time for America. The United States was simply too weak and unstable to become embroiled in European wars. Taking sides in the present conflict would be all the more disastrous in light of the intense political passions at home.

Washington believed that the United States would attain a stature of unassailable strength if allowed to develop peacefully. Just two decades, he thought, would probably be enough. He wrote, "Twenty years peace, with such an increase in population and respect as we have a right to expect . . . will in all probability enable us in a just cause to bid defiance to any power on earth."[2] (The War of 1812 was in fact twenty years in the future.) He rightly dreaded war in the 1790s. He reminded his minister to France that "unwise we should be in the extreme to involve ourselves in the contests of European Nations, where our weight could be but Small; tho' the loss to ourselves certain."[3] Washington's hope for his people was that "instead of being Frenchmen, or Englishmen, in Politics, they would be Americans; indignant at every attempt of either, or any other power to establish an influence in our Councils."[4]

At the same time, the neutrality proclamation was viewed by many as another unilateral augmentation of presidential power. Nowhere in the Constitution was the president given a power to issue proclamations that had the force of law. Congress had the sole power to make law. Moreover, Republicans argued that proclaiming neutrality was simply the reverse of declaring war and only Congress could declare war. (As Jefferson put it, "As the

Executive cannot decide the question of war on the affirm-
ative side, neither ought it to do so on the negative side.")[5]
At the least, the Senate should be allowed to "advise and
consent" on the proclamation, which was arguably similar to a treaty. Some also insisted that America was still
allied with France under the Revolutionary War treaty of
1778. And the French Revolution seemed to merit America's sympathy and support. Not only was it modeled on the
American example, but it also exalted the same ideals of
liberty and equality. It could represent the next, important
step in establishing republican government in the Atlantic
world. Madison said the neutrality proclamation "wounds
the popular feelings by a seeming indifference to the cause
of liberty."[6] Washington resolutely ignored all these arguments, insisting on strict neutrality.

A majority of the American people favored France over
Britain. The people's anger over President Washington's
refusal to support America's sister republic seemed for a
time to threaten to set off a revolution. Treason was openly
avowed. Pro-French mobs rampaged throughout the land.
Twenty years later, an aged John Adams still remembered
with a shudder "the Terrorism, excited by Genet, in 1793,
when ten thousand People in the Streets of Philadelphia,
day after day, threatened to drag Washington out of his
House, and effect a Revolution in the Government, or
compell it to declare War in favour of the French Revolution, and against England."[7]

The "Genet" Adams alluded to was Edmund-Charles
Genet, the new minister of the French Republic to the United
States. The brash, redheaded thirty-year-old Frenchman

was rapturously welcomed by huge crowds of pro-French Americans on his procession through the land. Unknown to his admirers, however, "Citizen Genet" had extraordinary secret plans. He came as a subversive provocateur. He planned to organize three military expeditions of American mercenaries and volunteers and set them on the attack. The first would try to reconquer Canada for France. The other two would attack Spanish Louisiana and Florida. That these invasions from America were likely to provoke war between the United States and Britain and Spain was but a useful concomitant of the scheme. Genet had brought no money. He was to finance his endeavors by peremptorily demanding immediate repayment of America's Revolutionary War debt to France, nearly $6 million. This demand the United States was both unwilling and unable to meet.

Genet landed in Charleston, South Carolina, on April 8, 1793. He was welcomed as a conquering hero. The governor of South Carolina, utterly defying constitutional authority, declared that, as an independent nation, his state would enter into a military alliance with the French Republic. Genet began commissioning privateers—government-sanctioned pirate ships—to prey on British commerce, in clear violation of American neutrality. He set up French courts on American soil to handle the legal aspects of the privateering. He did so in several American ports and with the connivance of many local officials. The Frenchman was predictably outraged by the neutrality proclamation, which was announced shortly after he arrived in America.

Genet proceeded north to present his diplomatic credentials to the president in Philadelphia. He was acclaimed by enthusiastic crowds of well-wishers in every town he passed through. "I live here in the midst of perpetual fetes," he boasted.[8] He was an eloquent orator. He gave inflammatory speeches extolling the French Revolution and the brotherhood of the French and American people, united in the holy crusade of spreading liberty across the globe. In his correspondence with his government, he condemned "the old Washington" as a reactionary enemy of republicanism. He insisted that both the treaty of 1778 and the debt of gratitude that America owed France for the winning of independence obliged the United States to take France's side. The adulation he received convinced him that the American people agreed. In this, he was probably right. Genet's privateers began bringing their prizes—British merchantmen captured on the high seas—into American ports. America now appeared to be helping France in its war. Britain threatened retaliation. Genet was enraged when the U.S. government told him he could commission no more privateers.

Genet was convinced that he could dictate to the American government. He wanted to overturn the neutrality proclamation. He intended to appeal directly to Congress and the people themselves. He believed that the House of Representatives was the supreme power in the United States, that the House could negate any presidential action. Genet was sure, Jefferson said, "that the people of the US. will disavow the acts of their government, and that he has an appeal from the Executive to Congress, and from both to the People."[9] Nevertheless, Jefferson remained the enthusiastic supporter of the French diplomat.

Washington received the flamboyant ambassador coolly,

but that meeting did bestow American recognition on the new French Republic. Genet was initially pleased with his reception by Washington, but when he saw that American policy was not shifting in favor of France, he became outraged. Staying on in Philadelphia, Genet seemed determined to intimidate Washington, as John Adams had reported. Pro-French mobs, joined by heavily armed French sailors from the fleet of warships that was in port, ruled the streets. A British diplomat thought that Genet was about to raise the French flag over Philadelphia. Adams got a crate of guns from the war department to defend his home against the mob attack he expected. The Republican press continued to extol Genet and the French Revolution while bitterly attacking the president.

Most brazen of his provocations was his commissioning and arming a formidable privateer, *La Petite Démocrate*, in the harbor of Philadelphia, the nation's capital. Washington was away at Mount Vernon; Jefferson in Philadelphia dealt ineptly with the crisis. When Washington returned, the cabinet met and decided to forbid the ship to sail. Genet seemed to agree to comply. (He would soon renege on his promise.) But he also threatened the administration—if the United States attempted to seize the ship, the crew would resist by force of arms. Some now argued that opposing Genet could provoke war with France. Others said that allowing the ship to put to sea could provoke war with Britain. Soon, in defiance of the administration, *La Petite Démocrate* sailed, embarking on a highly successful course of raiding British commerce. Even Jefferson, once Genet's ardent champion, was horrified.

Then, in the midst of the turmoil, a deadly epidemic broke out in Philadelphia. Adams thought that, given the crisis Genet had provoked, "nothing but the Yellow Fever . . . could have saved the United States from a total Revolution in Government."[10] For the lethal disease ravaged Philadelphia in the summer of 1793, killing a tenth of the population and emptying the city, as many of the survivors fled to seek safety in the countryside. Corpse-laden carts rolled through the streets to the cry of "Bring out your dead." (People commented on the prevalence of mosquitoes that summer, but no one made the connection.) Officials were gone, government was at a standstill, politics were suspended, the mobs vanished, and Genet was impotent. When word of Genet's provocations leaked out, indignant Americans rallied to Washington, further lessening the Frenchman's influence.

Finally, the administration demanded that France recall its troublesome minister. France was happy to oblige —there had been a change in that nation's government. The Girondins, the faction to which Genet belonged and the government that had dispatched him in the first place, had been overthrown and purged by a rival faction, the Jacobins. Genet's friends had gone to the guillotine. Back in France, Genet himself had a date with that dread instrument of death. The Frenchman appealed to President Washington for asylum. Washington, not feeling at all vindictive, agreed, and refused French demands to surrender the diplomat. So it came to pass that Citizen Genet, the man who had once imagined that he might overawe George Washington, married the daughter of a prominent

Republican, became a naturalized American, and spent the rest of his days in obscurity as a farmer in upstate New York.

One lingering result of Genet's bizarre American adventure was the creation of the so-called Democratic-Republican Societies. These were clubs of Jeffersonian Republicans that had come together to support Genet and the cause of France. Organized on the local level, mostly in big cities, the Democratic Societies held parades, rallies, and banquets; campaigned in local elections; drafted petitions; and worked closely with the opposition press. Thirty-five had sprung up by 1795. The societies were thoroughly Jeffersonian in philosophy. They favored states' rights and a weak federal government. They hated Hamilton's financial program. Most of all, they passionately supported the French Revolution and denounced what they saw as the pro-British policies of the Washington administration. Originally formed to help Genet, they were in no way weakened by that man's eventual self-destruction.

Washington disdainfully called them the "self-created societies," implying that they had no legitimacy. Indeed, he thought that any organized opposition to established government policy was illegitimate. For George Washington tended to see dissent as disloyalty. He believed that once government policy had been set, all citizens were obliged to give their support. He particularly deplored the Democratic Societies, believing them tools of France in that nation's campaign to subvert the American government. The societies' support of the Whiskey Rebellion in 1794 would only sharpen his aversion. He denounced them in 1795 in his Sixth Annual Address to Congress, the speech we now call the State of the Union Address. In their turn, Washington's critics charged that he was denying citizens the right to question the government, that he was even threatening free speech. They said that he was no longer the head of the nation but the head of a party—the Federalists.

Jefferson had resigned as secretary of state at the end of 1793. Bowing to Washington's entreaties, he had stayed on a year longer than he had originally intended. Out of government, permanently retired, he insisted, to his mountaintop retreat at Monticello, Jefferson remained the covert leader of the Republican opposition—chief strategist, theoretician and propagandist, organizer and inspiration. He acted and spoke through his followers, mainly Madison. All the while, he maintained that he was through with politics and finished with public life forever. The French Revolution's descent into bloody terror did nothing to shake the faith of Jefferson, who said he "would have seen half the earth desolated" so long as liberty triumphed.[11]

Trouble loomed in the West. The Treaty of Paris of 1783, which had confirmed the new nation's independence, also gave the fledgling republic a vast empire—half of North America, an expanse bounded by the Mississippi River on the west, Canada to the north, and the Spanish colonies of Louisiana and Florida to the south. But others coveted the region as well—Britain, Spain, and the native Americans themselves. They all reckoned that American weakness might allow them to seize the land. The Indians were particularly determined to resist American expansion. They had powerful allies in Great Britain and Spain.

The English continued to garrison the Ohio Valley forts they had pledged to give up in the Treaty of Paris. From their forts, they supplied the Indians with weapons and encouraged them to attack American settlements. Britain aimed at containing the new republic, keeping control of the fur trade, and even creating an Indian buffer state between the U.S. frontier and Canada. British agents in the Ohio Valley schemed to detach the western settlers from the United States and join them to Canada, putting them once again under crown sovereignty. Some of the settlers seemed willing to go along.

The fixed antagonism between the frontier people and the inhabitants of the settled coastward regions reached back into the colonial period. The easterners controlled the state governments, in which the western settlers were not fairly represented. Many continued to believe that the United States was simply too large and diverse to survive as a single nation. The splitting off of the Ohio region seemed a real possibility. Plenty of frontier folk would welcome independence.

For its part, Spain continued to deny to American settlers the use of the Mississippi River, the only practical way to move harvests to market. Spain encouraged the Creeks and its other Indian allies to attack the southern frontier. The settlers were desperate. The leaders of the new state of Kentucky alternated between plans to ally themselves with Spain and notions of attacking Spain in an unauthorized war. The settlers were furious with the Washington administration for its failure to secure for them the freedom of the Mississippi and crush the Ohio Indians once and for all. But Washington had different priorities. In fact, for a time, he did not even seek the right to use the Mississippi. He thought such trade would only bind the westerners to Spain and increase the risk of secession. In 1785, he wrote: "However singular the opinion may be, I cannot divest myself of it, that the Navigation of the Mississippi, at *this time*, ought to be no object with us; on the contrary, till we have a little time allowed to open & make easy the ways between the Atlantic States & the Western territory, the obstruction had better remain."[12] The grievances of the western people were real enough—their own president opposed their highest goal. As historian Thomas P. Slaughter has pointed out, "The immediate needs of the western settlers for markets must be sacrificed to the long-term benefits of eastern merchants, eastern canal investors, eastern speculators in western lands, and, of course, the nation itself."[13] The Whiskey Rebellion of 1794 would show soon just how angry the frontier people were.

To hold on to the West, the United States had to put an end to native American resistance. But the Indians were not about to give up without a fight. Coalitions of Ohio Valley warriors had convincingly defeated two American armies of about fifteen hundred men each in 1790 and 1791. The first army had been commanded by a drunk, the second by a cripple. The 1791 defeat, which resembled Braddock's 1755 debacle, was one of the worst in American history—nine hundred out of fourteen hundred men fell. The president, who knew something about Indian fighting, was enraged by the two generals' stupidity in allowing themselves to be surprised. He had strongly warned them against Indian ambushes. But it was Washington who took the blame. Now he was determined to crush the Ohio natives. The U.S. Army had numbered fewer than six hundred soldiers when he took office in 1789. Now, with the approval of Congress, he raised a new army of nearly five thousand regulars. The grant of authority to the president by Congress to raise the new army, the Militia Act, was yet another augmentation of executive power. The president put in command one of his most aggressive Revolutionary War generals, "Mad Anthony" Wayne. Wayne trained his "Legion of the United States" into a formidable fighting force. In August 1794, at the battle of Fallen Timbers, Wayne's army inflicted a crushing defeat on a final coalition of Ohio warriors. The British, though within earshot of the battle, refused to help their Indian allies. Soon the British would withdraw from their forts altogether under the terms of the Jay Treaty, dooming the native Americans' hopes. Fallen Timbers marked the end of effective resistance to the invasion of the Ohio country, now the Northwest Territory of the United States of America.

George Washington had promoted the settlement of the Ohio Valley for fifty years. He was convinced that the American future lay in the West. He held no illusions about the fate of the native populations: these people were to be dispossessed. Washington hoped that the takeover could be accomplished as peacefully as possible and that protected reservations would be set aside for the Indians. But he wanted nothing to stop the flood of settlers pouring over the mountains. The president himself owned tens of thousands of prime Ohio acres ready for settlement. Washington urged the Indians to abandon their traditional way of life, settle on the reservations the government provided, and take up agriculture. Most tribes were not interested. Those few who did in fact settle down and become farmers lost their land anyway. Washington issued the Proclamation of 1790, barring settlers and land speculators from the designated Indian reserves. The Proclamation of 1790 was reminiscent of the British Proclamation of 1763, which had closed the Ohio to white settlement, an enactment a younger Washington had both deplored and defied. The president's ban too was widely defied, by frontier settlers and state governments alike. The Indians were relentlessly driven west.

In the spring of 1793, a delegation from the Miami tribe paid an official visit on President Washington in Philadelphia. These people lived far to the west, on the banks of the Wabash River. Washington gave the Indians an imposing presidential proclamation, countersigned by Secretary of State Thomas Jefferson and adorned with the beribboned seal of the United States. The creamy parchment promised that the government would protect the tribe's "persons, towns, villages, lands, hunting-grounds and other rights and properties."[14] Washington handed out gleaming silver peace medals, engraved with the likeness of himself sharing a peace pipe with a chief. These they should wear as a sign of their allegiance to the United States. (Indians dearly loved such tokens, often taking them to their graves with them.) The president shook hands with each man and promised friendship.

But there was one other matter the president wished

to communicate to the tribesmen. The letter Washington also gave them, addressed to "My Children," contained this naked threat: "Most of you have been a long Journey to the Eastward where you have seen the numbers and Strength of a part of the United States. But you have seen only a part. . . . Judge then, what the bad Indians may expect in the end if they will not harken to the voice of peace!"[15] The definition of "bad Indians" adopted by the United States would prove exceedingly broad. The Miamis, like the other Ohio Valley tribes, would lose their homeland.

Included in Hamilton's 1791 fiscal program was an excise tax on alcoholic liquors, which in America usually meant whiskey distilled from grain. Excise taxes, or internal taxes, were odious to Anglo-American oppositional thinking. Prying tax collectors were hateful to many, seeming as they did to invade a man's private "home and castle." Excise taxes were unfair to the common people. And on the frontier, whiskey was a necessity of life. In addition to its matchless virtues as an inebriant, whiskey was a highly important commercial product, particularly in the back country, where it was cooked in countless little one-man stills. Whiskey solved the problem of getting agricultural harvests to market. Bulky wagonloads of wheat and corn could be distilled into compact, easy-to-move jugs of liquor. So essential was whiskey to the cash-poor frontier economy that it served as a medium of exchange, a substitute currency.

The frontiersmen, always an independent and cantankerous breed, did not take kindly to a federal tax on their favorite staple. Nor, as we have seen, did they have much affection for the federal government. Many of them didn't intend to pay. They were perfectly willing to oppose tax collection by force of arms. They saw no reason to subsidize a government that was doing nothing to help them. Defiance stopped all collection of the tax on the frontiers from Massachusetts south to Georgia. Federal tax collectors were threatened, forced to tear up and renounce their commissions. Compliance was violently discouraged. Those who were willing to pay had their stills wrecked, their houses and barns burned.

Particularly stubborn were the inhabitants of the four westernmost counties of Pennsylvania. They assembled in mobs and overran the courts. In September 1792, Washington issued a proclamation demanding enforcement of the law and the disbanding of "unlawful combinations." Things calmed down a bit and the rebellion smoldered on quietly for than a year, only to break out again with greater fury in summer of 1794.

The Whiskey Rebellion had taken on dimensions of a class, as well as a regional, struggle. The larger, commercial distillers were willing to pay the tax. They had the money and they expected that the tax burden would put many of their small-time, backcountry competitors out of business. The most violent rebels were men without property. Some of them were rumored to be "levelers," who wanted a social revolution against the rich and powerful. It seemed reminiscent of Shays' Rebellion in Massachusetts in 1786, the antigovernment outbreak that had so alarmed Washington and strengthened his resolve to bring about a strong central government.

At the same time, resistance to the whiskey tax flourished among the political classes in the cities as well as among pioneers on the frontier. In the same "Country-Court" language used in the run-up to the Revolution and the fight against the ratification of the Constitution, the opposition denounced the excise as a conspiracy of aristocratic moneymen, metropolitan easterners, against the agricultural people. Liberty hung in the balance. The question, said the tax's opponents, "is no longer between federalism and anti-federalism, but between republicanism and anti-republicanism."[16]

In 1793, concern over the whiskey tax was overshadowed by the passionate controversy over the French Revolution, Genet's provocations, and the gruesome yellow fever epidemic in Philadelphia. The entire frontier, from Massachusetts to Georgia, continued to defy the tax. The government gained no excise revenues. The frontier people began to think they had won the battle. They underestimated the resolve of Washington and Hamilton, however, men who had decided to single out the four counties of western Pennsylvania for enforcement.

New fighting broke out over the tax in western Pennsylvania in July 1794. Rioters defeated a small contingent of regulars. Defiant groups of tax protestors coalesced into mobs, and the mobs coalesced into a virtual army of more than seven thousand drawn up outside the walls of Pittsburgh, the little collection of two hundred log houses that was the largest town in the region. Many of them, "miserably poor" people, hoped to plunder and burn the town.[17] The president knew the area well: This was the spot Ma-

jor George Washington had identified as the ideal location for a fort on his perilous 1753 journey over the mountains. Nearby was "Braddock's Field," scene of the 1755
slaughter, where the soldiers' bones still lay unburied.
Washington also owned land outside Pittsburgh.

The rebels downed prodigious quantities of their favorite beverage, inflaming their defiance. Local authorities
were helpless; many fled. Washington thought the Whiskey
Rebellion actually threatened to destroy the republic. "What
may be the consequences of such violent & outrageous proceedings is painful in a high degree even in contempla-
tion," he wrote. "But if the laws are to be so trampled on
—with impunity—and a minority (a small one too) is to
dictate to the majority there is an end put, at one stroke,
to republican government; and nothing but anarchy and
confusion is to be expected hereafter."[18] Some rebels were
calling for secession. They devised a new six-striped flag
for their proposed new state—four stripes for four Pennsylvania counties, two for others in Virginia. Their success
could mean the dismemberment of the United States. Del-
egations claiming to represent the West made overtures to
British and Spanish officials. Washington was convinced
that the federal government had to suppress the rebellion. He decided to call out the militia of eastern Pennsylvania, New Jersey, Maryland, and Virginia, while at the
same time issuing an ultimatum demanding that the rebels stand down. Negotiations went nowhere. Washington
sent the whiskey army into western Pennsylvania in September 1794. For his part, Hamilton, the president's most
influential adviser, had strongly advocated military force for

months. Secretary of War Knox was absent from the seat of government, so Hamilton was given control of the war department. He asked Washington for command of the new army.

Nothing could be more terrifying to the Republican opposition than the vision of Alexander Hamilton at the head of a powerful army. He could use it for a coup d'état to create the monarchy they were sure he wanted. Washington knew better than to go along with Hamilton's request. He led the expedition himself. The 12,950-man army was larger than any he had commanded during most of the Revolutionary War. This remains the only time in American history that a president has actually taken on his constitutional role as commander in chief of the armed forces of the United States, leading an army in the field.

He moved his army west in September 1794. The result was an anticlimax. The rebels immediately folded. Despite all their drunken, defiant talk, they had no desire to fight against a real army. They simply went home. The dangerous Whiskey Rebellion had ended in a whimper. Contrary to the predictions of many, republican government had proved itself capable of exercising decisive authority. All the rebels were promptly given blanket amnesty and Washington pardoned two who had been condemned to death. But the government was never able to collect the whiskey tax.

The greatest crisis of Washington's presidency sprang from the Jay Treaty with Britain in 1795. War with England had threatened. Determined to enforce its naval blockade on France, the Royal Navy was seizing American merchant ships, confiscating their cargoes, and impressing American sailors into virtual slavery as seamen on British warships. British agents in the Ohio Valley continued their plotting to detach the western settlers from the United States. Washington knew the Union could not survive another war with Great Britain. It was also essential that the British be persuaded to leave their frontier outposts. The Americans could never hope to subdue the Ohio tribesmen so long as Britain was backing them. And besides, as Alexander Hamilton told a British diplomat in a secret and unauthorized meeting, *"We think in English."*[19]

In 1794, the president dispatched a special envoy, John Jay, to London. In addition to being chief justice of the Supreme Court, Jay was an experienced diplomat, one of the negotiators of the 1783 treaty that ended the American Revolution. The result of his negotiations, "Jay's Treaty," reached the president in March 1795. Washington was not pleased with the terms. Mighty Britain had conceded little to its former colonies. But adopting the "Treaty of Amity, Commerce and Navigation, between his Britannic Majesty, and the United States of America" would avert war and give American vessels more freedom to trade. And London had agreed to one important American demand— Britain would finally give up its military presence in the Northwest Territory.

Washington was not sure whether he should push for the treaty's ratification. Even the Federalists recognized that the British diplomats had handled Jay roughly. The Republicans, of course, vehemently opposed any agreement with England. Did not a peace treaty with one belligerent amount to a declaration of war against the other? The president sent the treaty to the Senate, where it was debated in secret session and ratified, twenty Federalist votes against ten Republican, the exact two-thirds required. (Washington did not decide to support the treaty himself until after Senate ratification.) Soon the text was leaked and published by the opposition. Furious denunciations, riots, even attacks on federal officials followed. John Jay was only half-joking when he said that his way could be lighted across nighttime America by the flames of his figure being burned in effigy. Hamilton's head was bloodied by a rock when he tried to speak to a crowd in favor of the treaty. "The cry against the Treaty," Washington said, "is like that against a mad dog."[20] Republicans charged that the administration was treacherously surrendering to England and betraying its ally and sister republic.

Federalists had shown that they had the votes in the Senate to ratify the treaty, but the opposition dominated the House of Representatives. By now Jefferson had managed to convince himself that the House, as the people's branch, had, under the Constitution, authority to veto any presidential action whatsoever, demonstrating that constitutional interpretation often has less to do with legality than with immediate political goals. The great mass of the American people, Jefferson reasoned, opposed the Jay Treaty. That meant it should not become law despite Senate ratification. Jefferson, of course, advanced these arguments anonymously, through his acolytes and his journalistic mouthpieces.

Jefferson was right about one thing—most Americans

were vehemently opposed to the Jay Treaty. A large majority favored France over Britain in the ongoing struggle. In 1795, the mob ruled Philadelphia again as it had in 1793. John Adams described "Washington's house . . . surrounded by an innumerable multitude, from day to day, huzzaing, demanding war against England, cursing Washington, and crying success to the French patriots and virtuous republicans."[21] The opposition press continued to attack the president savagely.

Amid the controversy over the Jay Treaty, there had been one rare bit of good news that strengthened the administration's hand. In October 1795, the United States had concluded a most favorable treaty with Spain. Spain had bowed to growing American numbers in the West. The agreement allowed Americans to use the Mississippi freely and to trade through the Spanish port of New Orleans. The westerners had been clamoring for this for years, some even threatening to secede if the U.S. government did not secure for them the freedom of the great river that formed the nation's western boundary.

When the House of Representatives demanded that Washington turn over secret diplomatic papers relating to the Jay Treaty, the president invoked (or discovered) executive privilege for the first time. He refused to surrender the papers. The proceedings of the Constitutional Convention were still held in strict secrecy. The Convention had entrusted Washington with the secret records. But Washington hardly needed to consult the record—he had been there. In his response to the House, Washington acidly observed that he had, after all, been present at the drafting of Constitution and knew as well as anyone that the document gave the lower house no role in the making of foreign policy. While this was true, the concept of executive privilege is to be found nowhere in the Constitution. It was another unilateral increase in presidential power by Washington.

The Republicans weren't ready to give up. The Senate may have ratified the treaty, but the opposition calculated that they could still kill it if the House refused to vote the funds needed to put it into effect. At first it seemed the opposition had the votes to pull off this de facto veto. Yet a change was in the air. Curiously, the American people had come around to the view that maybe the Jay Treaty wasn't so bad after all. It did prevent war, and it secured the Ohio Valley. Most now supported or at least accepted the agreement. Peace with England and the vastly increased trade that followed had proved a great boon to the American economy. Prosperity reigned. The Republicans' votes evaporated. On April 30, 1796, the House appropriated $80,800 to implement the Jay Treaty. The vote was close, 51 to 48.

The Republicans despaired and commiserated with one another on the impossibility of opposing George Washington's irresistible prestige in any political contest. Jefferson told an ally, "Congress has risen. You have seen by their proceedings the truth of what I always observed to you, that one man [Washington] outweighs them all in influence over the people who have supported his judgment against their own and that of their representatives. Republicanism must lie on its oars, resign the vessel to its pilot, and themselves to the course he thinks best for them."[22] Indeed, Washington had prevailed again, in "a great victory" that "established forever the principle of executive-branch leadership in foreign policy."[23] It was a most bitter defeat for James Madison and confirmed the enmity between him and George Washington. The two men never saw each other again and exchanged no more letters. It was by now well into 1796, the last full year of Washington's presidency.

Toward the end of his presidency, Washington was governing with a cabinet markedly inferior to his original one—that group of advisers he had extolled in 1790 as "able Co-adjutors, who harmonise extremely well together."[24] (Obviously that harmony was not long-lasting.) When Jefferson resigned the secretary of state's post, Washington replaced him by moving over Edmund Randolph, another Virginian and an old friend, from the justice department. He relied heavily on Randolph until that man was forced out in a scandal in 1795 that saw him accused, probably falsely, of traitorous intrigues with French agents. Randolph certainly was guilty, however, of massive indiscretions. At that point, the president had the humiliation of offering the office of secretary of state to six men in a row, each of whom turned him down. He ended up giving state to his last choice, his secretary of war, Timothy Pickering. Washington struggled to keep a balance in the cabinet. Now he needed to give equal representation not only to geographical regions but also to the Federalist and Republican factions. He tried to give posts to a balanced number of those Republicans who opposed his policies. For example, he named the radical Republican James Monroe minister to

France. Had he really been simply the head of the Federalist Party, as his enemies charged, he would certainly have packed his cabinet with like-minded statesmen.

When Hamilton resigned in 1795, the president replaced him with Oliver Wolcott, Jr., a treasury department official and a Federalist, who shared little of his predecessor's fiscal genius. He would also prove to be Hamilton's puppet. Henry Knox resigned as secretary of war. The president had to settle for his third choice, his old Revolutionary War aide, James McHenry, a friend and supporter but not a conspicuously able man. Of McHenry, Washington was unsparing: "I early discovered, after he entered upon the Duties of his Office, that his talents were unequal to great exertions."[25] The president had to take his third choice again when John Jay stepped down as chief justice. "The offices are once more filled," observed Vice President Adams, "but how differently than when Jefferson, Hamilton, Jay, etc., were here."[26]

By the end of his presidency, the opposition had abandoned all semblance of respect for Washington. The opposition press called him "a supercilious tyrant." "If ever a Nation was debauched by a man," the same paper informed its readers, "the American Nation has been debauched by Washington."[27] The harshest blast came from the Revolution's most celebrated pamphleteer. In the dark days of 1776, Thomas Paine had extolled General Washington as liberty's savior. Twenty years later, the radical revolutionary savaged the president in his widely circulated *Letter to George Washington*. "Elevated to the chair of the Presidency, you assumed the merit of everything to yourself,"

Paine hissed, "You commenced your Presidential career by encouraging, and swallowing, the grossest adulation. . . . As to you, sir, treacherous in private friendship . . . and a hypocrite in public life, the world will be puzzled to decide, whether you have abandoned good principles, or whether you ever had any."[28]

Early in 1796 the president dug out the valedictory Madison had written for him four years before. This time he would not be deterred. George Washington was going back to Mount Vernon when his second term ended in March 1797. He was old and tired and disillusioned, and he was right in thinking that he did not have many more years to live. Washington drafted a lengthy address, using the passages Madison had submitted. Quoting the earlier farewell address proved that he had never wanted a second term. He thought it needed rewriting. Madison was his enemy now, so the president sent it to Alexander Hamilton, who, although he was now a private citizen practicing law in New York City, had remained Washington's most important adviser. Over the next few months, the two men hammered out a version that satisfied Washington. While the document owed much to Hamilton as a prose stylist, the ideas were strictly Washington's own. He made public his decision to retire when the Farewell Address (as the untitled piece soon became known) was printed in the September 19, 1796, issue of the *Daily American Advertiser*, a Philadelphia newspaper. It began with the words "Friends, and Fellow-Citizens" and was signed "Go: Washington." The text was immediately reprinted hundreds of times throughout the land.

Washington's Farewell Address soon achieved a monumentality that has encouraged some to regard it as a source of timeless wisdom. But that was not really what its author had intended. The document was a product of the political passions of the 1790s. Washington's audience was his living countrymen, not the unborn Americans of future centuries. For George Washington did not know, and would die not knowing, whether the United States of America was destined to endure.

At first reading the Farewell Address seems to deal with three dominant themes—the preservation of the Union, foreign policy, and domestic politics. But foreign affairs and political factionalism at home were a single issue in Washington's mind, and the only issue that threatened to wreck the Union. Before long, Washington predicted again, the United States would be too strong for any foreign nation to threaten. The time is "not far off," he said, "when we may choose peace or war, as our interest, guided by justice, shall counsel." But now, the "passionate attachment" of the American political factions to one or the other of the warring powers was so intense that the Union could never survive if the United States allowed itself to become entangled in the European war. Nations do not have natural friends or enemies, Washington insisted, nations have only interests. The American people must be Americans first. They must avoid "an habitual hatred, or an habitual fondness" for any foreign nation. Neutrality, the president concluded, had been his "endeavour to gain time for our country to settle and mature its yet recent institutions."[29]

In speaking out against factions, Washington presented himself as the head of the government, not the head of a party. But many now considered him the chief Federalist. As the politically savvy could easily see, the address was not lacking in subtle slams against the Republican opposition. The Republicans themselves regarded it as little more than a Federalist position paper. Whatever the accuracy of this charge, Washington actually seemed to be doing something more—condemning any organized opposition to established government policy. The observation has been made that "it would be difficult to find an instance anywhere, from Washington's time to our own, of a new head of a revolutionary state who had much toleration for opposition."[30]

In spurning the entreaties of many Federalists that he stand for a third term, Washington set other important precedents. Many had hoped or feared that he would stay in office until the day he died. (Had he taken a third term, he would in fact have died in office.) As president-for-life, George Washington would then have set a standard that many of his successors would surely have aspired to match. The transfer of power to a new president confirmed the nation's republican character. And the peaceful transition was a novelty in a world in which heads of state were replaced only by natural death, assassination, foreign invasion, or domestic usurpation. The charges of Washington's enemies that he craved power and lusted after a crown were effectively refuted by the voluntary surrender. Washington's two-term presidency also set a precedent that not only stood for a century and a half but found eventual endorsement in a constitutional amendment. Instead of starting a third term, Washington handed the presidency over to John Adams on March 4, 1797. It was one of the happiest days of his life. He would have been surprised to learn that he wasn't quite finished yet.

≫ 12 ≪

"The Debt Which All Must Pay"

WASHINGTON'S RETURN to a neglected Mount Vernon in 1797 probably reminded him of his 1783 homecoming after the Revolution. He had sent hundreds of pages of instructions to his farm managers while president, more pages indeed than he had written on governmental matters during some months. Still, he found affairs at Mount Vernon in disarray. He began the work of putting things on course again with an outright exuberance: "I begin my diurnal course with the Sun," he wrote a friend. "If my hirelings are not in their places at that time I send them messages expressive of my sorrow for their indisposition; then having put these wheels in motion, I examine the state of things further; and the more they are probed, the deeper I find the wounds are which my buildings have sustained by an absence and neglect of eight years."[1] Mount Vernon, the inevitable throngs of visitors, and his endless letter writing kept Washington busy from sunrise until he retired at nine o'clock.

The first former president of the United States watched uneasily as events in Europe continued to convulse America. By 1798 war with France appeared likely. Washington came to regard the Republicans who supported France and opposed the policies of President John Adams as enemies of the Union. Swayed by the passions of that extraordinary moment in American history, Washington continued to confuse dissent with disloyalty. He called the Republicans "the French party" and the "disorganizing party." The figure who hated political parties hardly recognized that he himself had become a hard-line Federalist. At sixty-six, George Washington was an aged man. His body, his memory, and his hearing were failing him. Some of his sober moderation and impeccable judgment appear to have deserted him as well.

The "Quasi-War" with France now raged on the high seas. Many Americans feared further French aggression. Congress authorized the raising of a "Provisional Army" to meet the threat of an actual invasion of the United States by a French army. Without consulting Washington, President Adams commissioned the superannuated veteran a lieutenant general and gave him command of the New Army. Unfortunately, Washington believed he owed his country this final duty. His command of the New Army stands out as the most melancholy episode in his career. Washington behaved badly. He quarreled with the president and intrigued with Adams's cabinet behind his back. He allowed Alexander Hamilton to manipulate him. He forced Adams to make Hamilton de facto commander in chief of the New Army. Major General Hamilton had grandiose and dangerous plans for the army, projected to number ten or twenty thousand troops. He planned to march south, through Virginia and the other slaveholding states, to undertake the conquest of the Spanish colonies. Hamilton also hoped to cow pro-French southerners. The advance of a standing army, under the command of Alexander Hamilton, would surely have provoked civil war in Jeffersonian Virginia. (Washington didn't know about Hamilton's incendiary schemes.)

Then, in an act of heroic statesmanship, and in defiance of much of his own Federalist Party, President Adams made peace with France, thereby assuring his own defeat and Thomas Jefferson's victory in the forthcoming 1800 presidential election. The superfluous Provisional Army was abolished. Fortunately, only about two thousand soldiers had ever been enlisted. When peace broke out in 1799, Washington resigned his final commission. This time he did not bother with a farewell address.

When Connecticut governor Jonathan Trumbull, Jr., urged Washington to come out of retirement again, the old man's furious refusal revealed his utter disillusionment with the state of American political affairs. He believed the country far gone in iniquity. Federalists were arrayed against Republicans in a partisan battle that assured that faction alone commanded men's loyalties. Trumbull had begged Washington to consider standing in candidacy for a third presidential term in the 1800 election. Though he now strongly supported the Federalists, and as vehemently condemned the Republicans, Washington believed his return to the fray would be as futile as it would be personally abhorrent. No Republican would vote for him, the ex-president snarled: "Let that party set up a broomstick and call it a true son of Liberty; a Democrat, or give it any other epithet that will suit their purpose, and it will command their votes in toto!" Washington was "thoroughly convinced I should not draw a *single* vote from the Antifederal side."² The ongoing partisan conflict was the definitive repudiation of Washington's ideal of a republican nation governed by a concurring elite of virtuous statesmen.

In July 1799 Washington wrote a will. He provided for his wife, freed his slaves, left bequests to several educational institutions, and divided his remaining estate among a host of nieces, nephews, and Custis relations. In an appendix to the will, Washington inventoried his holdings and calculated his net worth at $530,000, a figure that entitled him to a rank among the richest men in America.

The most important provision of the thirty-page document was the emancipation of his 125 slaves. (More than 300 slaves lived at Mount Vernon in 1799, but most were the property of the Custis estate; Washington had no power to free those people. Neither did Martha—they belonged to the Custis heirs.) Washington's instructions for the future of his bondspeople appeared as the will's second clause, preceded only by the directive that his debts be paid:

> It is my Will and desire that all the Slaves which I hold in *my own right,* shall receive their freedom. . . . And whereas among those who will receive freedom according to this devise, there may be some, who from old age or bodily

infirmities, and others who on account of their infancy, that will be unable to support themselves; it is my Will and desire that all who come under the first and second description shall be comfortably cloathed and fed by my heirs while they live; and that such of the latter description as have no parents living, or if living are unable, or unwilling to provide for them, shall be bound by the Court until they shall arrive at the age of twenty five years. . . . The Negros thus bound, are (by their Masters or Mistresses) to be taught to read and write; and to be brought up to some useful occupation, agreeably to the Laws of the Commonwealth of Virginia, providing for the support of Orphan and other poor Children.[3]

The laws Washington cited for the support of orphans and poor children had of course been enacted for the benefit of Virginia's *white* children. His wish that the underage slaves be so educated was a bold statement of Washington's belief in the natural abilities of the enslaved. A certain egalitarianism was implicit in these provisions. He thought that the apparently improvident state of the enslaved people was the result of the oppressions of slavery itself. Washington's perception of the degrading effects of slavery was hardly new. On the eve of the Revolution he had predicted that if Americans did not resist British oppression, "custom and use, will make us as tame, & abject Slaves, as the Blacks we Rule over with such an arbitrary Sway." Slavery, then, and not any natural inferiority, had reduced the blacks to a state of dependency. If this is an accurate reconstruction of his views, Washington was more enlightened than most southern slaveholders. Thomas Jefferson had maintained that blacks were born inferior to whites in mind and body, and that they could never live in

American society as free people. Emancipation, Jefferson insisted, must be accompanied by a program of "colonization," the mass deportation of American blacks to an overseas colony. Colonization was simply a way of getting rid of slavery by getting rid of blacks. George Washington's visions were rather more expansive. The old man had come a long way from the callow young planter who once sold off a rebellious slave to the West Indies for a cargo of limes and molasses.

Washington left no doubt about the importance he attached to the provision for emancipation. Nor did he fail to recognize that it might go against the instincts of his survivors. "And I do moreover most pointedly, and most solemnly enjoin it upon my Executors," he continued, "to see that *this* clause respecting Slaves, and every part thereof be religiously fulfilled at the Epoch at which it is directed to take place; without evasion, neglect, or delay."[4] The Estate of George Washington, Deceased, would pay annual pensions to some of the freed people until 1833. Washington was the only one of the principal slaveholding founders to embrace emancipation.

Washington had been working toward this solution for decades. Yet even here he was not as successful as he might have wished. Unfortunately for the younger freed people, Virginia's restrictive laws prevented their being apprenticed or educated. Moreover, since Washington's own slaves had intermarried with the still-enslaved Custis family people over the forty years of George and Martha's marriage, the manumission broke up families. Washington's own blacks gained freedom while their husbands or wives or children remained in bondage. As former Mount Vernon staff member John Riley has remarked, not only was George Washington unable to bring about a general emancipation in the United States, he was not even able to arrange a satisfactory example for his own Mount Vernon estate.[5]

On December 12, 1799, Washington rode out in a winter storm for his customary inspection tour of the Mount Vernon farms. He was gone five hours. When the old man returned, his secretary remembered that he "appeared to be wet and the snow was hanging upon his hair."[6] The next day Washington complained of a sore throat. He woke in real distress in the middle of the night. His throat was so swollen that he could scarcely breathe.

Washington died an agonizing death.[7] Not only was the dying man slowly choked to death by the swelling in his throat, but he had to endure the tortures of eighteenth-century medicine. He was repeatedly bled until he had lost as much as half his blood volume. He was forced to vomit copiously. He was humiliated by the violent purging of his bowels. Burning chemicals were placed on his skin to blister him. At last, he thanked his physicians for their ministrations, but told them his case was hopeless and begged them please to leave him alone. Washington was resigned to death. "I find I am going," he rasped, "my breath cannot last long; I believed from the first that the disorder would prove fatal." He said that he was about to make good on "the debt which all must pay," and that "he looked to the event with perfect resignation."[8]

Martha sat at the foot of the bed, immured in grief.

Washington's secretary, Tobias Lear, did everything he could to help the dying man, lying beside him in the bed so that he might shift Washington into more comfortable positions. (Lear later recorded every detail of the death watch.) It was to Lear that Washington most often spoke, though speech came exceedingly hard. Uppermost in Washington's mind was completing the task of recording and copying his official papers. Several slaves were in the room. When Washington noticed that his black body servant, Christopher Sheels, was standing, he told the young man to sit down.

There was "a missing presence at the deathbed scene," Joseph Ellis has written, "there were no ministers in the room, no prayers uttered, no Christian rituals offering the solace of everlasting life. . . . He died as a Roman stoic rather than a Christian saint."[9] At the end, Washington struggled to make his last wish clear to Lear. He apparently had a horror of being buried alive. He ordered Lear not to put his body into the tomb until three days after his death. He made sure Lear understood, then spoke his last words: "'Tis well."[10] Ever the record taker, George Washington was counting his own pulse when he died. The lifeless hand fell from the pulseless wrist. It was half-past ten, the night of December 14, 1799.

Washington was sealed in a leaden coffin and entombed in the family vault at Mount Vernon. News of his passing united Americans in heartfelt grief. Devotion to the memory of their hero would continue to unite Americans for many years to come. The dead Washington's legacy proved nearly as precious to his country as had the living Washington's leadership. The United States was a new nation. In the year of Washington's death, the federal government was just ten years old. The Constitution had been signed twelve years before, while American independence, declared twenty-three years earlier, had been confirmed by treaty only sixteen years ago. Yet what had taken place in America during the scant generation since 1776 had changed history. For the United States was new also in its principles. First among those principles was the revolutionary belief that all people were created equal, and its corollary that governing power must derive from the people. The Americans had waged an ideological revolution— theirs was the first nation deliberately founded on ideas. Although Europe's powerful disdained the upstart republic, this leap of political faith had started monarchy and aristocracy on the road to oblivion.

Their brief, singular history had left America rather lacking in those attributes that traditionally serve to define nationhood. The country had recently been thirteen separate colonies. Americans descended from no ancestral tribe. They lacked a common religion, even, despite the dominance of English culture, a common language. George Washington remained the earliest and most powerful symbol of American nationalism. He had been there from the start, before the Confederation or the Constitution, before the eagle or the flag. The moment he took command of the Continental Army in 1775, George Washington became the vessel of America's hope and pride.

If death tended to cast Washington in godlike light, it also worked to further remove the remote hero from the living. George Washington remains remarkable for both his presence and absence in American memory. He is at once familiar and enigmatic, as conspicuous and yet as featureless as the sheer stone obelisk raised to his memory above a city he never saw.

As we have seen, "Parson" Mason Locke Weems, best-selling author of one of the first of Washington's biographies, invented such immortal legends as that of the contest of little George's hatchet with his father's prized cherry tree. Weems fabricated his pious fables in part to instill virtue in his youthful readers. But he also hoped to cast a glow of humanity across his subject's cold marble face. Weems and his imitators wanted to make Washington a real person. They ended up making him ridiculous and boring.

Like Parson Weems, most of those who have wrestled with the colossus over the past two centuries have hoped to reveal the living Washington hidden behind the mythological edifice. None has really succeeded. George Washington will continue to elude us. Of the countless memorials that Washington's death called forth, however, there may be a few passages that hint at the grandeur of his legacy. In his eulogy, Fisher Ames quietly suggested that George Washington had changed mankind's ideas of political greatness.[11] More quietly still, Abigail Adams said that "Simple Truth is his best, his Greatest Eulogy—She alone can render his Fame immortal."[12]

Notes

CHAPTER 1. Look Around You

1. GW to Sir Isaac Heard, May 2, 1792, Founders Online, National Archives [hereafter FO/NA] (http://founders.archives.gov/documents/Washington/05-10-02-0211-0001), *The Papers of George Washington*, Presidential Series, vol. 10, *1 March 1792–15 August 1792*, ed. Robert F. Haggard and Mark A. Mastromarino (Charlottesville: University Press of Virginia, 2002), 332–34.

2. GW to Edward Newenham, Aug. 29, 1788, FO/NA (http://founders.archives.gov/documents/Washington/04-06-02-0436), *The Papers of George Washington*, Confederation Series, vol. 6. *1 Jan. 1788–23 Sept. 1788*, ed. W. W. Abbot (Charlottesville: University Press of Virginia, 1997), 486–89.

3. Thomas Jefferson to Dr. Walter F. Jones, Jan. 2, 1814, FO/NA (http://founders.archives.gov/documents/Jefferson/05-02-07-02-0052), *The Papers of Thomas Jefferson*, Retirement Series, vol. 7, *28 Nov. 1813–30 Sept. 1814*, ed. J. Jefferson Looney (Princeton: Princeton University Press, 2010), 100–104.

4. GW to Tench Tilghman, April 24, 1783, Writings of George Washington from the original manuscripts [vol. 26], Electronic Text Center, University of Virginia Library, web.archive.org/web/20110220112332/http:/etext.lib.virginia.edu.

5. GW, "First Inaugural Address: Final Version, 30 April 1789," FO/

NA   (http://founders.archives.gov/documents/Washington/05-02-02-030
-0003), *The Papers of George Washington*, Presidential Series, vol. 2, *1 April
1789–15 June 1789*, ed. Dorothy Twohig (Charlottesville: University Press of
Virginia, 1987), 173–77.

6. Thomas Jefferson to Dr. Walter F. Jones, Jan. 2, 1814, FO/NA (http://
founders.archives.gov/documents/Jefferson/05-02-07-02-0052), *Papers of
Jefferson*, Ret. 7:100–104.

7. Thomas Jefferson to GW, April 16, 1784, FO/NA (http://founders.
archives.gov/documents/Jefferson/051-07-02-0102), *The Papers of Thomas
Jefferson*, vol. 7, *2 March 1784–25 Feb. 1784*, ed. Julian P. Boyd (Princeton:
Princeton University Press, 1953), 105–10.

8. GW to Catharine Sawbridge Macaulay Graham, Jan. 9, 1790, FO/NA
(http://founders.archives.gov/documents/Washington/05-02-02-030-0003),
The Papers of George Washington, Presidential Series, vol. 4, *8 Sept. 1789–15
Jan. 1790*, ed. Dorothy Twohig (Charlottesville: University Press of Virginia,
1993), 551–54.

9. Marcus Cunliffe, *George Washington: Man and Monument* (1958;
rpt. Mount Vernon, VA: Mount Vernon Ladies Assoc., 1998), 3.

10. Mason Locke Weems, *The Life of Washington: A New Edition with
Primary Documents and Introduction*, ed. Peter S. Onuf (Armonk, NY:
M. E. Sharpe, 1996), 2.

11. Cunliffe, *Washington*, 147.

12. Gordon S. Wood, "The Greatness of George Washington," *Revolutionary Characters* (New York: Penguin, 2006), 31, 63.

CHAPTER 2. Powerful Ambitions, Powerful Friends

1. GW to Sir Isaac Heard, May 2, 1792, Founders Online, National Archives [hereafter FO/NA] (http://founders.archives.gov/documents/Wash
ington/05-10-02-0211-0001), *The Papers of George Washington*, Presidential Series, vol. 10, *1 March 1792–15 Aug. 1792*, ed. Robert F. Haggard and
Mark A. Mastromarino (Charlottesville: University Press of Virginia, 2002),
332–34.

2. According to the Julian calendar in use at the time of his birth, he
was born on February 11, 1732 (or 1731/2). Replacing that defective calendar

with the Gregorian calendar in 1752 added eleven days to all dates in the year 1732, making George Washington's actual birthday February 22, 1732.

3. The family record entered in Mary Washington's Bible is illustrated as the frontispiece of the first volume of Douglas Southall Freeman's seven-volume *George Washington: A Biography* (1948–57). Freeman's caption says that the writing is "by an unknown hand." In 1896, Paul L. Ford, in *The True George Washington*, had correctly identified the writer as Washington.

4. W. W. Abbot, "An Uncommon Awareness of Self: The Papers of George Washington," *Prologue: The Quarterly Journal of the National Archives*, Spring 1989, 7–19; passage cited, 7.

5. Edmund S. Morgan, "The Genuine Article," *New York Review of Books*, Feb. 29, 1996, 14.

6. Douglas Southall Freeman, *George Washington: A Biography*, 7 vols., vol. 7 completed by John A. Carroll and Mary W. Ashworth (New York: Scribner's, 1948–57), 1:76, 1:201 ff.

7. Thomas Jefferson to Dr. Walter F. Jones, Jan. 2, 1814, FO/NA (http://founders.archives.gov/documents/Jefferson/05-02-07-02-0052), *The Papers of Thomas Jefferson*, Retirement Series, vol. 7, *28 Nov. 1813–30 Sept. 1814*, ed. J. Jefferson Looney (Princeton: Princeton University Press, 2010), 100–104.

8. William Rasmussen and Robert Tilton, *George Washington: The Man Behind the Myths* (Charlottesville, University Press of Virginia, 1999), 21.

9. Freeman, *George Washington*, 1:xi.

10. GW to Sarah Cary Fairfax, Sept. 12, 1758, FO/NA (http://founders .archives.gov/documents/Washington/02-06-02-0013), *The Papers of George Washington*, Colonial Series, vol. 6, *4 Sept. 1758–26 Dec. 1760*, ed. W. W. Abbot (Charlottesville: University Press of Virginia, 1988), 10–13.

11. "Heaven, in giving him the higher qualities of the soul, had given also the tumultuous passions which accompany greatness, and frequently tarnish its lustre. With them was his first contest, and his first victory was over himself. So great the empire he had there acquired, that calmness of manner and conduct distinguished him through life"; Gouverneur Morris, "An oration on the death of General Washington, delivered at the request of the Corporation of the City of New York, December 31, 1799," extracted in *Life Portraits of Washington . . .*, comp. William Spohn Baker (Philadelphia, 1887), 73.

12. Douglass Adair, "Fame and the Founding Fathers," in *Fame and the Founding Fathers: Essays by Douglass Adair*, ed. Trevor Colburn (New York: Norton, 1974), 8, 11–12, and passim.

13. GW, "A Journal of my Journey over the Mountains begun Friday the 11th of March 1747/8," FO/NA (http://founders.archives.gov/documents/Washington/01-01-02-0001-0002), *The Diaries of George Washington*, vol. 1, *11 March 1748–13 Nov. 1765*, ed. Donald Jackson (Charlottesville: University Press of Virginia, 1976), 6–16.

14. Philander D. Chase, "A Stake in the West: George Washington as Backcountry Surveyor and Landholder," in *George Washington and the Virginia Backcountry*, ed. Warren Hofstra (Madison, WI: Madison House, 1998), 170 ff.

15. GW to Lawrence Washington, May 5, 1749, FO/NA (http://founders.archives.gov/documents/Washington/02-01-02-0003), *The Papers of George Washington*, Colonial Series, vol. 1, *7 July 1748–14 Aug. 1755*, ed. W. W. Abbot (Charlottesville: University Press of Virginia, 1983), 6–8.

16. GW, Barbados diary, 1751–52, FO/NA (http://founders.archives.gov/documents/Washington/01-01-02-0001-0002), *Diaries of GW*, 1:35–117.

17. GW to Robert Dinwiddie, June 10, 1752, FO/NA (http://founders.archives.gov/documents/Washington/02-01-02-0003), *Papers of GW*, Col. 1:50–51.

18. GW, cash account, Oct. 23, 1754, FO/NA (http://founders.archives.gov/documents/Washington/02-01-02-0003), *Papers of GW*, Col. 1:217–18.

CHAPTER 3. War for North America

1. Kenneth P. Bailey, *Christopher Gist* (Hamden, CT: Archon, 1976), 35.

2. Francis Jennings, *Empire of Fortune* (New York: Norton, 1988), 52.

3. John R. Alden, *Robert Dinwiddie: Servant of the Crown* (Charlottesville: University Press of Virginia, 1973), 20.

4. Ibid., 42.

5. Douglas Southall Freeman, *George Washington: A Biography*, 7 vols., vol. 7 completed by John A. Carroll and Mary W. Ashworth (New York: Scribner's, 1948–57), 1:56.

6. GW, "Remarks, 1787–1788" [comments on David Humphreys's biography of Washington], Founders Online, National Archives [hereafter FO/NA] (http://founders.archives.gov/documents/Washington/02-05-02-0463), *The Papers of George Washington, Confederation Series,* vol. 5, *1 Feb. 1787–31 Dec. 1787,* ed. W. W. Abbot (Charlottesville: University Press of Virginia, 1997), 515–26.

7. Gary B. Nash, *Red, Black, and White: The Peoples of Early North America* (New York: Prentice Hall, 1974), 261.

8. John Ferling, *The First of Men: A Life of George Washington* (Knoxville: University of Tennessee Press, 1990), 84.

9. GW, "Remarks, 1787–1788" [comments on Humphreys's biography].

10. Freeman, *George Washington,* 1:58.

11. "Editorial Note," FO/NA (http://founders.archives.gov/documents/Washington/01-01-02-0001-0002), *The Diaries of George Washington,* vol. 1, *11 March 1748–13 Nov. 1765,* ed. Donald Jackson (Charlottesville: University Press of Virginia, 1976), 118–29.

12. Jennings, *Empire of Fortune,* 234.

13. William A. Hunter, "Tanagrisson," *Dictionary of Canadian Biography,* vol. 3, *1741 to 1770* (Toronto: University of Toronto Press, 1974), 613–14.

14. Michael N. McConnell, *A Country Between: The Upper Ohio Valley and Its People, 1724–1774* (Lincoln: University of Nebraska Press, 1992), passim.

15. GW, "Journey to the French Commandant: Narrative," FO/NA (http://founders.archives.gov/documents/Washington/01-01-02-0003-0002), *Diaries of GW,* 1:130–61.

16. Ibid.

17. Ibid.

18. Ibid.

19. Ibid.

20. Ibid.

21. Freeman, *George Washington,* 1:325.

22. GW, "Journey to the French Commandant."

23. Ibid.

24. Ibid.

25. Ibid.

26. Ibid.

27. The 1754 Williamsburg edition of *The Journal of Major George Washington* is one of the rarest of American imprints. Only seven copies are known—those in the Huntington Library, the New York Public Library, the Newberry Library, the John Carter Brown Library, the Historical Society of Pennsylvania, the Scheide Library at Princeton University, and Colonial Williamsburg. There is no copy in the British Library, as erroneously stated in standard bibliographies.

28. David L. Preston, *Braddock's Defeat: The Battle of the Monongahela and the Road to Revolution* (New York: Oxford University Press, 2015), 352.

29. Ibid., 352.

30. Fred Anderson, *Crucible of War: The Seven Years' War and the Fate of Empire in British North America* (New York: Knopf, 2000), 56–58.

31. GW to John Augustine Washington, May 31, 1755, FO/NA (http://founders.archives.gov/documents/Washington/02-01-02-0003), *The Papers of George Washington*, Colonial Series, vol. 1, *7 July 1748–14 Aug. 1755*, ed. W. W. Abbot (Charlottesville: University Press of Virginia, 1983), 118–19.

32. Horace Walpole, cited in FO/NA (http://founders.archives.gov/documents/Washington/02-01-02-0003), *Papers of GW*, Col. 1:199n.

33. GW, "Journey to the French Commandant."

34. Freeman, *George Washington*, 1:381, 388, 403.

35. Ange de Menneville, marquis de Duquesne, to Claude Pierre Contrecoeur, Sept. 8, 1754, *Papers of GW*, Col. 1:165–68 [print edition only].

36. James T. Flexner, *Washington: The Indispensable Man* (Boston: Little, Brown, 1974), 18.

37. Freeman, *George Washington*, 1:415.

38. Rupert Hughes, *George Washington: The Human Being and the Hero* (New York: Scribner's, 1926), 156–57.

39. Freeman, *George Washington*, 1:379.

40. The British gleefully resurrected the Jumonville affair during the War for Independence as proof of the treachery of the man who now commanded the rebel armies.

41. GW to Richard Corbin, Feb.–March 1754, FO/NA (http://founders

.archives.gov/documents/Washington/02-06-02-0013), *Papers of GW,* Col. 1:70–71.

42. George II, *Orders for Settling the Rank of the Officers of HM's Forces, When Serving with the Provincial Forces in North America* (London, 1754).

43. Paul K. Longmore, *The Invention of George Washington* (Berkeley: University of California Press, 1988), 21.

44. Bernard Knollenberg, *George Washington, the Virginia Period, 1732–1775* (Durham, NC: Duke University Press, 1964), 29.

45. GW to Robert Dinwiddie, March 10, 1757, FO/NA (http://founders .archives.gov/documents/Washington/02-04-02-0062), *The Papers of George Washington,* Colonial Series, vol. 4, *9 Nov. 1756–24 Oct. 1757,* ed. W. W. Abbot (Charlottesville: University Press of Virginia, 1984), 112–15.

CHAPTER 4. The Rise of George Washington

1. GW to Augustine Washington, May 14, 1755, Founders Online, National Archives [hereafter FO/NA] (http://founders.archives.gov/docu ments/Washington/02-06-02-0013), *The Papers of George Washington,* Colonial Series, vol. 1, *7 July 1748–14 Aug. 1755,* ed. W. W. Abbot (Charlottesville: University Press of Virginia, 1983), 171–73.

2. Benjamin Franklin, "Autobiography," *Benjamin Franklin: Writings,* ed. J. A. Leo LeMay (New York: Library of America, 1987), 1441.

3. Paul E. Kopperman, *Braddock at the Monongahela* (Pittsburgh: University of Pittsburgh Press, 1977), 15.

4. Stanley Pargellis, "Braddock's Defeat," *American Historical Review,* Jan. 1936, 253–69.

5. GW to John Campbell, Earl of Loudoun, Jan. 10, 1757, FO/NA (http:// founders.archives.gov/documents/Washington/02-04-02-0045), *The Papers of George Washington,* Colonial Series, vol. 4, *9 Nov. 1756–24 Oct. 1757,* ed. W. W. Abbot (Charlottesville: University Press of Virginia, 1984), 79–93.

6. Kopperman, *Braddock at the Monongahela,* 29.

7. Thomas A. Lewis, *For King and Country: George Washington, the Early Years* (New York: Wiley, 1993), 178–79.

8. Ibid., 182.

9. GW to Robert Dinwiddie, July 18, 1755, FO/NA (http://founders

.archives.gov/documents/Washington/02-06-02-0013), *Papers of GW,* Col. 1:339–42.

10. GW, "Remarks, 1787–1788" [comments on David Humphreys's biography of Washington], FO/NA (http://founders.archives.gov/documents/ Washington/02-05-02-0463), *The Papers of George Washington,* Confederation Series, vol. 5, *1 Feb. 1787–31 Dec. 1787,* ed. W. W. Abbot (Charlottesville: University Press of Virginia, 1997), 515–26.

11. GW to Robert Dinwiddie, July 18, 1755, FO/NA (http://founders. archives.gov/documents/Washington/02-06-02-0013), *Papers of GW,* Col. 1:339–42.

12. Ian Steele, *Betrayals: Fort William Henry and the Massacre* (New York: Oxford University Press, 1990), 189.

13. Nicholas Cresswell, *Journal of Nicholas Cresswell, 1774–1777,* ed. Lincoln MacVeagh, (New York: Dial, 1924), 65.

14. Robert Dinwiddie to GW, July 26, 1755, FO/NA (http://founders/ archives.gov/documents/02-01-02-0185), *Papers of GW,* Col. 1:344.

15. GW to John Augustine Washington, July 18, 1755, *George Washington: Writings,* ed. John Rhodehamel (New York: Library of America, 1997), 59–60.

16. Kopperman, *Braddock at the Monongahela,* 112.

17. Samuel Davies, *Religion and Patriotism the Constituents of a Good Soldier* (Philadelphia, 1755), 8–9.

18. Paul K. Longmore, *The Invention of George Washington* (Berkeley: University of California Press, 1988), 30.

19. Dinwiddie's commission appointing Washington "Colonel of the Virga Regimt & Commander in Chief of all Forces" was dated August 14, 1755. Washington probably accepted about September 1.

20. GW to Charles Lewis, Aug. 14, 1755, FO/NA (http://founders.archives .gov/documents/Washington/02-01-02-0185), *Papers of GW,* Col. 1:364.

21. Longmore, *Invention,* 40 and passim.

22. Ibid., passim.

23. Douglas Southall Freeman, *George Washington: A Biography,* 7 vols., vol. 7 completed by John A. Carroll and Mary W. Ashworth (New York: Scribner's, 1948–57), 2:110.

24. Adam Stephen to GW, Oct. 4, 1755, FO/NA (http://founders.archives
.gov/documents/Washington/02-02-02-0668), *Papers of GW*, Col. 4:72–75.

25. GW to John Campbell, Earl of Loudoun, Jan. 10, 1757, FO/NA
(http://founders.archives.gov/documents/Washington/02-04-02-0045),
Papers of GW, Col. 4:79–93.

26. The only record of the crucial meeting is a note in Loudoun's crabbed
hand in a memorandum filed among his voluminous papers in the Huntington
Library: "Called then Col. Washington and made of new disposition of the Virginia troops"; March 20, 1757, LO 1717. Lack of documentation did not prevent
one eminent Washington biographer from painting a dramatic confrontation
that so perfectly captures the irrepressible conflict between raw American
pride and British aristocratic intransigence that the imaginative reader can almost smell the gun smoke of the 1770s; James T. Flexner, *George Washington:
The Forge of Experience, 1732–1775* (Boston: Little, Brown, 1965), 174–75. The
story has been repeated and embellished by subsequent biographers.

27. GW to Robert Dinwiddie, March 10, 1757, FO/NA (http://founders
.archives.gov/documents/Washington/02-04-02-0062), *Papers of GW*, Col.
4:112–15.

28. Francis Jennings, *Empire of Fortune* (New York: Norton, 1988),
204–22 and passim.

29. GW to Richard Washington, April 15, 1757, FO/NA (http://founders
.archives.gov/documents/Washington/02-04-02-0045), *Papers of GW*, Col.
4:132–34.

30. Flexner, *George Washington: The Forge of Experience*, 185.

31. Freeman, *George Washington*, 2:266.

32. W. W. Abbot, "An Uncommon Awareness of Self: The Papers of
George Washington," *Prologue: The Quarterly Journal of the National Archives*, Spring, 1989, 8.

33. GW to Sarah Cary Fairfax, Sept. 12, 1758, FO/NA (http://founders
.archives.gov/documents/Washington/02-06-02-0013), *The Papers of George
Washington*, Colonial Series, vol. 6, *4 Sept. 1758–26 Dec. 1760*, ed. W. W. Abbot
(Charlottesville: University Press of Virginia, 1988), 10–13.

34. GW to Sarah Cary Fairfax, Sept. 25, 1758, FO/NA (http://founders.
archives.gov/documents/Washington/02-06-02-0033), *Papers of GW*, Col.
6:41–43.

35. Early in the twentieth century, Woodrow Wilson alluded to the romance circumspectly, neither quoting the letters nor naming Sally. In 1926, novelist-turned-biographer Rupert Hughes wrote of it at length, exuberantly, and to the outrage of the historical profession. It seems to have been the distinguished historian Samuel Eliot Morison, however, in a speech at Harvard marking the bicentennial of Washington's birth in 1932, who first gave respectability to the conceit that his secret love for a married woman was the crucial formative experience of Washington's life. Morison called the episode "the most beautiful thing in Washington's life."

36. GW to John Stanwix, April 10, 1758, FO/NA (http://founders.archives.gov/documents/Washington/02-05-02-0087), *The Papers of George Washington,* Colonial Series, vol. 5, ed. W. W. Abbot (Charlottesville: University Press of Virginia, 1988), 117–20.

37. GW, "Journey to the French Commandant: Narrative," FO/NA (http://founders.archives.gov/documents/Washington/01-01-02-0003-0002), *The Diaries of George Washington,* vol. 1, *11 March 1748–13 Nov. 1765,* ed. Donald Jackson (Charlottesville: University Press of Virginia, 1976), 130–61.

38. "Address of the Officers of the Virginia Regiment," Dec. 31, 1758, FO/NA (http://founders.archives.gov/documents/Washington/02-06-02-0013), *Papers of GW,* Col. 6:178–80.

39. Thomas Jefferson to Dr. Walter F. Jones, Jan. 2, 1814, FO/NA (http://founders.archives.gov/documents/Jefferson/05-02-07-02-0052), *The Papers of Thomas Jefferson,* Retirement Series, vol. 7, *28 Nov. 1813–30 Sept. 1814,* ed. J. Jefferson Looney (Princeton: Princeton University Press, 2010), 100–104.

40. Freeman, *George Washington,* 2:370–71.

41. Rupert Hughes, *George Washington: The Human Being and the Hero* (New York: Scribner's, 1926), 375–76.

42. Jennings, *Empire of Fortune,* 220.

43. Benjamin Franklin to William Strahan, Aug. 19, 1784, *Not Your Usual Founding Father: Selected Readings from Benjamin Franklin,* ed. Edmund S. Morgan (New Haven: Yale University Press, 2006), 250–51.

44. Jennings, *Empire of Fortune,* 206.

45. GW to Richard Washington, Sept. 20, 1759, FO/NA (http://founders.archives.gov/documents/Washington/02-06-02-0013), *Papers of GW,* Col. 6:358–59.

46. GW to Charles Mynn Thruston, March 12, 1773, FO/NA (http://founders.archives.gov/documents/Washington/02-09-02-0147), *The Papers of George Washington*, Colonial Series, vol. 9, *8 Jan. 1772–18 March 1774*, ed. W. W. Abbot and Dorothy Twohig (Charlottesville: University Press of Virginia, 1994), 194–98.

47. GW to William Crawford, Sept. 21, 1767, FO/NA (http://founders.archives.gov/documents/Washington/02-08-02-0020), *The Papers of George Washington*, Colonial Series, vol. 8, *24 June 1767–25 Dec. 1771*, ed. W. W. Abbot and Dorothy Twohig (Charlottesville: University Press of Virginia, 1993), 26–32.

48. Fred Anderson, "The Man Behind the Myth," review of John Rhodehamel, ed., *George Washington: Writings*, in *Los Angeles Times Book Review*, Feb. 23, 1997.

CHAPTER 5. "Because We Are Americans"

1. "I never forgot your declaration when I had the pleasure of being at your House in 1768 that you were ready to take your Musket on your Shoulder whenever your Country call'd on you, I heard that declaration with great satisfaction"; Arthur Lee to GW, June 15, 1777, Founders Online, National Archives [hereafter FO/NA] (http://founders.archives.gov/documents/Washington/02-10-02-0043), *The Papers of George Washington*, Revolutionary War Series, vol. 10, *11 June 1777–18 Aug. 1777*, ed. Frank E. Grizzard, Jr. (Charlottesville: University Press of Virginia, 2000), 43–45. I am grateful to Peter R. Henriques for citing this important letter in his essay "Taking Command: George Washington and the Beginning of the War for American Independence," in *Realistic Visionary: A Portrait of George Washington* (Charlottesville: University Press of Virginia, 2006), 34.

2. GW to George Mason, April 5, 1769, FO/NA (http://founders.archives.gov/documents/Washington/02-08-02-0132), *The Papers of George Washington*, Colonial Series, vol. 8, *24 June 1767–25 Dec. 1771*, ed. W. W. Abbot and Dorothy Twohig (Charlottesville: University Press of Virginia, 1993), 177–81.

3. GW to Robert Cary and Company, Sept. 20, 1765, FO/NA (http://founders.archives.gov/documents/Washington/02-07-02-0252-0001), *The Papers of George Washington*, Colonial Series, vol. 7, *1 Jan. 1761–15 June*

1767, ed. W. W. Abbot and Dorothy Twohig (Charlottesville: University Press of Virginia, 1990), 398–402.

4. GW to George William Fairfax, June 10, 1774, FO/NA (http://founders .archives.gov/documents/Washington/02-10-02-0097), *The Papers of George Washington,* Colonial Series, vol. 10, *21 March 1774–15 June 1775,* ed. W. W. Abbot and Dorothy Twohig (Charlottesville: University Press of Virginia, 1995), 94–101.

5. Jeremy Black, *George III: American's Last King* (New Haven: Yale University Press, 2006), 215.

6. GW to Bryan Fairfax, Aug. 24, 1774, FO/NA (http://founders.ar chives.gov/documents/Washington/02-10-02-0097), *Papers of GW,* Col. 10:154–56.

7. GW to George William Fairfax, May 31, 1775, FO/NA (http://found ers.archives.gov/documents/Washington/02-10-02-0097), *Papers of GW,* Col. 10:367–68.

8. GW, "Address to the Continental Congress," June 16, 1775, FO/NA (http://founders.archives.gov/documents/Washington/03-01-02-0001), *The Papers of George Washington,* Revolutionary War Series, vol. 1, *16 June 1775–15 Sept. 1775,* ed. Philander D. Chase (Charlottesville: University Press of Virginia, 1985), 1–3.

9. Douglas Southall Freeman, *George Washington: A Biography,* 7 vols., vol. 7 completed by John A. Carroll and Mary W. Ashworth (New York: Scribner's, 1948–57), 3:433.

10. GW to Martha Washington, June 18, 1775, FO/NA (http://founders .archives.gov/documents/Washington/03-01-02-0003), *Papers of GW,* Rev. 1:3–6.

11. Fisher Ames, *An Oration on the Sublime Virtues of General George Washington, Pronounced at the Old South Meeting-House in Boston, before his Honor the Lieutenant-Governor, the Council, and the Two Branches of the Legislature of Massachusetts, at their Request, on Saturday, the 8th of February, 1800* (Denham, [MA]: Printed by H. Mann, 1800), 4.

12. GW to Burwell Bassett, June 19, 1775, FO/NA (http://founders .archives.gov/documents/Washington/03-01-02-0006), *Papers of GW,* Rev. 1:12–14.

13. Freeman, *George Washington,* 3:439–40.

14. John Adams to Abigail Adams, June 17, 1775, in *The American Revolution: Writings from the War of Independence*, ed. John Rhodehamel (New York: Library of America, 2001), 32–33.

15. Don Higginbotham, *The War of American Independence: Military Attitudes, Policies, and Practice, 1763–1789* (New York: Macmillan, 1971), 85.

16. "Address from the New York Provincial Congress," June 26, 1776, FO/NA (http://founders.archives.gov/documents/Washington/03-01-02-0018), *Papers of GW*, Rev. 1:40–41.

17. GW, "Address to the New York Provincial Congress," June 26, 1775, FO/NA (http://founders.archives.gov/documents/Washington/03-01-02-0018), *Papers of GW*, Rev. 1:41.

18. Garry Wills, *Cincinnatus: George Washington and the Enlightenment* (New York: Doubleday, 1984), xxiv.

19. GW, "General Orders," July 4, 1775, FO/NA (http://founders.archives .gov/documents/Washington/03-01-02-0027), *Papers of GW*, Rev. 1:54–58.

20. GW to Lund Washington, Aug. 20, 1775, FO/NA (http://founders .archives.gov/documents/Washington/03-01-02-0234), *Papers of GW*, Rev. 1:334–40.

21. James T. Flexner, *George Washington in the American Revolution* (Boston: Little, Brown, 1967), 35.

22. The account has to be regarded with some skepticism since it derives from the testimony, given seventy years later, of one Israel Trask, all of ten years old in 1775. Still, Stephen Brumwell asserts that "it likely preserves at least some semblance of truth"; Stephen Brumwell, *George Washington: Gentleman Warrior* (New York: Quercus, 2012), 206.

23. Edward G. Lengel, *General George Washington: A Military Life* (New York: Random House, 2007), 114.

24. GW, "Circular to General Officers," Sept. 9, 1775, FO/NA (http://founders.archives.gov/documents/Washington/03-01-02-0327), *Papers of GW*, Rev. 1:432–34.

25. GW to John Hancock, Jan. 4, 1776, FO/NA (http://founders.archives.gov/documents/Washington/03-03-02-0013), *The Papers of George Washington*, Revolutionary War Series, vol. 3, *1 Jan. 1776–31 March 1776*, ed. Philander D. Chase (Charlottesville: University Press of Virginia, 1988), 18–21.

26. GW to John Hancock, Feb. 9, 1776, FO/NA (http://founders.ar chives.gov/documents/Washington/03-03-02-0201), *Papers of GW,* Rev. 3:274-77.

27. Francis Jennings, *Empire of Fortune* (New York: Norton, 1988), 208-9.

28. Freeman, *George Washington,* 2:373.

29. Ibid., 2:189.

30. GW to John Augustine Washington, Sept. 22, 1776, FO/NA (http:// founders.archives.gov/documents/Washington/03-06-02-0290), *The Papers of George Washington,* Revolutionary War Series, vol. 6, *13 Aug. 1776-20 Oct. 1776,* ed. Philander D. Chase and Frank E. Grizzard, Jr. (Charlottesville: University Press of Virginia, 1994), 371-74.

31. GW to John Hancock, Sept. 3, 1776, FO/NA (http://founders.ar chives.gov/documents/Washington/03-06-02-0162), *Papers of GW,* Rev. 6:199-201.

32. GW to John Banister, April 21, 1778, FO/NA (http://founders.ar chives.gov/documents/Washington/03-14-02-0525), *The Papers of George Washington,* Revolutionary War Series, vol. 14, *1 March 1778-30 April 1778,* ed. David R. Hoth (Charlottesville: University Press of Virginia, 2004), 573-79.

33. GW to John Hancock, Sept. 25, 1776, FO/NA (http://founders .archives.gov/documents/Washington/03-06-02-0305), *Papers of GW,* Rev. 6:393-401.

34. GW to Joseph Reed, Jan. 14, 1776, FO/NA (http://founders.archives .gov/documents/Washington/03-03-02-0062), *Papers of GW,* 3:87-92.

35. GW to Joseph Reed, Feb. 10, 1776, FO/NA (http://founders.archives .gov/documents/Washington/03-03-02-0209), *Papers of GW,* 3:286-91.

CHAPTER 6. Winter Soldier

1. GW to Joseph Reed, Jan. 31, 1776, Founders Online, National Ar chives [hereafter FO/NA] (http://founders.archives.gov/documents/Wash ington/03-03-02-0163), *The Papers of George Washington,* Revolutionary War Series, vol. 3, *1 Jan. 1776-31 March 1776,* ed. Philander D. Chase (Char lottesville: University Press of Virginia, 1988), 215-19.

2. *Thomas Paine: Collected Writings,* ed. Eric Foner (New York: Library of America, 1995), 5.

3. Ibid.

4. Joseph J. Ellis, *His Excellency: George Washington* (New York: Random House, 2004), 13.

5. GW to John Hancock, July 10, 1776, FO/NA (http://founders.ar chives.gov/documents/Washington/03-06-02-0188), *The Papers of George Washington*, Revolutionary War Series, vol. 5, *16 June 1776–12 Aug. 1776*, ed. Philander D. Chase (Charlottesville: University Press of Virginia, 1993), 258–61.

6. Christopher Ward, *The War of the Revolution*, 2 vols. (New York: Macmillan, 1952), 1:226.

7. Ambrose Serle, diary entry of Aug. 27, 1776, in *The American Revolution: Writings from the War of Independence*, ed. John Rhodehamel (New York: Library of America, 2001), 197.

8. Ellis, *His Excellency*, 95.

9. GW to John Hancock, Sept. 8, 1776, FO/NA (http://founders.ar chives.gov/documents/Washington/03-06-02-0305), *The Papers of George Washington*, Revolutionary War Series, vol. 6, *13 Aug. 1776–20 Oct. 1776*, ed. Philander D. Chase and Frank E. Grizzard, Jr. (Charlottesville: University Press of Virginia, 1994), 248–56.

10. Ambrose Serle, diary entry of Sept. 15, 1776, in Rhodehamel, *The American Revolution*, 218.

11. Ward, *War of the Revolution*, 1:243.

12. GW to Lund Washington, Oct. 6, 1776, FO/NA (http://founders .archives.gov/documents/Washington/03-06-02-0305), *Papers of GW*, Rev. 6:493–95.

13. David Hackett Fischer, *Washington's Crossing* (New York: Oxford University Press, 2004), 114.

14. Ward, *War of the Revolution*, 1:281.

15. GW to Samuel Washington, Dec. 18, 1776, FO/NA (http://founders .archives.gov/documents/Washington/03-07-02-0299), *The Papers of George Washington*, Revolutionary War Series, vol. 7, *21 Oct. 1776–5 Jan. 1777*, ed. Philander D. Chase (Charlottesville: University Press of Virginia, 1997), 369–72.

16. GW to John Augustine Washington, Sept. 22, 1776, FO/NA (http://

founders.archives.gov/documents/Washington/03-07-02-0290), *Papers of GW*, Rev. 6:371-74.

17. GW to Lund Washington, Sep. 30, 1776, FO/NA (http://founders .archives.gov/documents/Washington/03-07-02-0299), *Papers of GW*, Rev. 6:440-43.

18. Edward G. Lengel, *General George Washington: A Military Life* (New York: Random House, 2007), 189.

19. James T. Flexner, *George Washington in the American Revolution* (Boston: Little, Brown, 1967), 163.

20. Fischer, *Washington's Crossing*, 228.

21. Ron Chernow, *Washington: A Life* (New York: Penguin, 2010), 280.

22. Fischer, *Washington's Crossing*, 334.

23. Stephen Brumwell, *George Washington: Gentleman Warrior* (New York: Quercus, 2012), 294.

24. Douglas Southall Freeman, *George Washington: A Biography*, 7 vols., vol. 7 completed by John A. Carroll and Mary W. Ashworth (New York: Scribner's, 1948-57), 4:362.

25. Flexner, *Washington in the Revolution*, 189.

26. GW, General Orders, Dec. 27, 1776, FO/NA (http://founders.archives .gov/documents/Washington/03-07-02-0351), *Papers of GW*, Rev. 7:448-49.

27. Chernow, *Washington*, 278.

28. Don Higginbottom, *George Washington and the American Military Tradition* (Athens: University of Georgia Press, 1985), 75.

29. Elizabeth A. Fenn, *Pox Americana: The Great Smallpox Epidemic of 1775-81* (New York: Hill and Wang, 2001), 134.

CHAPTER 7. Brandywine, Germantown, and Monmouth

1. Douglas Southall Freeman, *George Washington: A Biography*, 7 vols., vol. 7 completed by John A. Carroll and Mary W. Ashworth (New York: Scribner's, 1948-57), 4:463-64.

2. Ibid., 4:488.

3. Christopher Ward, *The War of the Revolution*, 2 vols. (New York: Macillan, 1952), 1:354.

4. GW to John Hancock, Sept. 11, 1777, Founders Online, National Archives [hereafter FO/NA] (http://founders.archives.gov/documents/Washington/03-11-02-0190-0009), *The Papers of George Washington*, Revolutionary War Series, vol. 11, *19 Aug. 1777-25 Oct. 1777*, ed. Philander D. Chase and Edward Lengel (Charlottesville: University Press of Virginia, 2001), 200-201.

5. Freeman, *George Washington*, 4:493.

6. Robert Middlekauff, *The Glorious Cause: The American Revolution, 1763-1789* (New York: Oxford University Press, 1982), 393.

7. Ira D. Gruber, ed., *John Peebles' American War: The Diary of a Scottish Grenadier, 1776-1782* (Mechanicsburg, PA: Stackpole, 1998), 140.

8. GW to John Banister, April 21, 1778, FO/NA (http://founders.archives.gov/documents/Washington/03-14-02-0525), *The Papers of George Washington*, Revolutionary War Series, vol. 14, *1 March 1788-30 April 1788*, ed. David R. Hoth (Charlottesville: University Press of Virginia, 2004), 573-79.

9. GW to Patrick Henry, Dec. 27, 1777, FO/NA (http://founders.archives.gov/documents/Washington/03-13-02-0015), *The Papers of George Washington*, Revolutionary War Series, vol. 13, *26 Dec. 1777-28 Feb. 1778*, ed. Edward G. Lengel (Charlottesville: University Press of Virginia, 2003), 17-18.

10. *The American Revolution: Writings from the War of Independence*, ed. John Rhodehamel (New York: Library of America, 2001), 404.

11. GW to Henry Laurens, Dec. 23, 1777, FO/NA (http://founders.archives.gov/documents/Washington/03-12-02-0628), *The Papers of George Washington*, Revolutionary War Series, vol. 12, *26 Oct. 1777-25 Dec. 1777*, ed. Frank E. Grizzard, Jr., and David R. Hoth (Charlottesville: University Press of Virginia, 2002), 683-87.

12. Ibid.

13. GW, General Orders, May 5, 1778, FO/NA (http://founders.archives.gov/documents/Washington/03-15-02-0039), *The Papers of George Washington*, Revolutionary War Series, vol. 15, *May-June 1778*, ed. Edward G. Lengel (Charlottesville: University Press of Virginia, 2006), 38-41.

14. Mark M. Boatner, III, *Encyclopedia of the American Revolution* (New York: David McKay, 1974), 278.

15. John Adams to Abigail Adams, Oct. 26, 1777, FO/NA (http://found

ers.archives.gov/documents/Adams/04-02-02-0289), *The Adams Papers,* Adams Family Correspondence, vol. 2, *June 1776–March 1778,* ed. L. H. Butterfield (Cambridge: Harvard University Press, 1963), 360–61.

16. Edward G. Lengel, *General George Washington: A Military Life* (New York: Random House, 2005), 294.

17. Ward, *War of the Revolution,* 2:577.

18. Ibid., 2:581.

19. Ibid.

20. Middlekauff, *Glorious Cause,* 429.

21. GW to Thomas Nelson, Aug. 20, 1778, FO/NA (http://founders .archives.gov/documents/Washington/03-16-02-0373), *The Papers of George Washington,* Revolutionary War Series, vol. 16, *1 July–14 Sept. 1778,* ed. David R. Hoth (Charlottesville: University Press of Virginia, 2006), 340–42.

22. Benjamin Franklin to GW, March 5, 1780, *Papers of Benjamin Franklin,* vol. 32, *March 1 through June 30, 1780,* ed. Barbara Oberg (New Haven: Yale University Press, 1996), 56–57.

23. Jean François, Chevalier de Chastellux, *Travels in North America,* 2 vols., ed. Howard C. Rice, Jr. (Chapel Hill: University of North Carolina Press, 1963), 1:106.

CHAPTER 8. The Great Man

1. Douglas Southall Freeman, *George Washington: A Biography,* 7 vols., vol. 7 completed by John A. Carroll and Mary W. Ashworth (New York: Scribner's, 1948–57), 5:238.

2. GW to John Laurens, Jan. 30, 1781; original letter reproduced in John Rhodehamel, *The Great Experiment: George Washington and the American Republic* (New Haven: Yale University Press, 1998), 72.

3. GW to James McHenry, Oct. 17, 1782, in *George Washington: Writings,* ed. John Rhodehamel (New York: Library of America, 1997), 476.

4. Gouverneur Morris to John Jay, quoted in James T. Flexner, *George Washington in the American Revolution* (Boston: Little, Brown), 1967, 493.

5. James T. Flexner, *Washington: The Indispensable Man* (Boston: Little, Brown, 1969), 169.

6. Alexander Hamilton to GW, Feb. 13, 1783, Founders Online, National

Archives [hereafter FO/NA] (http://founders.archives.gov/documents/Hamil
ton/01-03-02-0155), *The Papers of Alexander Hamilton*, vol. 3, *1782–1786*, ed.
Harold C. Syrett (New York: Columbia University Press, 1962), 253–55.

7. GW to Alexander Hamilton, March 4, 1783, Writings of George Washington from the original manuscript sources [vol. 26], Electronic Text Center, University of Virginia Library, web.archive.org/web/20110220112332/http:/etext.lib.virginia.edu.

8. GW to Alexander Hamilton, April 4, 1783, Writings of George Washington from the original manuscripts [vol. 26], Electronic Text Center, University of Virginia Library, web.archive.org/web/20110220120246/http:/etext.lib.virginia.edu.

9. GW, "Speech to the Officers of the Army," March 15, 1783, in Rhodehamel, *Washington: Writings*, 500.

10. Rhodehamel, *Great Experiment*, 84–85.

11. GW, "Circular to the State Governments," June 8, 1783, in Rhodehamel, *Washington: Writings*, 518.

12. Ibid., 517.

13. Ibid.

14. Ibid., 518.

15. James HcHenry to Margaret Caldwell, Dec. 23, 1783, in *The American Revolution: Writings from the War of Independence*, ed. John Rhodehamel (New York: Library of America, 2001), 796.

16. GW, Resignation Speech to the Continental Congress, Dec. 23, 1783, in Rhodehamel, *The American Revolution*, 794.

17. Ibid., 794–95.

18. Thomas Jefferson to GW, April 16, 1784, FO/NA (http://founders.archives.gov/documents/Jefferson/051-07-02-0102), *The Papers of Thomas Jefferson*, vol. 7, *2 March 1784–25 Feb. 1784*, ed. Julian P. Boyd (Princeton: Princeton University Press, 1953), 105–10.

19. Ron Chernow, *Washington: A Life* (New York: Penguin, 2010), 454.

CHAPTER 9. "The Destiny of Unborn Millions"

1. GW to Henry Knox, Feb. 20, 1784, Founders Online, National Archives [hereafter FO/NA] (http://founders.archives.gov/documents/Wash

ington/04-01-02-0099), *The Papers of George Washington*, Confederation Series, vol. 1, *1 Jan. 1784–17 July 1784*, ed. W. W. Abbot (Charlottesville: University Press of Virginia, 1992), 136–38.

2. One of Custis's daughters told a story that illustrates the man's character. When she was a little girl of four or five, her father taught her to sing dirty songs. When Custis was deep in drink with his friends, he would bring in the little girl, stand her on a table, and make her sing the lewd ditties for the amusement of his drunken pals. He also cheated his stepfather in business dealings.

3. GW to James Craik, Aug. 4, 1788, FO/NA (http://founders.archives .gov/documents/Washington/04-06-02-0386), *The Papers of George Washington*, Confederation Series, vol. 6, *1 Jan. 1788–23 Sept. 1788*, ed. W. W. Abbot (Charlottesville: University Press of Virginia, 1997), 423.

4. GW, "Last Will and Testament, Enclosure: schedule of property," July 9, 1799, FO/NA (http://founders.archives.gov/documents/Washing ton/06-04-02-0404-0002), *The Papers of George Washington*, Retirement Series, vol. 4, *20 April 1799–13 Dec. 1799*, ed. W. W. Abbot (Charlottesville: University Press of Virginia, 1999), 512–27.

5. Thomas P. Slaughter, *The Whiskey Rebellion: Frontier Epilogue to the American Revolution* (New York: Oxford University Press, 1986), 85.

6. GW, diary entry, Oct. 4, 1784, FO/NA (http://founders.archives .gov/documents/Washington/04-04-02-0001-0002-0004), *The Diaries of George Washington*, vol. 4, *1 Sept. 1784–30 June 1786*, ed. Donald Jackson and Dorothy Twohig (Charlottesville: University Press of Virginia, 1978), 57–71.

7. GW to James McHenry, Aug. 22, 1785, FO/NA (http://founders.ar chives.gov/documents/Washington/04-03-02-0184), *The Papers of George Washington*, Confederation Series, vol. 3, *19 May 1785–31 March 1786*, ed. W. W. Abbot (Charlottesville: University Press of Virginia, 1994), 197–99.

8. Ibid.

9. GW to Henry Knox, Feb. 3, 1787, FO/NA (http://founders.archives .gov/documents/Washington/04-05-02-0006), *The Papers of George Washington*, Confederation Series, vol. 5, *1 Feb. 1787–31 Dec. 1787*, ed. W. W. Abbot (Charlottesville: University Press of Virginia, 1997), 7–9.

10. GW to Benjamin Lincoln, Nov. 7, 1786, FO/NA (http://founders.ar

chives.gov/documents/Washington/04-04-02-0304), *The Papers of George Washington*, Confederation Series, vol. 4, *2 April 1786–31 Jan. 1787*, ed. W. W. Abbot (Charlottesville: University Press of Virginia, 1995), 339.

11. GW to Henry Knox, Feb. 25, 1787, FO/NA (http://founders.archives .gov/documents/Washington/04-05-02-0006), *Papers of GW*, Confed. 5:52–53.

12. Notably Douglas Southall Freeman.

13. GW to Henry Knox, March 8, 1787, FO/NA (http://founders.ar chives.gov/documents/Washington/04-05-02-0072), *Papers of GW*, Confed. 5:74–75.

14. Henry Knox to GW, March 19, 1787, FO/NA (http://founders.ar chives.gov/documents/Washington/04-05-02-0095), *Papers of GW*, Confed. 5:95–98.

15. GW to Henry Knox, April 27, 1787. FO/NA (http://founders.ar chives.gov/documents/Washington/04-05-02-0149), *Papers of GW*, Confed. 5:157–59.

16. GW to Edmund Randolph, March 28, 1787, FO/NA (http://found ers.archives.gov/documents/Washington/04-05-02-0110), *Papers of GW*, Confed. 5:112–14.

17. GW to John Francis Mercer, Sept. 9, 1786, FO/NA (http://founders .archives.gov/documents/Washington/04-04-02-0232), *Papers of GW*, Confed. 4:243–44.

18. GW, "Reflection on Slavery," c. 1788–89, in *George Washington: Writings*, ed. John Rhodehamel (New York: Library of America, 1997), 701–2.

19. GW to Robert Lewis, Aug. 17, 1799, FO/NA (http://founders.ar chives.gov/documents/Washington/06-04-02-0211), *Papers of GW*, Ret. 4:256–58.

20. GW to Tobias Lear, May 6, 1794, FO/NA (http://founders.archives .gov/documents/Washington/05-16-02-0023), *The Papers of George Washington*, Presidential Series, vol. 16, *1 May–30 Sept. 1794*, ed. David R. Hoth and Carol S. Ebel (Charlottesville: University Press of Virginia, 2011), 22–28.

21. James Monroe to Thomas Jefferson, July 12, 1788, FO/NA (http:// founders.archives.gov/documents/Jefferson/01-13-02-0256), *The Papers of Thomas Jefferson*, vol. 13, *March–7 Oct. 1788*, ed. Julian P. Boyd (Princeton: Princeton University Press, 1956), 351–55.

22. Thomas Jefferson to John Adams, Aug. 30, 1787, FO/NA (http://

founders.archives.gov/documents/Jefferson/04-09-02-0278), *The Papers of Thomas Jefferson*, vol. 12, *7 Aug. 1787–31 March 1788*, ed. Julian P. Boyd (Princeton: Princeton University Press, 1955), 66–69.

23. Max Farrand, ed., *The Records of the Federal Convention*, rev. ed., 4 vols. (New Haven: Yale University Press, 1937, 1966), 3:303 (May 5, 1788).

24. GW, diary entry, July 31, 1787, FO/NA (http://founders.archives .gov/documents/Washington/01-05-02-0002-0007-0031), *The Diaries of George Washington*, vol. 5, *1 July 1786–31 Dec. 1789*, ed. Donald Jackson and Dorothy Twohig (Charlottesville: University Press of Virginia, 1979), 179.

25. James Madison, "The Slave Trade and Slaveholders' Rights," June 17, 1788 [debated in the Virginia ratification convention], FO/NA (http:// founders.archives.gov/documents/Madison/01-11-02-0091), *The Papers of James Madison*, vol. 11, ed. Robert A. Rutland and Charles F. Hobson (Charlottesville: University Press of Virginia, 1977), 150–51.

26. Farrand, *Records*, 2:354, 364 (August 21).

27. Jonathan Eliot, ed., *The Debates in the Several State Conventions on the Adoption of the Federal Constitution*, 2nd ed., 5 vols. (Philadelphia: J. B. Lippincott, 1891), 4:285–86.

CHAPTER 10. "On Untrodden Ground"

1. John Adams to Abigail Adams, Dec. 19, 1793, Founders Online, National Archives [hereafter FO/NA] (http://founders.archives.gov/doc uments/Adams/04-09-02-0278), *The Adams Papers*, Adams Family Correspondence, vol. 9, *Jan. 1790–Dec. 1793*, ed. C. James Taylor et al. (Cambridge: Harvard University Press, 2009), 476–77.

2. GW to Henry Knox, April 1, 1789, FO/NA (http://founders.archives .gov/documents/Washington/05-02-02-0003), *The Papers of George Washington*, Presidential Series, vol. 2, *1 April 1789–15 June 1789*, ed. Dorothy Twohig (Charlottesville: University Press of Virginia, 1987), 2–3.

3. GW to Benjamin Lincoln, Oct. 26, 1788, FO/NA (http://founders.ar chives.gov/documents/Washington/05-01-02-0054), *The Papers of George Washington*, Presidential Series, vol. 1, *24 Sept. 1788–31 March 1789*, ed. Dorothy Twohig (Charlottesville: University Press of Virginia, 1987), 70–74.

4. GW to Edward Rutledge, May 5, 1789, FO/NA (http://founders

NOTES TO PAGES 222–25

.archives.gov/documents/Washington/05-02-02-0158), *Papers of GW*, Pres. 1:217–18.

5. Don Higginbottam, *George Washington: Uniting a Nation* (New York: Rowman and Littlefield, 2002), 52.

6. GW, diary entry, April 16, 1789, FO/NA (http://founders.archives. gov/documents/Washington/01-05-02-0005-0001-0001), *The Diaries of George Washington*, vol. 5, *1 July 1786–31 Dec. 1789*, ed. Donald Jackson and Dorothy Twohig (Charlottesville: University Press of Virginia, 1979), 445–47.

7. Ibid., 5:447–48.

8. Edward G. Lengel, *Inventing George Washington: America's Founder, in Myth and Memory* (New York: HarperCollins, 2011), 102–5.

9. *The Diary of William Maclay and Other Notes on Senate Debates*, ed. Kenneth R. Bowling and Helen E. Veit (Baltimore: John Hopkins University Press, 1988), 13.

10. GW, "First Inaugural Address: Final Version, 30 April 1789," FO/NA (http://founders.archives.gov/documents/Washington/05-02-02-030-0003), *Papers of GW*, Pres. 2:173–77.

11. Douglas Southall Freeman, *George Washington: A Biography*, 7 vols., vol. 7 completed by John A. Carroll and Mary W. Ashworth (New York: Scribner's, 1948–57), 6:184.

12. Ron Chernow, *Washington: A Life* (New York: Penguin, 2010), 586.

13. James T. Flexner, *George Washington and the New Nation* (Boston: Little Brown, 1969), 212.

14. Ibid., 245.

15. GW to David Stuart, June 15, 1790, FO/NA (http://founders.ar chives.gov/documents/Washington/05-05-02-0334), *The Papers of George Washington*, Presidential Series, vol. 5, *16 Jan. 1790–30 June 1790*, ed. Dorothy Twohig et al. (Charlottesville: University Press of Virginia, 1996), 523–28.

16. GW to Catherine Sawbridge MaCauly Graham, Jan. 9, 1790, FO/NA (http://founders.archives.gov/documents/Washington/05-04-02-0363), *The Papers of George Washington*, Presidential Series, vol. 4, *8 Sept. 1789–15 Jan. 1790*, ed. Dorothy Twohig (Charlottesville: University Press of Virginia, 1993), 551–54.

17. James McHenry to GW, March 29, 1789, FO/NA (http://founders

.archives.gov/documents/Washington/05-01-02-0357), *Papers of GW,* Pres. 1:461–62.

18. See Kathleen Bartoloni-Tuazon, *For Fear of an Elective King: George Washington and the Presidential Title Controversy of 1789* (Ithaca, NY: Cornell University Press, 2014), particularly 149–53.

19. GW to David Stuart, July 26, 1789, FO/NA (http://founders.ar chives.gov/documents/Washington/05-03-02-0180), *The Papers of George Washington,* Presidential Series, vol. 3, *15 June 1789–5 Sept. 1789,* ed. Dorothy Twohig (Charlottesville: University Press of Virginia, 1989), 321–27.

20. Thomas Jefferson to Dr. Walter Jones, Jan. 2, 1814, in *Thomas Jefferson, Writings,* ed. Merrill D. Peterson (New York: Library of America, 1984), 1319.

21. See T. H. Breen, *George Washington's Journey: The President Forges a New Nation* (New York: Simon and Schuster, 2016).

22. Frank E. Grizzard, Jr., *George Washington: A Biographical Companion* (Santa Barbara, CA: ABC-CLIO, 2002), 236.

23. GW to James Madison, Aug. 5, 1789, FO/NA (http://founders.ar chives.gov/documents/Washington/05-03-02-0225), *Papers of GW,* Pres. 3:387.

24. Bowling and Veit, *Diary of William Maclay,* 130.

25. The emphasis throughout this chapter on Washington's efforts to augment the powers of the presidency is influenced by Harlow Giles Unger, *"Mr. President:" George Washington and the Making of the Nation's Highest Office* (Boston: Da Capo, 2013).

26. "Notes on the State of Virginia," in Peterson, *Jefferson, Writings,* 290.

27. W. W. Abbot, "The Young George Washington and His Papers: A Lecture Presented at the University of Virginia in Commemoration of the Bicentennial of Washington's Death," Charlottesville, 1999, 16.

28. Thomas Jefferson, "Notes on a Conversation with Edmund Randolph, [after 1795]," FO/NA (http://founders.archives.gov/documents/ Jefferson/01-28-02-0441), *The Papers of Thomas Jefferson,* vol. 28, *1 Jan. 1794–29 Feb. 1796,* ed. John Catanzanti (Princeton: Princeton University Press, 2000), 568–69.

29. Thomas Jefferson to GW, Sept. 9, 1792, FO/NA (http://founders

.archives.gov/documents/Jefferson/01-24-02-0330), *The Papers of Thomas Jefferson*, vol. 24, *1 June–31 Dec. 1792*, ed. John Catanzanti (Princeton: Princeton University Press, 1990), 351–60.

30. Alexander Hamilton to Gouverneur Morris, Feb. 27, 1802, FO/NA (http://founders.archives.gov/documents/Hamilton/01-28-02-0441), *The Papers of Alexander Hamilton*, vol. 25, *July 1800–April 1802*, ed. Harold C. Syrett (New York: Columbia University Press, 1977), 544–46.

31. Jerry McCaffery and L. R. Jones, *Budgeting and Financial Management in the Federal Government* (n.p.: Information Age Publishing, 2001), 90, note 4.

32. Stanley Elkins and Eric McKitrick, *The Age of Federalism: The Early American Republic, 1788–1800* (New York: Oxford University Press, 1993), 118.

33. Ibid., 128.

34. James Madison to Edward Carrington, March 14, 1790, FO/NA (http://founders.archives.gov/documents/Madison/01-13-02-0072), *The Papers of James Madison*, vol. 15, *March 24, 1793–April 20, 1795*, ed. Charles F. Hobson and Robert A. Rutland (Charlottesville: University Press of Virginia, 1981), 103–5.

35. Lance Banning, *The Sacred Fire of Liberty: James Madison and the Founding of the Federal Republic* (Ithaca, NY: Cornell University Press, 1995).

36. Kenneth R. Bowling, *The Creation of Washington, D.C.: The Idea and Location of the American Capital* (Fairfax, VA: George Mason University Press, 1991), 3.

37. TJ to GW, Sept. 9, 1792, FO/NA (http://founders.archives.gov/documents/Jefferson/01-24-02-0330), *Papers of Jefferson*, 24:351–60.

38. GW to Anne-Cesar, chevalier de la Luzern, Aug. 10, 1790, FO/NA (http://founders.archives.gov/documents/Washington/05-10-02-0268), *The Papers of George Washington*, Presidential Series, vol. 10, *1 March 1792–15 August 1792*, ed. Robert F. Haggard and Mark A. Mastromarino (Charlottesville: University Press of Virginia, 2002), 229–30.

39. Bowling, *Creation of Washington, D.C.*, 106 ff.

40. Elizabeth S. Kite, *L'Enfant and Washington, 1791–1792* (Baltimore: Johns Hopkins University Press, 1929), 34.

41. Bowling, *Creation of Washington, D.C.*, 6.

42. "L'Enfant, Charles Pierre," *Dictionary of American Biography* (New York: Scribner's, 1933), 11:167.

43. William Seale, *The President's House: A History*, 2 vols. (Washington, DC: White House Historical Society, 1986), 1:19.

44. Elkins and McKitrick, *Age of Federalism*, 172.

45. Thomas Jefferson, "Conversations with the President, Oct. 1, 1792," "Anas," in Peterson, *Jefferson, Writings*, 681–82.

46. Thomas Jefferson, "Conversations with the President, July 10, 1792," ibid., 679.

47. Thomas Jefferson "Conversations with the President, Aug. 6, 1793," FO/NA (http://founders.archives.gov/documents/Jefferson/01-26-02-0571), *The Papers of Thomas Jefferson*, vol. 26, *11 May–31 Aug. 1793*, ed. John Catanzariti (Princeton: Princeton University Press, 1995), 627–30.

48. Thomas Jefferson, "Conversations with the President, Feb. 7, 1792," "Anas," in Peterson, *Jefferson, Writings*, 683.

49. Thomas Jefferson, "Conversations with the President, Feb. 19, 1792," ibid., 677.

50. Thomas Jefferson to James Madison, June 9, 1793, FO/NA (http://founders.archives.gov/documents/Madison/01-15-02-0027), *The Papers of James Madison*, vol. 15, *24 March 1793–20 April 1793*, ed. Thomas Mason et al. (Charlottesville: University Press of Virginia, 1985), 26–28.

51. Thomas Jefferson, "Notes of Cabinet Meeting on Edmond Charles Genet, 2 Aug. 1793," FO/NA (http://founders.archives.gov/documents/Jefferson/01-26-02-0595), *Papers of Jefferson*, 26:601–3.

52. "Thomas Jefferson's Memorandum of Conversations with Washington, March 1, 1792," FO/NA (http://founders.archives.gov/documents/Washington/05-10-02-0004), *Papers of GW*, Pres. 105–10.

53. Thomas Jefferson to GW, May 23, 1793, FO/NA (http://founders.archives.gov/documents/Washington/05-10-02-0268), *Papers of GW*, Pres. 10:408–14.

54. Alexander Hamilton to GW, July 30–[Aug. 3], 1792, FO/NA (http://founders.archives.gov/documents/Hamilton/01-12-02-0109), *The Papers of Alexander Hamilton*, vol. 12, *July 1792–Oct. 1792*, ed. Harold C. Syrett (New York: Columbia University Press, 1967), 137–39.

55. GW to James Madison, May 20, 1792, FO/NA (http://founders .archives.gov/documents/Washington/05-10-02-0260), *Papers of GW*, Pres. 10:339–403.

56. GW to Henry Lee, Jan. 20, 1793, FO/NA (http://founders.archives .gov/documents/Washington/05-12-02-0012), *The Papers of George Washington*, Presidential Series, vol. 12, *16 Jan. 1793–31 May 1793*, ed. Christine Sternberg Patrick and John C. Pinheiro (Charlottesville: University Press of Virginia, 2006), 30–31.

57. Thomas Jefferson, "Conversations with the President, Feb. 7, 1792," "Anas," in Peterson, *Jefferson, Writings*, 683.

58. Thomas Jefferson, "Notes of Cabinet Meeting on Edmond Charles Genet, Aug. 2, 1793," FO/NA (http://founders.archives.gov/documents/Jef ferson/01-26-02-0595), *Papers of Jefferson*, 26:601–3.

CHAPTER 11. The Age of Passion

1. See Edmund S. Morgan, *The Genius of George Washington* (New York: Norton, 1980), passim.

2. GW to Charles Carroll, May 1, 1796, Founders Online, National Archives [hereafter FO/NA] (http://founders.archives.gov/documents/Wash ington/99-01-02-00480); this is an Early Access document from *The Papers of George Washington*.

3. GW to Gouverneur Morris, March 25, 1793, FO/NA (http://found ers.archives.gov/documents/Washington/05-12-02-0302), *The Papers of George Washington*, Presidential Series, vol. 12, *16 Jan. 1793–31 May 1793*, ed. Christine Sternberg Patrick and John C. Pinheiro (Charlottesville: University Press of Virginia, 2006), 380–81.

4. GW to William Heath, May 20, 1797, FO/NA (http://founders.archives .gov/documents/Washington/06-01-02-0118), *The Papers of George Washington*, Retirement Series, vol. 1, *4 March 1797–30 Dec. 1797*, ed. W. W. Abbot (Charlottesville: University Press of Virginia, 1998), 148–50.

5. Thomas Jefferson to James Madison, March 29, 1793, FO/NA (http://founders.archives.gov/documents/Jefferson/01-25-02-0480), *The Papers of Thomas Jefferson*, vol. 25, *Jan. 1–May 10, 1793*, ed. John Catanzariti (Princeton: Princeton University Press, 1992), 442–43.

6. James Madison to Thomas Jefferson, June 19, 1793, FO/NA (http://

founders.archives.gov/documents/Madison/01-15-02-0032), *The Papers of James Madison*, vol. 15, *March 24, 1793–April 20, 1795*, ed. Thomas A. Mason, Robert A. Rutland, and Jeanne K. Sisson (Charlottesville: University Press of Virginia, 1985), 33–34.

7. John Adams to Thomas Jefferson, June 30, 1813, *The Adams-Jefferson Letters: The Complete Correspondence between Thomas Jefferson and Abigail and John Adams*, ed. Lester J. Cappon (Chapel Hill: University of North Carolina Press, 1959), 346–47.

8. Stanley Elkins and Eric McKitrick, *The Age of Federalism: The Early American Republic, 1788–1800* (New York: Oxford University Press, 1993), 343.

9. Thomas Jefferson to James Monroe, June 28, 1793, FO/NA (http://founders.archives.gov/documents/Jefferson/01-26-02-0358), *The Papers of Thomas Jefferson*, vol. 26, *May 11–Aug. 31, 1793*, ed. John Catanzariti (Princeton: Princeton University Press, 1995), 392–93.

10. John Adams to Thomas Jefferson, June 30, 1813, in Cappon, *Adams-Jefferson Letters*, 346–47.

11. Thomas Jefferson to William Short, Jan. 3, 1793, FO/NA (http://founders.archives.gov/documents/Jefferson/01-25-02-0016), *Papers of Jefferson*, 25:14–17.

12. GW to Richard Henry Lee, Aug. 22, 1785, FO/NA (http://founders.archives.gov/documents/Washington/04-03-02-0183), *The Papers of George Washington*, Confederation Series, vol. 3, *19 May 1785–31 March 1786*, ed. W. W. Abbot (Charlottesville: University Press of Virginia, 1994), 195–97.

13. Thomas P. Slaughter, *The Whiskey Rebellion: Frontier Epilogue to the American Revolution* (New York: Oxford University Press, 1986), 87.

14. GW, "Attachment: Letter of Protection, May 7, 1793," FO/NA (http://founders.archives.gov/documents/Washington/05-12-02-0435), *Papers of GW*, Pres. 12:553–54. The document is reproduced in John Rhodehamel, *The Great Experiment: George Washington and the American Republic* (New Haven: Yale University Press, 1998), 134.

15. GW to the Chiefs and Warriors of the Wabash and Illinois Indians, May 7, 1793, FO/NA (http://founders.archives.gov/documents/Washington/05-12-02-0434), *Papers of GW*, Pres. 12:551–53.

16. Slaughter, *Whiskey Rebellion*, 131.

17. Ibid., 186-87.

18. GW to Charles Mynn Thruston, Aug. 10, 1794, FO/NA (http://founders.archives.gov/documents/Washington/05-16-02-0376), *The Papers of George Washington*, Presidential Series, vol. 16, *May 1-Sept. 30, 1794*, ed. David R. Hoth and Carol S. Ebel (Charlottesville: University Press of Virginia, 2011), 47-48.

19. Elkins and McKitrick, *Age of Federalism*, 125.

20. GW to Alexander Hamilton, July 29, 1795, FO/NA (http://founders.archives.gov/documents/Hamilton/01-18-02-0318), *The Papers of Alexander Hamilton*, vol. 18, *Jan. 1795-July 1795*, ed. Harold C. Syrett (New York: Columbia University Press, 1973), 524-26.

21. John Adams to William Cunningham, Oct. 15, 1808, FO/NA (http://founders.archives.gov/documents/Adams/99-02-02-5265); this is an Early Access document from *The Adams Papers*.

22. Thomas Jefferson to James Monroe, June 13, 1796, FO/NA (http://founders.archives.gov/documents/Jefferson/01-29-02-0088), *The Papers of Thomas Jefferson*, vol. 29, *March 1, 1796-Dec. 31, 1797*, ed. Barbara B. Oberg (Princeton: Princeton University Press, 2002), 123-25.

23. Ron Chernow, *Alexander Hamilton* (New York: Penguin, 2004), 499.

24. GW to Lafayette, June 3, 1790, FO/NA (http://founders.archives.gov/documents/Washington/05-05-02-0292), *The Diaries of George Washington*, vol. 5, *1 July 1786-31 Dec. 1789*, ed. Donald Jackson and Dorothy Twohig (Charlottesville: University Press of Virginia, 1979), 467-69.

25. GW to Alexander Hamilton, Aug. 9, 1798, FO/NA (http://founders.archives.gov/documents/Hamilton/01-22-02-0042), *The Papers of Alexander Hamilton*, vol. 22, *July 1798-March 1799*, ed. Harold C. Syrett (New York: Columbia University Press, 1975), 62-64.

26. Quoted in James T. Flexner, *George Washington: Anguish and Farewell* (Boston: Little, Brown, 1972), 251.

27. Rhodehamel, *Great Experiment*, 139.

28. Ibid.

29. John Rhodehamel, ed., *George Washington: Writings* (New York: Library of America, 1997), 973, 977.

30. Elkins and McKitrick, *Age of Federalism*, 497.

CHAPTER 12. "The Debt Which All Must Pay"

1. GW to James McHenry, May 29, 1797, Founders Online, National Archives [hereafter FO/NA] (http://founders.archives.gov/documents/Washington/06-01-02-0128), *The Papers of George Washington*, Retirement Series, vol. 1, *March 4, 1797–Dec. 30, 1797*, ed. W. W. Abbot (Charlottesville: University Press of Virginia, 1998), 159–60.

2. GW to Jonathan Trumbull, Jr., July 21, 1799, FO/NA (http://founders.archives.gov/documents/Washington/04-02-0404-0001), *The Papers of George Washington*, Retirement Series, vol. 4, *April 20, 1799–Dec. 13, 1799*, ed. W. W. Abbot (Charlottesville: University Press of Virginia, 1999), 201–4.

3. GW, Last Will and Testament, July 9, 1799, FO/NA (http://founders.archives.gov/documents/Washington/04-02-0404-0001), *Papers of GW*, Ret. 4:459–511.

4. Ibid.

5. Interview in PBS-WGBH documentary, *Africans in America*, 1999.

6. Tobias Lear's account of GW's last hours, quoted in James T. Flexner, *George Washington: Anguish and Farewell* (Boston: Little, Brown, 1972), 456.

7. Historian Peter R. Henriques has described Washington's painful death in "He Died as He Lived: The Death of George Washington," in *Realistic Visionary: A Portrait of George Washington* (Charlottesville: University Press of Virginia, 2006), 187–204.

8. Flexner, *Anguish and Farewell*, 459.

9. Joseph J. Ellis, *His Excellency: George Washington* (New York, Vintage, 2004), 269.

10. Flexner, *Anguish and Farewell*, 460.

11. Fisher Ames, *An Oration on the Sublime Virtues of General George Washington, Pronounced at the Old South Meeting-House in Boston, before his Honor the Lieutenant-Governor, the Council, and the Two Branches of the Legislature of Massachusetts, at their Request, on Saturday, the 8th of February, 1800* (Denham, [MA]: Printed by H. Mann, 1800), 4.

12. Abigail Smith Adams to Mary Smith Cranch, Jan. 28, 1800, FO/NA (http://founders.archives.gov/documents/Adams/99-03-02-0564); this is an Early Access document from *The Adams Papers*.

Index

ancestry and genealogy of Washington, 1–2, 11–13
Anderson, Fred, *Crucible of War*, 50
André, John, 175
Annapolis, Maryland, Washington resigns commission at, 191
Antifederalists, 217, 296
Appalachian Mountains, 33, 39
aristocracy, aristocrats, 1–3, 20, 22–23, 90, 125, 137; condemnations of, 125, 279, 301; of Virginia, 146, 237
Arnold, Benedict: as American military hero, 120, 153–54, 172; as traitor, 174–76, 180
Arnold, Margaret (Peggy) Shippen, 175
Articles of Confederation, 169, 199, 200, 219, 236; Philadelphia Convention to amend, 202, 210
assumption of Revolutionary War debt, 244–45

Bache, Benjamin Franklin, 260
Ball, Mary. *See* Washington, Mary Ball
Baltimore, Maryland: Continental Congress in, 138; Washington in, 101
Banister, John, Washington writes to, 118–19, 157, 316n32, 319n8
Bank of England, 240, 255
Bank of the United States, 242, 255–56, 258
Banning, Lance, 245
Barbados, Washington's trip with Lawrence to, 27
Bartram, William, 212
Bassett, Burwell, Washington writes to, 112, 314n12
Battle of Fallen Timbers, 275
Beaujeu, Daniel Liénard, 65–67
Belvoir, 15–16, 19–20, 22, 23, 36, 79

Bill of Rights, 217, 231
biographers of Washington: Abbot, 13–14; Chernow, 146; Cunliffe, 8, 9; Ellis, 126, 300; Flexner, 186, 311n26; Freeman, 13, 36, 90, 110, 150, 177; Higginbottam, 222; Irving, 136; Lengel, 223; Morgan, 17; Morison, 312n35; Riley, 299; on Sally Fairfax, 83, 312n35; separate man from myth, 8–9; Weems, 8–9, 159, 302; Wills, 113
blacks: Washington's views on, 00, 297–98
Boston, 104–5, 148; British abandon, 121–22; siege of, 108–9, 114, 120, 122, 126; Washington in, 87, 112, 229
Boston Massacre (1770), 104
Boston Port Bill (1774), 105
Boston Tea Party (1773), 104–5
Bowling, Kenneth, 249
boycotts and nonimportation, 103, 104
Braddock, Edward, 61, 62, 63, 91, 117; builds road, 62, 64, 67, 68, 69
Braddock's Defeat, 64–70, 105, 118; site of, 280
Brandywine Creek, 147, 150, 151–53
Breed's Hill, 108
Bridges Creek, Virginia, first Washingtons settle at, 11
British Army, 40, 61, 200; amphibious operations of, 127; Arnold and, 175–76; attacked in Massachusetts, 108–9; in Boston, 104, 121–22; colonists' experience with, 91–92; Lawrence Washington in, 16; in New Jersey, 144, 167; in New York, 122, 126–37, 173; regular commissions in, 58–60; in southern theater, 171, 180. *See also* redcoats

Madison, James, 17, 214, 252; advocates strong presidency, 230–31;
Bill of Rights and, 231; Compromise of 1790 and, 247–48; drafts
Farewell Address, 261–62, 288;
drafts first inaugural address,
224; ends friendship with Washington, 286; *The Federalist No.
10*, 217–18; Hamilton and, 245;
hates England, 243; ideological
shift of, 245; opposes Bank of
United States, 255; opposes discrimination in Congress, 244;
in opposition to Washington,
256, 259–60; on Proclamation
of Neutrality, 266; proportional representation and, 211;
Virginia Plan and, 210, 213;
Washington and, 203–4, 245;
Washington writes to, 326n23,
329n55
Maine, 120
manufacturing, Hamilton and, 242,
246
Marblehead, Massachusetts, 131
Marin de la Malgue, Paul, 35, 37,
41, 42
Maryland, 33, 149, 218, 247, 280;
in French and Indian War, 49,
73; regiments of, 129, 166; tidewater, 11, 12
Mason, George, 106, 215, 216;
Washington writes, 102, 313n2
Massachusetts, 104, 105–6, 108,
201, 202, 218. *See also* Boston;
Intolerable Acts; Maine
Massachusetts Government Act
(1774), 105
McHenry, James, 191, 287; Wash-
ington writes to, 185, 200, 293,
320n3, 322n7, 332n1; writes to
Washington, 225, 325n17
Mercer, John Francis, Washington
writes to, 206, 323n17

meritocracy, 2, 77, 200–201
Miami Indians, visit President
Washington, 276–77
Middlebrook, New Jersey, Continental Army winters in, 176
Middlekauff, Robert, 154
militia, 127, 132, 140, 153–54, 155,
180, 280–81; becomes Continental Army, 110, 112; minutemen as, 108, 114; mythic view
of, 118, 126; Washington and,
116–18, 119
Militia Act (1792), 275
Mississippi River, 41, 198; Spain
and, 273, 284
mob violence, 7, 103: in Philadelphia, 266, 269, 270, 284; in
Whiskey Rebellion, 278, 279
Mohawk Indians, 32, 105
monarchy, 191, 235, 264; Americans reject, 7, 125, 184–85, 301;
constitutional, 237–38; Democratic-Republicans' fear of, 241,
259; Jefferson's hypersensitivity
to, 234, 257; presidency resembled, 217, 225–26
Monongahela River, 40, 65, 66, 69
Monroe, James, 286
Montgomery, Richard, 120
Monticello, 239, 272
Montreal, 41, 56, 120
Morgan, Edmund S., 17
Morison, Samuel Eliot, 312n35
Morris, Gouverneur, 102, 213,
305n11; Washington writes to,
265, 329n3
Morris, Robert, 255
Morristown, New Jersey, 144, 146,
176–77
Mount Vernon, 6, 19, 71, 101, 182,
195, 220, 222, 261; agricultural
experimentation at, 95–96,
194; federal district and, 249;
as Lawrence and Anne Fairfax

344

Ohio River, 32, 41; canals and, 197,
250; Forks of, 40, 48, 53, 62, 64,
70, 97; French forts on, 34, 39,
42; Washington on, 44; Washington's lands on, 97
Ohio Valley, 33–34, 40, 52, 98;
Britain and, 61, 96, 273, 282;
Indians in, 274–77; Jay's Treaty
and, 285; Marin's expedition to,
35, 37, 41, 42; Potomac site for
federal city and, 247; settlement
of, 198–99; Treaty of Paris and,
197; Washington considers
retreating to, 137
opposition ideology, of Democratic-
Republican party, 240–41, 256
opposition press, 269, 284, 287. *See
also* newspapers and magazines
Oxford University, 12

Paine, Thomas: *Common Sense*,
125; *Letter to George Washington*, 287–88
Pamunkey River, Virginia, 79, 80
Paris, 55, 169, 209
Parliament, 3, 105, 161, 240; taxation and, 103, 104, 107–8
parties, 295–96; creation of,
234–48; in Farewell Address,
289–90; Washington on evils
of, 236
peace negotiations, with Britain,
184, 187, 189
Peale, Charles Willson, 212, 213
Peebles, John, 155–56
Pennsylvania, 35, 218, 280;
Continental Army in, 137–38,
142; Ohio country and, 32;
State House in, 109, 209; 13th
Regiment of, 166; Washington's
lands in, 97; Whiskey Rebel-
lion in, 278, 280, 281. *See also*
Philadelphia
Pennsylvania Line, mutiny of, 177

people, the: in Constitution, 216;
Genet and, 268; militia and,
118; monarchy and, 7; popular
government and, 3–4, 5; in
republics, 5, 209, 225, 230, 241,
283, 301; Washington and, 4,
185, 203, 227, 228, 266, 285
Philadelphia, 34, 70, 71, 82, 101,
147, 148, 288; Arnold in, 174–75;
British in, 75, 78, 87, 101, 107,
125, 138, 147, 149, 156, 161, 162;
Continental Army and, 150, 177;
Genet and, 266, 269; Miami
Indians visit, 276; mobs in, 266,
269, 270, 284; as seat of federal
government, 247, 249, 255; Valley Forge and, 157; Washington
in, 101, 205; yellow fever in, 270
Philadelphia Convention, 209, 210,
237; debates in, 209–15; exceeds
authority, 202, 210; Great Compromise in, 211; secrecy of, 217;
Virginia Plan in, 209–10, 213;
Washington and, 202, 208. *See
also* U.S. Constitution
Pickering, Timothy, 286
Pinckney, Charles C., 215–16
Pitt, William, 84, 85, 90
Pittsburgh, Pennsylvania, 40; Whiskey Rebellion and, 279–81. *See
also* Fort Duquesne; Fort Pitt
Potomac River: canals and, 96,
197, 199, 254; federal city and,
247–55; Mount Vernon and,
19, 194; Potomac Fever and,
249–50
Potomac River Navigation Company, 199, 254
presidency, 220; designed with
Washington in mind, 208;
foreign policy and, 233; as monarchy, 225–26; titles and, 226;
Washington increases power of,
230–31, 265, 285

Washington, George, in French
and Indian War (*continued*)
doun and, 74–77; military and
political education of, 86–89;
military reputation of, 86–87;
mistakes and failures of, 86–88;
political skills undeveloped in,
87; rise of, 97–98; turning point
of life in, 76–77. *See also* Virginia
Regiment; *and "Ohio" entries*
Washington, George, General, 103,
145; appointment of, 8, 110–13;
Arnold and, 174, 175; assumes
command of Continental Army,
112–13; Battle of Brandywine
and, 150–52; Battle of Germantown and, 154–56; Battle of
Monmouth and, 162–68; Battle
of Trenton and, 139–42; boldness of, 156, 182; Boston and,
120–21, 122; Charles Lee and,
165–66, 167; commitment of,
137, 188; Continental Congress
and, 2, 87, 138, 170, 219–20;
Conway Cabal and, 162; defensive
war of, 182; defers to civilian
power, 191–92; discouragement
of, 121, 136; enforces discipline,
115; enters New York City,
190–91; errors of, 126, 128, 132,
135–36, 150–51, 155, 164; on
front lines, 143–44; Gates and,
161–62; greatest achievement in
preserving Continental Army,
169; Newburgh Conspiracy and,
184–88; New Jersey campaign
of, 137–46; New York campaign
of, 125–36; offers pardons to
Crown allegiants, 144–45;
orders of, 140–41, 145–46;
as realist, 119; refuses salary,
110; reluctance of, to accept
command, 72; resigns commission, 6, 191; scorecard of, 169;

stagecraft of, 187, 188; successful
retreats of, 131; as successful
statesman, 87, 169–70, 205,
219–20; supports strong central
government, 186, 190; sup-
presses mutinies, 178–79; as
symbol of national unity, 170;
uniform of, 101, 109–10, 159;
at Valley Forge, 157; Yorktown
campaign and, 181–84. *See also*
Continental Army; Revolutionary War battles
Washington, George, health and
physique of: anthrax, 224–25;
deafness, 228; dysentery, 64–65,
78; effects of aging on, 204–5,
261, 294; eyes, 22, 38; final
illness, 299–300; hemorrhoids,
65; illness after Braddock's
Defeat, 71, 72; illnesses after
1757 Philadelphia trip, 78; physique of, 21, 109; pneumonia,
225; smallpox and, 27; teeth, 9,
204; tuberculosis, 78
Washington, George, papers of:
correspondence with Continental Congress, 116, 117–18, 119,
128, 132, 152; correspondence
with department secretaries,
186–87, 201; correspondence
with Martha, 110–11; diaries
and journals, 25–26, 28, 41,
55, 213, 222–23; earliest, 17,
24, 25–26; legal documents,
296–97; letters to Sally Fairfax,
82–83; Mount Vernon record
books, 206; official presidential
records, 271–72, 277; private
correspondence, 114, 221, 248;
total volume of, 17; at Washington's death, 299
Washington, George, President:
addresses to Congress, 271–72;
cabinet of, 231, 232, 260, 269,

1